BATTLE OF THE BULGE
ST. VITH, THE NORTHERN SHOULDER AND BASTOGNE

American History Archives™

The Battle of the Bulge
St. Vith, the Northern Shoulder and Bastogne

3 4 5 6 7 11 10 09 08
ISBN 978-1-58159-248-1

The History Channel Club
c/o North American Membership Group
12301 Whitewater Drive
Minnetonka, MN 55343
www.thehistorychannelclub.com

Published by North American Membership Group under license from Osprey
Publishing, Ltd.

Previously published as Campaign 115: Battle of the Ardennes 1944 (1) St Vith
and the Northern Shoulder and Campaign 145: Battle of the Bulge 1944 (2)
Bastogne by Osprey Publishing, Midland House, West Way, Botley, Oxford
OX2 0PH, United Kingdom.

© 2005 Osprey Publishing Ltd.   OSPREY
PUBLISHING

Editor: Lee Johnson
Design: The Black Spot
Index by Fineline Editorial Services
Maps by The Map Studio
3D bird's-eye views by The Black Spot
Originated by The Electronic Page Company, Cwmbran, UK
Printed in China through World Print Ltd.

FRONT COVER
**Riflemen of the 393rd Infantry, 99th Division during
the fighting around Rocherath (NARA).**

Author's Note

The author would like to thank the staff of the US Army's Military
History Institute at the Army War College at Carlisle Barracks, PA,
for their kind assistance in the preparation of this book, especially
Mr. Randy Hackenburg and Jay Graybeal of Special Collections.
The photos in this book are primarily from the US Army's Signal
Corps collections at the US National Archives and Records
Administration (NARA) in College Park, MD. Other photos were
located at the special collections branch of the Military History
Institute, including the 28th Division veterans' collections. Special
thanks also to Rob Plas, Ron Volstad and the other participants
of the TWENOT 2001 Ardennes battlefield tour.
For brevity, the usual conventions have been used when referring
to American and German units. In the case of US units, 1/393rd
Infantry refers to the 1st Battalion, 393rd Infantry Regiment. In the
case of German units, GR.27 refers to Grenadier Regiment 27.

Glossary

AFAB: Armored Field Artillery Battalion
AIB: Armored Infantry Battalion
CCA, CCB, CCR: Combat Command A, B, Reserve (US armored
divisions)
GR: Grenadier Regiment
Jabo: German term for American fighter-bombers
KG: Kampfgruppe (battle group)
PIR: Parachute Infantry Regiment
PzGR: Panzergrenadier Regiment
TF: Task Force
VG Div.: Volksgrenadier Division

KEY TO MILITARY SYMBOLS

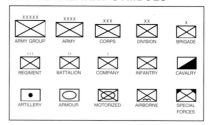

STEVEN J ZALOGA has his BA in history from Union College and his MA from Columbia
University. He is currently a senior analyst for the aerospace research firm, Teal Group
Corp. and an adjunct staff member with the Strategy, Forces, and Resources division
of the Institute for Defense Analyses, a federal think-tank in Washington, DC. He has
written over 50 books on military history and technology, as well as many television
documentaries.

HOWARD GERRARD studied at the Wallasey School of Art and has been a freelance
designer and illustrator for over 20 years. He has won both the Society of British
Aerospace Companies Award and the Wilkinson Sword Trophy and has illustrated
a number of books for Osprey including Campaign 69: *Nagashino 1575* and
Campaign 72: *Jutland 1916*. Howard lives and works in Kent.

PETER DENNIS was born in 1950 and, having been inspired by contemporary
magazines such as 'Look and Learn', studied illustration at Liverpool Art College.
He has since contributed to hundreds of books, predominantly on historical subjects.
He is a keen wargamer and modelmaker.

BATTLE OF THE BULGE
St. Vith, the Northern Shoulder and Bastogne

CONTENTS

INTRODUCTION

By the autumn of 1944, the war in northwestern Europe had ground to a standstill both literally (heavy autumn rains hampered troop movements for both sides) and figuratively (the battle lines on both sides were relatively stagnant).

But Hitler was ready for something to happen and, despite advice to the contrary from his senior commanders, he decided to go on the offensive. His goal? Break the Allied lines. His tool? The vaunted Sixth Panzer Army. The place? St. Vith and the Elsenborn ridge – the northern shoulder of the "bulge" in German lines. If the Germans could break through, they would separate the Allied Armies.

But the Allies held strong. And when it was clear that a breakthrough wouldn't be achieved to the North, the Wehrmacht shifted its efforts south, toward Bastogne. Here, the German Fifth Panzer Army overwhelmed the "green" U.S. 106th division and moved toward the river Meuse. But in their way was the crossroads town of Bastogne, which had been reinforced at the last minute by the "Screaming Eagles" of the 101st Airborne. And so began an epic struggle that began the end of the war … the battle for Bastogne.

Hitler wrote the destiny for his Wehrmacht fighting machine when he decided to go on the offensive. Both sides paid a high price during The Battle of the Bulge, in places like St. Vith, the Northern Shoulder and Bastogne. Here is the complete story of this huge and costly battle – the largest one fought by the U.S. Army in World War II, and the one that sealed the fate of the German Empire forever.

The defeat of the 6th Panzer Army's breakthrough attempts in the St Vith sector shifted the focus of the German Ardennes offensive to the south in the second week of the offensive, with attention increasingly focused on Bastogne. This PzKpfw IV Ausf J from the spearhead of Kampfgruppe Peiper was knocked out by US M10 tank destroyers on the road from Bullingen to Wirtzfeld on 17 December. (NARA)

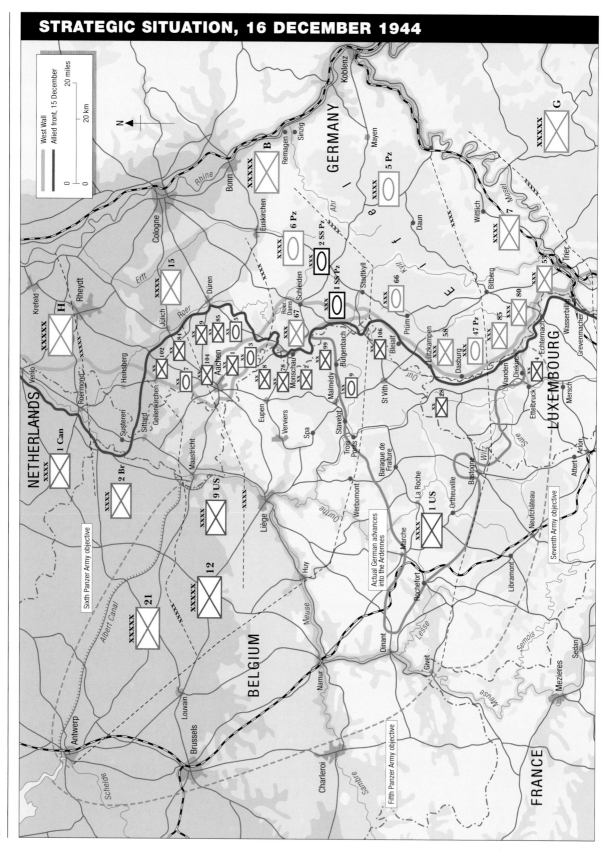

West Wall
Allied front, 15 December

0   20 km
0   20 miles

N

GERMANY

NETHERLANDS

BELGIUM

LUXEMBOURG

FRANCE

Koblenz

Sinzig

Remagen

Mayen

Bonn

Euskirchen

Cologne

Rhine

Erft

Krefeld

Rheydt

Roer

Düren

Jülich

Heinsberg

Venlo

Roermond

Susteren

Sittard

Geilenkirchen

Maastricht

Aachen

Roer Dams

Schleiden

Stadtkyll

Daun

Wittlich

Mosel

Trier

Bitburg

Prüm

Bleialf

St Vith

Bütgenbach

Monschau

Malmédy

Eupen

Verviers

Spa

Stavelot

Trois
Ponts

Baraque de
Fraiture

Werbomont

La Roche

Ortheuville

Marche

Rochefort

Dinant

Givet

Liège

Huy

Namur

Louvain

Brussels

Antwerp

Charleroi

Albert Canal

Meuse

Ourthe

Lesse

Semois

Meuse

Sambre

Scheldt

Mézières

Sedan

Libramont

Neufchâteau

Bastogne

Wiltz

Diekirch

Wianden

Vianden

Echternach

Wasserbillig

Grevenmacher

Luxembourg

Ettelbruck

Mersch

Arlon

Attert

Dasburg

Lützkampen

Daleiden

Ahr

Kyll

Our

Sûre

Witz

Attert

B

XXXXX

15

XXXX

H

XXXXX

1 Can

XXXX

2 Br

XXXX

9 US

XXXX

12

XXXXX

21

XXXXX

6 Pz

XXXX

5 Pz

XXXX

7

XXXX

G

XXXXX

2 SS Pz

XXXX

1 SS Pz

67
XXX

66
XXX

58
XXX

47 Pz
XXX

85
XXX

80
XXX

53
XXX

1 US

XXXX

Sixth Panzer Army objective

Fifth Panzer Army objective

Seventh Army objective

Actual German advances
into the Ardennes

PART 1
ST. VITH AND THE
NORTHERN SHOULDER

Long overshadowed by the legendary defense of Bastogne, the battles around St Vith in the northern sector of the Ardennes front were the most decisive to the outcome of the German offensive of December 1944. The prime objective of Hitler's desperate gamble was to split the Allied front by assaulting across the Meuse River to the vital port city of Antwerp. The shortest route was in the northern sector, and Hitler assigned his favored Waffen-SS Panzer divisions to this mission. Spearheaded by Oberstgruppenführer "Sepp" Dietrich's 6th Panzer Army, the northern thrust contained almost two-thirds of the German armored strength. The 7th Army opposite Bastogne was assigned the dregs of the German infantry with practically no armored support. The failure of 6th Panzer Army in the opening ten days of the offensive doomed Hitler's plans. With their best routes blocked, the momentum shifted to General Hasso von Manteuffel's 5th Panzer Army in the center of the front, which attempted to redeem the offensive using a less direct approach further south near Bastogne. But by Christmas, the initiative had shifted to the American side and it was no longer a question of whether the German offensive would be defeated, but simply of when. This book focuses on the northern shoulder of the Battle of the Bulge in the vital first ten days of the campaign, concentrating on the attack by 6th Panzer Army and the American defense from St Vith to the Elsenborn Ridge.

The 9th Infantry, 2nd Infantry Division pass though the Krinkelt woods on 13 December 1944 on their way to attack towards the Roer dams. A few days later, the 1/9th Infantry would return to the area, serving as a breakwater against the 12th SS-Panzer Division at the Lausdell crossroads outside Krinkelt. (NARA)

In the autumn of 1944, the campaign on the Western Front had degenerated into a miserable slogging match along the German frontier. After the destruction of the German army in France in the summer of 1944 and the race into the Low Countries in September, the logistical support for the Allied armies became exhausted. Until Field Marshal Bernard L. Montgomery's 21st Army Group could clear the approaches to the port of Antwerp, the Allies nibbled away at German defenses. By early December Antwerp was finally operating, and the Allies began building up supplies for offensives in the new year.

Lieutenant General Bradley's 12th Army Group stretched along the German Westwall fortifications from Aachen to the Saar. The key objective in this sector was to seize the Roer dams east of Aachen. Until they were captured, they would pose a threat to any Allied attempt to cross the Roer River, since the Germans could open the dams and flood the plains to the south. There were repeated attempts to reach the Roer in November, including armored attacks on the muddy plains east of Aachen and a bloody attempt to secure the approaches to the dams through the Hürtgen forest. By mid-December Lieutenant General Courtney Hodges' First Army had succeeded in reaching the western banks of the Roer, but at an appalling cost in men and machines. The Ardennes was a "ghost front" for most of the autumn with little combat, while to the south, Lieutenant General George S. Patton's Third Army pushed out of Lorraine towards the Saar.

For the German army, the prospects were forbidding. Although the Western Front had almost collapsed completely in September, the strained Allied logistics had provided just enough breathing space for the Germans to strengthen defenses along the Westwall. These defenses held through October and November, aided in no small measure by the wretched weather, which limited Allied mobility and restricted air operations. Yet no German commander, except Hitler, had much hope that these defenses would remain viable once the Allies resumed their offensives in earnest. In the east, the main front in Poland had been dormant since August as the Red Army reinvigorated its forces for the final push into Germany. Most of the activity in the autumn was on the peripheries, especially Hungary, but there was little doubt that the New Year would bring a dreaded Soviet offensive.

CHRONOLOGY

September 1944: Hitler first mentions plans for Ardennes offensive.

11 October: Jodl submits first draft of Ardennes plan, codenamed *Wacht am Rhein*, to Hitler.

22 October: Senior German commanders are briefed on the Ardennes plan.

Early November: First German units begin moving into the Eifel for the offensive.

Mid-November: US 99th Division arrives in Ardennes, takes over Monschau sector mid-November.

9–10 December: US Army G-2 intelligence sees no immediate threat of German offensive operations.

10 December: US Army begins another offensive against Roer dams with first objectives near Wahlerscheid.

11 December: US 106th Division arrives near St Vith and takes over Schnee Eifel defense from 2nd Infantry Division.

0400, 16 December: Infantry in 5th Panzer Army sector begins infiltration past Schnee Eifel.

0430, 16 December: Operation *Herbstnebel* (Autumn Mist) begins with opening barrages against forward US positions in Ardennes.

0700, 16 December: German preparatory artillery ends.

0700–0800: Infantry begins advancing.

Afternoon, 16 December: Major General Robertson begins moving 2nd Infantry units back towards Krinkelt to reinforce flank. 3rd Fallschirmjäger Division takes Lanzerath; Krewinkel–Losheim Gap open.

Afternoon–Evening, 16 December: Major General Middleton commits CCB/9th Armored Division to 106th Division; Lieutenant General Omar Bradley allots 7th Armored Division to VIII Corps; Eisenhower agrees to shift XVIII Airborne Corps to Ardennes.

Evening, 16 December: After 277th Volksgrenadier Division fails to penetrate Krinkelt woods, Gruppenführer Hermann Preiss orders 12th SS-Panzer Division *Hitlerjugend* to commit armor to make breakthrough.

0330, 17 December: Kampfgruppe (KG) Peiper begins drive at Buchholz.

0900, 17 December: 106th Division encircled as 18th Volksgrenadier Division reaches Schönberg.

1500, 17 December: 12th Volksgrenadier Division finally takes Losheimergraben.

1500, 17 December: Massacre of US POWs by KG Peiper at Baugnez crossroads.

1800, 17 December: KG Peiper halts on approaches to Stavelot.

2400, 17 December: 12th Volksgrenadier Division takes Mürringen.

0700, 18 December: KG Peiper begins attack on Stavelot.

1000, 18 December: KG Peiper passes through Stavelot by this time.

1200, 18 December: Bridges blown at Trois Ponts, forcing KG Peiper to La Gleize.

Afternoon, 18 December: KG Peiper reaches La Gleize, probes sent west to find route to Werbomont.

Evening, 18 December: 12th SS-Panzer Division *Hitlerjugend* fails to take Krinkelt-Rocherath, Gruppenführer Preiss orders division to move west instead. Major General Robertson decides to pull back from Krinkelt-Rocherath to Elsenborn Ridge.

0230, 19 December: First major attack by 12th SS-Panzer Division *Hitlerjugend* against 1st Infantry Division at Dom Bütgenbach crossroads.

19 December: Eisenhower meets with senior US commanders to plan further responses to German attack.

1200, 19 December: US troops retake control of Stavelot, cutting off KG Peiper.

Afternoon, 19 December: CCB/7th Armored Division begins deploying near St Vith.

21 December: 12th SS-Panzer Division *Hitlerjugend* abandons attacks on Dom Bütgenbach.

0800, 22 December: Obersturmbannführer Skorzeny's Panzer Brigade 150 launches attack on Malmedy but fails.

22 December: Montgomery takes command of US units in northern shoulder of the Ardennes.

0600, 23 December: US forces begin withdrawal from St Vith salient.

0200, 24 December: KG Peiper begins escape from La Gleize.

OPPOSING PLANS

GERMAN PLANS

The idea for the Ardennes offensive came to Hitler in mid-September 1944 during his recuperation from the 20 July 1944 bomb plot. Albert Jodl, the chief of the Wehrmacht operations staff, made a casual mention that the Ardennes was the most weakly held sector of the Allied front. Hitler immediately connected this remark with the bold Panzer drive across the Meuse in 1940 that had led to the stunning victory over France. Given Germany's desperate circumstances Hitler convinced himself that a success in the west could change the course of the war. In his fevered mind, the alliance between Britain and the United States was fragile, and if their forces could be separated by an assault to the sea, the Allied front would collapse. Hitler dreamed that a third to a half of the Allied divisions on the western front could be destroyed. A similar offensive in other theaters held out no opportunity. Jodl was assigned the task of elaborating Hitler's plans and he submitted the first draft on 11 October 1944.

The Ardennes offensive was shaped by earlier German counter-offensives. Two previous Panzer operations against the advancing US Army – near Mortain in early August and in Lorraine in September – had failed. Although the attacking German forces had modest numerical

A 9th Infantry squad huddles in a snowy ditch during the fighting on the approaches to "Heartbreak Crossroads" near Wahlerscheid on 13 December 1944. (NARA)

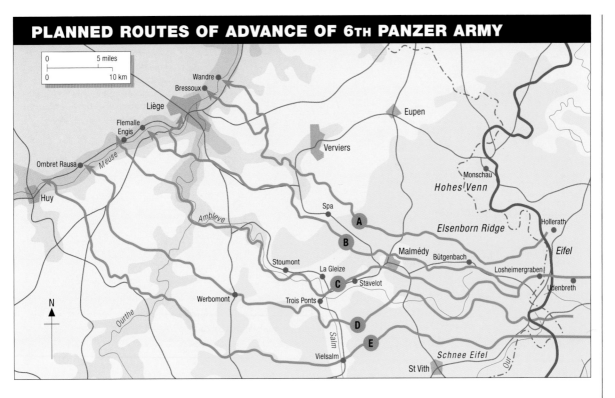

superiority in both battles, this was not enough when faced by American artillery and air power. Hitler concluded that the Ardennes operation would require substantial superiority in men and materiel. Since only four American divisions were holding the Ardennes, Hitler calculated that a total of about 30 German divisions would be needed. Given the weakened state of the Wehrmacht after the summer disasters, such a force could not be assembled until late November 1944, but the poor weather in the late autumn would hobble Allied air power. An essential element of the plan, first dubbed *Wacht am Rhein* (Watch on the Rhine), was total secrecy. Since the attempted military coup of July 1944, Hitler had a pathological distrust of the commanders of the regular army. Details of the plan were kept to an absolute minimum of planners, and the movement of troops and materiel to the German frontier in the late autumn was explained as an effort to prepare for Allied offensives over the Rhine that were expected in the New Year.

The offensive was aimed at the Ardennes sector most weakly held by the US Army from Monschau in the north to Echternach in the south, a distance of about 60km. The neighboring German sector in the Eifel was heavily wooded, shielding fresh German units from aerial observation. The offensive would be conducted by three armies: two Panzer armies in the north and center and a relatively weak infantry army on the southern flank to block counterattacks against this shoulder. Hitler would have preferred to use only his trusted Waffen-SS Panzer divisions, but there were not enough. So he settled on an attack by the 6th (SS) Panzer Army in the vital northern sector with a parallel assault by the 5th Panzer Army in the center. The 6th Panzer Army sector from Monschau to St Vith was the most important, since success here would secure the shortest route over the Meuse through Liège to

The farm roads leading out of the Eifel in the northern sector were churned up by the advancing columns of Panzers and quickly became channels of mud, trapping this captured jeep being used by an officer of 1st SS-Panzer Corps. (MHI)

Antwerp. German planners believed that the main logistics network for the First US Army was in this area and its capture would assist the German attack by providing supplies as well as weakening the American response. The weakest of the attacking German armies, the 7th Army, would strike towards Bastogne. Unlike the two Panzer forces to the north, the 7th Army had virtually no armored support. Bastogne had little role in the original Ardennes plan since it was quite distant from any strategic objectives. The Waffen-SS Panzer commanders were fairly confident they could reach the Meuse river in a day or two, and the plan considered that it might be possible to reach Antwerp by the seventh day of the offensive.

In the 6th Panzer Army sector, Hitler wanted two special operations to seize vital bridges over the Meuse before they could be destroyed by retreating American forces. Operation *Grief*, led by Hitler's favorite adventurer, Obersturmbannführer Otto Skorzeny, would consist of a special brigade of English-speaking German troops disguised as Americans which would surreptitiously make its way through the American lines to capture vital objectives ahead of the main Panzer force. Operation *Stösser* was a paratroop drop to seize vital objectives deep behind the American lines while paralyzing any attempts to reinforce the northern sector.

The plan for the 6th Panzer Army was based around the use of two SS Panzer corps. After the lead infantry divisions had penetrated the American defenses, the first of these corps would secure bridgeheads over the Meuse after which the second Panzer corps would be committed to exploit towards Antwerp. Hitler allotted priority in assault guns and tank destroyer units to this sector, since the American response would be to divert forces from the Aachen area and move them south against the 6th Panzer Army's right flank. He directed that this sector receive the best infantry formations including two Fallschirmjäger (paratrooper) divisions and the 12th Volksgrenadier Division, which had distinguished itself in the recent Aachen fighting. Hitler stressed that the lead Panzer corps was to avoid becoming entangled in fighting along its right flank with counterattacking American units, a mission that should be left to a blocking force of infantry and separate tank destroyer units.

Nicknamed "Obersepp" by his troops, Oberstgruppenführer Josef "Sepp" Dietrich was the commander of the 6th Panzer Army. (NARA)

The senior commanders were brought in for their first briefing on *Wacht am Rhein* on 22 October 1944. The Western Front commander, Generalfeldmarshall Gerd von Rundstedt, and Army Group B commander, Generalfeldmarshall Walter Model, were aghast at the details of the plan which they viewed as wildly impractical. Knowing that Hitler would not be amused by their doubts, they approached Jodl with a "small solution": an alternative offensive aimed at enveloping the US forces around the recently fallen city of Aachen. Jodl was unwilling to even the broach the idea with Hitler, knowing he was determined to embark on this desperate final gamble for the fate of Germany.

Wacht am Rhein was foolhardy with few realistic chances for success. The quality of German forces in the late autumn of 1944 had plummeted drastically since the summer, due to the catastrophic losses in France and eastern Europe. The plan could only succeed if the initial American defenses could be rapidly breached and if the US Army dawdled as the Panzers raced for the Meuse. This was pinned on Hitler's exaggerated estimation of German combat power and a dismissive underestimation of American battlefield prowess. Any delays in reaching key objectives would doom the plan, since many key routes through the wooded hill country of the Ardennes could be blocked by relatively small forces at choke points and key river crossings. Delays of only a few days would be fatal since the Americans could use their better mobility to reinforce the Ardennes. The plan's logistical underpinning was suspect. Fuel and ammunition were in short supply and once the offensive began, the rail

Commander of the 5th Panzer Army, General Hasso von Manteuffel on the left confers with the Army Group B commander, Generalfeldmarshall Walter Model (right) and the inspector of the Panzer force on the western front, Generalleutnant Horst Stumpf (center). (MHI)

lines running into the Eifel would be relentlessly bombed regardless of weather, preventing re-supply.

At the tactical level, the two principal armies had different approaches to the initial break-in operation. The 5th Panzer Army commander, Hasso von Manteuffel was an energetic commander who had fought against US forces since the summer. As German commanders put it, he had an intuitive "finger-feel" for the battlefield based on a sharp intellect and experience. Contrary to Hitler's orders, he permitted scouting along his front, and after donning a colonel's uniform, he scouted the frontlines himself in the days before the offensive. This convinced him that there was a major gap in the American lines in the Losheim area. He also determined that American patrols were very active at night, but that they returned to base before dawn and did not resume patrols until mid-morning. Manteuffel was convinced that the planned artillery preparation would do little good against the forward US trenches and would only serve to alert the Americans. Since Hitler would not agree to an abandonment of the barrage, he won approval for an initial infiltration of American lines by assault groups followed by the artillery. Dietrich paid little attention to the details of his sector, and remained convinced that an initial barrage would soften the American defenses and make them easy to overrun. Unlike Manteuffel, he had no experience of the infernal combat in the Hürtgen forest, and had no appreciation of the challenges posed by the wooded areas that had to be breached on the first day.

AMERICAN PLANS

Allied planning in December 1944 was in a period of transition since the opening of the port of Antwerp would permit the renewal of major Allied offensive operations within a month. A meeting of the senior leadership on 7 December was inconclusive. Montgomery reiterated his proposal for a single thrust into the Ruhr, under his command of course. Having accepted Montgomery's argument in September which resulted in the disaster at Arnhem, Eisenhower no longer had much patience and reminded him that their central objective was not territorial but the defeat of the German army. To the north of the Ardennes, Bradley hoped for a repeat of the July breakout from Normandy, but until the Roer dams were seized, the US forces would have no freedom of maneuver. After attacks by specialized RAF bombers failed to bring down the dams, two corps launched another set of ground attacks on 10 December. When the second corps joined the offensive on 13 December, it ran into fierce resistance, little realizing that it had encountered the northern shoulder of the German Ardennes attack force. Although the key Wahlerscheid crossroads were taken, the American attacks stalled. To the south of the Ardennes, Patton's Third Army had finally overcome the obstinate German resistance in the fortified city of Metz, and had pushed out of Lorraine and into the Saar. The Third Army was planning an offensive on 19 December through the Westwall towards Frankfurt. In the British 21st Army Group area to the north, Field Marshal Montgomery was planning his Rhine offensive.

There were no immediate plans for operations from the "ghost front" in the Ardennes, as the mountainous Eifel area to the east promised to be every bit as difficult as the Hürtgen forest, with no strategic objectives worth the cost. First Army used the Ardennes to rest battle-weary infantry divisions and to acquaint green divisions with life at the front. In mid-December, there were four infantry divisions in the Ardennes. In the north opposite the 6th Panzer Army were the 99th Division and the 106th Division, both green units recently arrived from the United States. Further south were two veteran divisions, the 4th and 28th Divisions that had been badly mauled during the savage fighting in the Hürtgen forest in November. Portions of another green division, 9th Armored Division, were in reserve to the rear of these units.

The senior US commanders, Omar Bradley of 12th Army Group, and Courtney Hodges of First Army, both recognized that the divisions in the Ardennes were stretched much too thinly along the frontier. Middleton's VIII Corps was stretched over three times what US doctrine considered prudent but there was no expectation of a major attack in the area. This intelligence failure resulted from two major factors: the success of the Germans in strategic deception and the conviction by senior Allied commanders that the Ardennes was unsuitable for a winter offensive.

Until the Ardennes offensive, Allied signals intelligence had provided the high command with such a steady stream of reliable intelligence data that the senior leadership had come to depend upon it. There was no evidence in the top-secret Enigma traffic of a German offensive. This was a testament to the success of the Wehrmacht in maintaining a signals blackout prior to the attack. The 12th Army Group weekly intelligence summary of 9 December 1944 concluded that the Germans were in a situation analogous to late July before the Operation Cobra breakout from Normandy. German forces were unable to replace their losses and the reserve 6th Panzer Army would be kept around Cologne to eventually respond to a breakout by either the US First or Third Army. The First Army's G-2 summary of 10 December placed greater emphasis on the possibility of a German counter-offensive but again expected it against First Army after it had crossed the Roer. General K. Strong, Eisenhower's G-2, was so alarmed by accumulating if inconclusive evidence of German reinforcement of the Ardennes that he visited Bradley in early December to express his misgivings. Bradley heard him out but repeated his belief that no strategic objectives were in the path of an attack through the Ardennes.

Colonel Oscar Koch, the Third Army G-2, convinced Patton of the likelihood of a German attack against the First Army's VIII Corps in the Ardennes, with the 6th Panzer Army as its likely spearhead. Koch and Patton did not share the view that the Germans were waiting for a First Army offensive, arguing that the likely breakthrough of the Westwall in the Third Army sector in mid-December should have caused the Germans to move part of their reserve towards the Saar in response. The fact that they had not moved suggested that they had more immediate plans to the north. On 13 December 1944, Patton sent a message to Eisenhower's headquarters warning of an Ardennes attack, and echoing Strong's concerns.

Bradley didn't think that the Germans were foolhardy enough to launch a winter attack in an area with such a restricted road network with very strong American forces on either flank. Such an assessment was the

Standartenführer Hugo Kraas commanded the 2nd SS-Panzergrenadier Regiment until assigned to command the 12th SS-Panzer Division *Hitlerjugend*. (NARA)

classic intelligence error of mirror-imaging an enemy's intentions based on one's own inclinations. The senior American commanders like Eisenhower, Bradley, and Hodges, were conservative and risk-averse in their operational planning and so could not imagine the perspective of someone as desperate and reckless as Hitler. Audacious commanders such as Patton made a more astute assessment of German intentions. In the end, Bradley was proven correct that the German attack was a foolish adventure. But the risky deployment of such a thin cover force in the Ardennes should have been accompanied by a more deliberate intelligence effort, especially in view of the accumulating evidence of German activity in the Eifel area in the days prior to the offensive. Bradley's G-2, Brigadier General Edwin Sibert, was later sacked.

After nearly three months of bloody fighting in the mud and forests along the Westwall, Bradley continued to voice the hope that the Germans would emerge from their Westwall fortifications for an all-out fight. He got far more than he wished.

Weather and Terrain

Wacht am Rhein was strongly affected by weather and terrain conditions. Weather would prove a very mixed blessing for the German attack. On the one hand, early December was overcast which limited Allied air reconnaissance before the offensive began, and Allied air attacks after the attack started. But this also meant that Luftwaffe attempts to provide air support for the offensive would be frustrated by the weather.

In terms of ground conditions, the weather had generally adverse effects on the initial phase of the German attack. The autumn weather in Belgium had been wetter than usual and the soil was saturated and muddy. Temperatures for the first week of the offensive were slightly above freezing during the day, though often below freezing at night. There was a thaw on 18 December, and the temperatures were not cold enough until 23 December to actually freeze the soil to any depth. This severely limited German mobility since vehicles, even tanks, became bogged down after they left the roads. US forces had dubbed the condition "a front one tank wide" since all traffic was road-bound. The muddy fields channeled German attack forces down available roads, and made towns and road junctions especially important. German schemes to bypass centers of resistance were impossible for the Panzer columns and their essential support vehicles. A divisional commander later recalled that the mud "played a decisive role since even undamaged tracked vehicles stuck fast. This was decisive because, towards the end of the war, our own infantry attacked unwillingly and reluctantly if there was no armored support."

Although the popular image of the Battle of the Bulge is of a snow-covered terrain, in fact, snow cover was not predominant in the first week of the fighting. Snow began to fall in the second week of November, but it did not cling due to frequent daylight thaws. The exception was in the shady forested areas, where the snow often endured. Significant snow falls did not begin until after Christmas. The weather during the first few days of the fighting was characterized by clinging ground fog especially in the early morning hours with frequent spells of rain or freezing rain, and occasional snow at night.

The northern Ardennes consists of rolling hills with woods interspersed with open farm land. The forests were often cultivated pine stands,

Major General Troy Middleton commanded the VIII Corps from Bastogne to the Schnee Eifel. (NARA)

harvested for wood. As a result, the spacing of the trees was uniform, with little undergrowth, and a pattern of fire breaks and narrow forest trails for logging. But some of the rougher hill terrain in the river valleys were pine barrens[1], with thick undergrowth. The roads from the German border into Belgium were mostly graveled. While adequate for infantry, the tanks and tracked vehicles churned them into glutinous mud trenches, trapping subsequent vehicle columns.

The initial attack area for the 6th Panzer Army was forested, varying in depth from about three to six kilometers. Beyond this was a band of open farm terrain with better roads. To the north was the Elsenborn Ridge, a shallow plateau with the upland moors of the Hohes Venn further north. This meant that once the German forces had broken out of the woods, there was a relatively open area to deploy mechanized units. The best roads out of the area towards Liège were on the Elsenborn Ridge and through Malmédy. Access via the Amblève river valley was problematic as the roads were very narrow and winding, with forested slopes on one side, and wooded drops towards the river on the other side. If this could be rapidly traversed, the region beyond was more suitable for advance.

The attack area in the 5th Panzer Army sector was significantly different since the attack was launched from farmlands towards the forested plateau of the Schnee Eifel. However, there were open areas to either side, most notably the Losheim Gap, which was a traditional access route westward. This permitted a relatively quick passage in the initial stages of the offensive, but the terrain became progressively more difficult to the west with wooded ravines and hills nearer the Meuse.

---

1 Areas where the soil is so barren (usually sandy) that pines are the only thing that will grow.

OPPOSING COMMANDERS

GERMAN COMMANDERS

Wacht am Rhein was the brainchild of Adolf Hitler. Most senior Wehrmacht commanders regarded the campaign as foolhardy. However, their influence on strategic issues had declined precipitously since the army bomb plot against Hitler of July 1944. Hitler played a central role in all the planning of *Wacht am Rhein*, and his increasingly delusional views underlay the unrealistic expectations of the campaign. Hitler's main aide in planning the Ardennes offensive was **Generaloberst Alfred Jodl**, the chief of the Wehrmacht Operations Staff. Conditioned by his traditional training to value loyalty, Jodl's unassuming manner helped him survive Hitler's irascible temper. He was injured in the bomb explosion in July 1944 and so was one of the few senior German generals to retain the Führer's confidence until the end of the war.

Field command of the German forces in the Ardennes campaign was under **Generalfeldmarshall Gerd von Rundstedt** who commanded the western theater. Rundstedt was respected by Hitler for his competence, but was outside Hitler's circle of intimates due to his blunt honesty on military matters. Unlike Jodl, Rundstedt was not afraid to tell Hitler his misgivings about his more outlandish schemes, and so he was kept out of the planning until Jodl had completed the essential details. When finally handed a copy of the draft, Hitler had personally marked it "Not to be altered". Although the American press often referred to the Ardennes attack as the "Rundstedt Offensive", in fact he had little connection to its planning or execution. After studying the plan, he concluded that the Wehrmacht would be very lucky indeed if it even reached the Meuse, never mind Antwerp.

The senior field commander for the offensive was **Generalfeldmarshall Walter Model**, commander of Army Group B. By 1944, Model had become Hitler's miracle worker. When all seemed hopeless and defeat inevitable, Hitler called on the energetic and ruthless Model to save the day. After a distinguished career as a Panzer commander during the Russian campaign, in March 1944 he became the Wehrmacht's youngest field marshal when assigned to the key position of leading Army Group North Ukraine. When Army Group Center was shattered by the Red Army's Operation Bagration in the summer of 1944, Model was assigned by Hitler the almost hopeless task of restoring order, which he accomplished. In mid-August, after German forces in France had been surrounded in the Falaise Gap, Hitler recalled Model from the eastern front and assigned him command of Army Group B. During the Ardennes offensive Model commanded the assault force: 7th Army, 5th Panzer Army, and 6th Panzer Army. Model was equally skeptical of the plan calling it "damned fragile", but he understood Germany's

A Volksgrenadier captured during the fighting around Bütgenbach in January 1945. Many of the Volksgrenadier units were provided with snowsuits or other forms of winter camouflage prior to the Ardennes offensive. (NARA)

The Panzergrenadiers of 1st SS-Panzer Div. were still wearing their autumn-pattern camouflage jackets during the initial phase of the Ardennes attack. This NCO is armed with a StG44 assault rifle, an innovation in infantry small arms and forebear of modern assault rifles. This photo is from a well-known series staged along the Poteau-Recht road on 17 December after a column from the 14th Cavalry Group had been ambushed. (NARA)

desperate situation and set about trying to execute the plan to the best of his ability.

The army commander most central in the attack in the northern sector was **SS Oberstgruppenführer Josef "Sepp" Dietrich**. Unlike the other senior German commanders, he had little formal officer training. Senior German commanders regarded him as an uncouth lout and a dim sycophant of the Führer. His military talents were damned with faint praise as those of a "splendid sergeant". He was a jovial, hard-drinking, and down-to-earth commander who was very popular with his troops. Brutal to opponents, Dietrich was maudlin and sentimental with his own soldiers. Dietrich had won the Iron Cross in World War I in a storm troop unit, and served in one of the few German tank units during 1918. He fought against the Poles with the Silesian militias in 1921 and returned to Bavaria to serve as a policeman since there were few opportunities in the army. Dietrich joined the Nazi party in 1928 and was promoted to command of the Munich SS (*Schutzstafflen*), a group of toughs formed as a personal guard for Hitler in the rough and tumble street politics of the fractious Weimar Republic. Hitler's trust in Dietrich as a reliable enforcer led to his appointment as the head of the enlarged *SS Leibstandarte Adolf Hitler* after he became Chancellor in 1933. He demonstrated his loyalty to Hitler by rounding up his brown-shirt comrades for summary execution in the "Night of the Long Knives" in 1934 when Hitler ordered the SA (*Sturmabteilung*) crushed to curry favor with the army. The *Leibstandarte* was committed to combat for the first time during the 1939 Polish campaign, gradually shaking off their reputation as "asphalt soldiers". Dietrich was a charismatic fighter, but unprepared in intellect or training to command a large formation. So the practice began of placing him in a prominent position while at the same time assigning a talented officer as his chief of staff to carry out the actual headquarters and staff functions. Dietrich was Hitler's alter ego – a common soldier of the Great War, a man of the people, a man of action, and a polar opposite to the type of intellectual, aristocratic Prussian staff officer that Hitler so despised. Dietrich was awarded the Iron Cross 1st and 2nd Class for the undistinguished performance of the *Leibstandarte* in Poland, and the Knight's Cross for their role in the French campaign. These were the first of many preposterous awards and rank increases which Hitler used as much to rankle the blue-bloods of the German military establishment as to reward Dietrich. In 1943, he was ordered to form the 1st SS-Panzer Corps, with the considerable help of his new right hand man, Colonel Fritz Kraemer, a talented staff officer who would serve with him in the Ardennes. The 1st SS-Panzer Corps was first committed to action in Normandy where it earned a formidable reputation for its obstinate and skilled defense of Caen against British tank assaults. On 1 August 1944, Dietrich was elevated to SS Oberstgruppenführer, and a few days later, Hitler added Diamonds to his Iron Cross, one of only 27 soldiers so decorated during the war. On 14 September 1944, Hitler instructed him to begin the formation of the 6th Panzer Army. Dietrich had grown increasingly despondent over the conduct of the war, but he was too inarticulate to convey his views, and too beholden to his Nazi sponsors to press his complaints with any conviction. He vaguely blamed the setbacks at the front on "sabotage", unwilling to recognize the source of the problem was the regime he so ardently served.

Dietrich's counterpart in command of the 5th Panzer Army was **General der Panzertruppen Hasso von Manteuffel**. He had none of Dietrich's political connections and started the war commanding an infantry battalion in Rommel's 7th Panzer Division in France in 1940. He won the Knight's Cross in Russia in 1941, and while still a colonel led an improvised division in Tunisia so ably that General von Arnim described him as one of his best divisional commanders. Hitler liked the brash young officer and assigned him to command the 7th Panzer Division in June 1943, and the elite *Grossdeutschland* Panzergrenadier Division later in the year. Hitler took personal interest in his career and on 1 September 1944 he was given command of 5th Panzer Army, leapfrogging to army commander in a single step, and by-passing the usual stage as a Panzer corps commander. Manteuffel learned the task the hard way during tough fighting against Patton's Third Army in Lorraine through the early autumn. His units were in continual combat with the US Army through December 1944.

AMERICAN COMMANDERS

The senior American field commander was **Lieutenant General Omar Bradley**, who commanded the 12th Army Group. This consisted of Lieutenant General William H. Simpson's Ninth Army which abutted Montgomery's 21st Army Group on the Dutch frontier, LtGen Courtney Hodges' First Army in the center from Aachen through the Ardennes, and LtGen George Patton's Third Army in the Saar. Although Bradley was junior to his three army commanders, he had formed a better impression with the Army chief of staff, George Marshall, and his immediate superior, Dwight Eisenhower who led the Supreme Headquarters Allied Expeditionary Force (SHAEF). Bradley's elevation to command over more dynamic leaders such as George Patton was in no small measure due to his better managerial talents in mastering the complexities of senior command where an appreciation for logistics was as important as tactics. Bradley was a cool infantryman in an army which was uncomfortable with the flamboyant histrionics of a charismatic cavalryman like Patton.

When Bradley was booted upstairs to command 12th Army Group in August, command of First Army fell to his aide, **Lieutenant General Courtney Hodges**. Hodges was older than Bradley and Patton, having dropped out of the US Military Academy at West Point for academic reasons. But he enlisted in the army and earned his lieutenant's bar shortly after he would have graduated. Bradley had considerable confidence in Hodges, though other American commanders felt he was not assertive enough and that he might be overly influenced by his dynamic chief of staff, Major General William Kean. His inactivity in the first days of the Ardennes fighting is something of a mystery – in the charitable view being attributed to the flu, and in the more skeptical view, to nervous exhaustion. However, he had an able staff, and Bradley played a central role in the first few days of fighting. Hodges also benefited from having some of the Army's best officers serving under him. The two corps in the northern sector near St Vith were the V Corps to the north, and the VIII Corps to its south. **Major General Leonard Gerow** of the V Corps had commanded Eisenhower in 1941 while heading the war plans division of the general staff, and was regarded as the quintessential staff officer, comfortable with planning combat operations but not leading them. To the surprise of many, he proved a very able corps commander, leading V Corps during the liberation of Paris through the Rhineland campaign. **Major General Troy Middleton** of the VIII Corps had commanded the corps since Normandy. Middleton had entered the army as a private in 1909 and had risen through the ranks to become the army's youngest regimental commander in World War I. Although he had retired before the outbreak of World War II to become a college administrator, he returned to the Army and commanded the 45th Division in Italy with distinction. Old for a corps commander, the army chief of staff remarked that he would "rather have a man with arthritis in the knee than one with arthritis in the head." When the issue of retirement was raised in 1944, Eisenhower quipped that he wanted him back in command even if he had "to be carried on a stretcher".

Of the US Army tactical commanders in this sector of the Ardennes fighting, none made a stronger impression than **Brigadier General Bruce C. Clarke**. He began his career in the National Guard and received an appointment to the Military Academy at West Point. He spent most of the inter-war years as an engineer officer, and was transferred to the new armor branch at the beginning of the war. He commanded one of the early armored engineer battalions and was instrumental in the development of a treadway pontoon bridge that could be used easily by armored units. In 1943, he became chief of staff of the 4th Armored Division, a unit that would later become the spearhead of Patton's Third Army. By the time of the Normandy fighting in July 1944, he had been appointed to lead the division's Combat Command A (CCA). He became famous for his skilled leadership in Normandy and in the subsequent

The shortage of manpower led the Waffen-SS to abandon their recruitment of volunteers and depend instead on draftees and transfers from the Luftwaffe and Kriegsmarine. Age restrictions were also loosened, as these two young soldiers from 12th SS-Panzer Div. suggest. They were captured during the fighting around Bütgenbach and a few prisoners were as young as ten. (NARA)

The workhorse of the German infantry divisions was the Sturmgeschütz III Ausf. G assault gun. These provided direct fire support for infantry units, but were usually in short supply. (MHI)

fighting in Lorraine where he often commanded the tank columns from the back seat of a Piper Cub observation aircraft. His unit was responsible for the defeat of the German Panzer counter-offensive around Arracourt. As an engineer rather than an infantryman, Clarke endured very slow career advancement. Patton jokingly told him that he was a "nobody" since the army chief of staff, George C. Marshall, had not recognized his name when he had pushed to get him a general's star. A similar situation befell another gifted engineer, **Brigadier General William Hoge**, who ended up commanding the CCB of 9th Armored Division alongside Clarke at St Vith. Patton succeeded in advancing Clarke to brigadier general, but he was obliged to switch units since there were no slots in the 4th Armored Division. Bradley had been very unhappy with the performance of the 7th Armored Division, and to rejuvenate the unit he elevated Robert Hasbrouck to command, and shifted Clarke to lead its Combat Command B. Hasbrouck and Clarke straightened out the problems in the division during November 1944 shortly before it was put to its greatest test at St Vith. There were a number of other excellent commanders in this sector as well, such as Major General Walter Robertson of the 2nd Infantry Division.

OPPOSING ARMIES

GERMAN FORCES

Dietrich's 6th Panzer Army, although it would later be redesignated as the 6th SS-Panzer Army, was in fact an amalgam of units from three combat arms – the regular army, the Waffen-SS, and the Luftwaffe's ground combat formations. This conglomeration was the result of the factional in-fighting of Hitler's cronies as they sought greater personal power in the final years of the Third Reich.

The shock force of the 6th Panzer Army was the 1st SS-Panzer Corps, composed of the 1st SS-Panzer Division *Leibstandarte Adolf Hitler* and the 12th SS-Panzer Division *Hitlerjugend*. The Waffen-SS was the Praetorian Guard of the Nazi regime and allotted the best equipment. The diminishing fighting power of these once formidable formations was evidence of the steady erosion of German military capabilities in 1944. Even though German industry was at its peak in the production of tanks and other weapons, the German armed forces were unable to transform this industrial windfall into increased combat power due to shortages of fuel and trained personnel. As a result, these Panzer divisions were significantly weaker than their American counterparts in most respects. So for example, the 1st SS-Panzer Division had only 34 PzKpfw IV, 37 Panther and 30 Kingtiger tanks for a total of 101 tanks, and the 12th SS-Panzer Division only 39 PzKpfw IV and 38 Panthers for a total of 77 tanks. A comparable American division at the time such as the 9th Armored Division had 186 M4 medium tanks, while the two heavy armored divisions (2nd and 3rd) had about 230 medium tanks. The 12th SS-Panzer Division

Aside from tanks, one of the most common German armored vehicles during the fighting on the northern shoulder was the Jagdpanzer IV/70 tank destroyer. This one from 1st SS-Panzerjäger Abteilung is seen in action with Kampfgruppe Hansen during the fighting with the 14th Cavalry Group along the Recht-Poteau road on 18 December 1944. (NARA)

was so weak in tanks that a tank destroyer formation, 560th schweres Panzerjäger Abteilung, equipped with Jagdpanzer IV and Jagdpanther tank destroyers, was attached. The Panzergrenadier battalions were supposed to be equipped with SdKfz 251 half-tracks, but in fact only one-in-four battalions were so equipped.

A more significant problem was the declining quality of troops in these units. This affected the units from top to bottom, from the officers to the ranks. Both divisions had been destroyed in the summer 1944 fighting and reconstituted in November 1944. One of the corps' officers later wrote "The level of training of the troop replacements was very poor. The Panzergrenadiers had been soldiers for only four to six weeks but instead of receiving basic training in this period, they had been employed cleaning away debris in towns damaged by air raids. Replacements in the Panzer regiments had never ridden in a tank, let alone driven one, or fired from one, or sent messages from one by radio. Furthermore, the majority of the drivers have not had more than one or two hours driving lessons before obtaining their driver's license. The casualties in officers had been exceptionally high during the hard battles of the summer, so that including the battalion and regimental commanders, it was mostly officers inexperienced in combat who had to lead these troops." Previously, the Waffen-SS had relied on volunteers but, by the autumn of 1944, it was forced to accept transfers from Luftwaffe ground personnel as well as underage recruits. The training problem was exacerbated by restrictions imposed by the lack of fuel, preventing any significant formation training above platoon level after the units were re-equipped in mid-November. There was also very little firing practice with live ammunition. The two Panzer divisions were rated only as *Kampfwert III*, that is suitable for defensive operations, *Kampfwert I* indicating suitability for offensive operations. The Waffen-SS divisions had won their reputation for stubborn defensive fighting and had far less experience in offensive Panzer operations. Due to the declining training, tactics were unsophisticated and tended towards the

brute force approach. The chief of staff of the neighboring 5th Panzer Army complained that their lack of road discipline was a major cause of the traffic jams that hindered the initial advance, and that their reconnaissance skills were poor. Commanders of the Panzer spearheads such as Peiper were remarkably indifferent to the requirements for bridging and other engineering support during offensive operations.

If the situation in the elite formations was discouraging, it was even worse in the three infantry divisions of 1st SS-Panzer Corps that were expected to make the initial breakthrough. The best of the three divisions was the 12th Volksgrenadier Division (VGD), which was personally selected by Hitler to lead the attack due to its excellent performance in the defense of Aachen. Having suffered heavy casualties in the autumn fighting, it had been withdrawn into Germany only on 2 December for hasty refitting prior to the offensive. The other Volksgrenadier divisions had been created to fill the growing gap in infantry divisions in the German order of battle. They were easier and cheaper to raise, having less support equipment than normal infantry divisions, and older personnel of very mixed quality with an average age of 35 years. Some of their troops were drawn from the barrel-scrapings of the personnel pool, others were transfers from idle support units of the navy and air force. The 277th VGD had been gutted in the Normandy fighting and reconstituted in Hungary in September 1944 after absorbing the remains of the shattered 374th VGD. It was fleshed out with young Austrian conscripts who lacked the usual German basic training, ethnic German *volksdeutche* from eastern Europe, and Alsatians. The latter two groups were characterized by the divisional commander as "an untrustworthy element". It was rated as *Kampfwert III*, suitable for defense. Though still under strength, the division was deployed for static defense along the Westwall for most of the autumn and gradually brought up to strength with transfers from the navy and air force with no infantry training. The US Army had faced the 3rd Fallschirmjäger Division in the hedgerows of Normandy the previous summer and considered the paratroopers to be some of the toughest opponents they had ever fought.

A major advantage enjoyed by US forces in the Ardennes campaign was superior artillery. This is a 155mm howitzer of the 254th Field Artillery Battalion providing support to the 82nd Airborne Division near Werbomont on 2 January 1945. (NARA)

As in the case of the Waffen-SS Panzer divisions, this division had been decimated in the Normandy fighting and was a shadow of its former self. Replacement troops came mainly from Luftwaffe support units with no infantry training to say nothing of paratroop training. Casualties among the officers and troop leaders had been crippling, and some senior command positions had been filled by Luftwaffe staff officers with no infantry experience. It had been further weakened by almost continual combat through the late autumn, and arrived in the Ardennes with little opportunity to rebuild.

Dietrich's 6th Panzer Army had two more corps, the 2nd SS-Panzer Corps, and the 67th Infantry Corps. The 2nd SS-Panzer Corps, including the 2nd SS-Panzer Division *Das Reich* and the 9th SS-Panzer Division *Hohenstaufen* was in army reserve waiting until the 1st SS-Panzer Corps completed the breakthrough to the Meuse. It saw no fighting in the initial stage of the campaign. The 67th Army Corps was located on the northern flank and consisted of Volksgrenadier units intended to serve as a blocking force.

Fuel would be a constant problem. At the outset of the campaign, the divisions carried enough fuel with them to travel 100km under normal conditions. But in the move from staging areas to the front in the days before the attack, the divisions found that the terrain and the drivers' inexperience led to such high consumption that only 50–60km could be covered with the remaining fuel. A resupply of another 100km-worth was brought up on the morning of 16 December 1944. Although a significant stockpile of fuel had been built up for the offensive, it was far behind the frontlines and difficult to move forward. The fuel situation was exacerbated by the use of tanks such as the Panther and Kingtiger that consumed 350 and 500 liters of fuel per 100km of road travel. By comparison, the PzKpfw IV consumed only 200 to 210 liters of fuel – between 40 and 60 per cent of a Panther's or Kingtiger's consumption.

Long range firepower for the US Army was provided by the 155mm gun, which was assigned to separate battalions at corps or army level. This is a 155mm gun of the 981st Field Artillery Battalion in action near Heppenbach in the Schnee Eifel towards the end of the Ardennes campaign in late January 1945. (NARA)

The quality of artillery support was mixed. Besides the divisional artillery, each of the three corps had an additional heavy artillery battalion with guns of between 150mm and 210mm caliber. The 1st SS-Panzer Corps also had two Nebelwerfer rocket artillery brigades, three heavy artillery batteries and two to three *Volksartillerie* corps. These later formations each had six battalions of artillery, but were formed from a wide range of artillery types including captured foreign designs, presenting an ammunition headache. The artillery was supposed to be allotted a 14-day supply of ammunition but in fact received about ten days supply. Resupply after the start of the offensive was very meager since the dumps were near Bonn and subject to Allied air interdiction.

AMERICAN FORCES

The principal US units opposite the 6th Panzer Army were two green infantry divisions, the 99th and 106th Divisions. The 99th Division, the "Battlin' Babes", was the southernmost unit of Gerow's V Corps, stretching along the Siegfried Line from Hofen to Lanzerath. It had arrived in Belgium in mid-November, replaced the 9th Division on the frontline, and had become reasonably well acclimatized to the front. The division had been formed in 1942, but in March 1944, 3,000 riflemen were pulled from its ranks to make up for combat losses in Italy. Their places were filled by young men from the ASTP program.

The Army Specialized Training Program (ASTP) was an effort by the army chief of staff, General George C. Marshall, to divert the smartest young soldiers into advanced academic training. At a time when less than five per cent of young men went to college, Marshall did not want to waste their talents and had them sent for further schooling rather than to the battlefield. ASTP came to abrupt end in 1944 when rising casualties created an immediate need for troops, so 100,000 ASTP college students were transferred to active service. Some were sent as

engineers to the secret atomic bomb program, others to technical branches of the army, but most ended up as riflemen.

Although the Ardennes was a quiet front compared to the Hürtgen forest, the division suffered moderate casualties during its first month at the front. The US Army had not paid enough attention to the need for winter clothing or boots, and what resources were available in Europe were scandalously mismanaged. Some of the division's rifle platoons had suffered 30 per cent casualties in the latter half of November, more than half due to trench foot. On the positive side, the division's forward rifle companies had time to dig in, creating a network of foxholes and shelters with log roofs that would reduce artillery casualties in the ensuing battle. The division covered a 12-mile wide sector from the hilly Monschau forest, south to the more open country near Losheim.

The 106th Division had a less fortunate experience. The division was formed in early 1943 and by the spring of 1944 was ready to take the field. However, from April to August 1944, the division was gutted as more than 7,000 of its riflemen were shipped off to serve as replacements. They were replaced at the last minute by a mixture of ASTP students, gunners from anti-aircraft and coastal artillery units, military policemen and service personnel. This process had hardly ended when the division was shipped off to England in October 1944. Not only did the 106th Division have less unit cohesion than the 99th Division, but it arrived much later. It took over the northern sector of Middleton's VIII Corps from the 2nd Infantry Division on 11 December, a few days before the German attack. To make matters worse, the division was thinly spread along a 15-mile front projecting into German lines on the Schnee Eifel plateau. The previous tenants of this position, the 2nd Infantry Division, had complained about its precarious location, but higher headquarters were reluctant to pull the units back as they sat within the German Westwall defensive belt.

This was one of five Panthers of the first company of 12th SS-Panzer Regiment that fought their way into Krinkelt around 0730 on 18 December. Four were knocked out by bazooka teams and anti-tank guns and this vehicle escaped down the Büllingen road where it was knocked out by a M10 3in. GMC of the 644th Tank Destroyer Battalion around 1100hrs. It had 11 bazooka hits, several 57mm hits and three 3in. impacts in the rear. (NARA)

The 99th and 106th Divisions sat on the boundary between Gerow's V Corps to the north, and Middleton's VIII Corps to the south. Between them was the eight mile Losheim Gap. This area was covered by the 14th Cavalry Group with two armored cavalry reconnaissance squadrons. These cavalry groups, as their name suggests, were intended for scouting and not positional defense. Although they had considerable firepower for such small units, this was mostly mounted on the squadrons' jeeps and light armored vehicles and was of little use when the unit was deployed in a dismounted defensive position. The squadrons' tactics were summarized as "sneak and peek", and they were spread much too thinly to create any sort of credible barrier. It was not unusual for a cavalry group to be placed along a corps boundary during offensive operations, since they could be used for mobile screening, but they were not well suited to this role when the mission became defensive. The first of its squadrons deployed on 10 December and the second did not follow until 15 December. As a result, the corps boundary, which happened to be situated on a traditional invasion route, was weakly protected by a unit very ill-suited to a defensive role. It was no coincidence that the German plan aimed its heaviest strike force through this area.

In view of the composition of the attacking German forces, it is worth mentioning the anti-tank capabilities of the US Army. The organic anti-tank defense of the infantry divisions was a license copy of the British 6-pdr, the 57mm anti-tank gun. There were 57 in each division, with 18 in each regiment. By 1944 this gun was obsolete, and the official history of the campaign pungently describes them as "tank fodder". A more useful weapon was the 2.35in. anti-tank rocket launcher, more popularly called the bazooka. There were 557 in each division, and they were generally allotted on a scale of one per rifle squad. Their warhead

An aerial view of Krinkelt (to the left) and Rocherath (to the right). This view looks westward. (MHI)

was not as effective as comparable German weapons such as the *Panzerfaust* or *Panzerschreck*, but in the hands of a brave soldier, they could disable German tanks by a well-placed side or rear hit. Most infantry divisions had an attached tank destroyer battalion equipped with 36 3in. anti-tank guns. Unfortunately, in the spring of 1943, the organization of these units was changed, and a portion of the force was converted from self-propelled M10 3in. gun motor carriages to towed 3in. guns based on a mistaken assessment of the Tunisian campaign. These towed battalions proved to be poorly suited to conditions in the European theater, and the two battalions attached to the infantry in the St Vith sector were this configuration, as was the battalion attached to the unfortunate 14th Cavalry Group.

There were a few bright spots in the American dispositions. The battle-hardened 2nd Infantry Division had been pulled off the Schnee Eifel in early December with the arrival of the 106th Division, and had been shifted northward to take part in the V Corps offensive against the Roer dams in mid-December. Some elements of the division were still intermixed with the 99th Division or stationed on the nearby Elsenborn Ridge. The proximity and combat readiness of this unit would play a crucial role in the US Army's subsequent ability to hold the northern shoulder of the Bulge.

ORDER OF BATTLE – NORTHERN SECTOR

GERMAN FORCES

6th Panzer Army
1st SS-Panzer Corps
1st SS-Panzer Division
12th SS-Panzer Division
12th Volksgrenadier Division
277th Volksgrenadier Division
3rd Fallschirmjäger Division
Panzer Brigade 150

Oberstgruppenführer Josef Dietrich
Gruppenführer Hermann Preiss
Oberführer Wilhelm Mohnke
Standartenführer Hugo Kraas
Generalmajor Gerhard Engel
Oberst Wilhelm Viebig
Generalmajor Walther Wadehn
Obersturmbannführer Otto Skorzeny

5th Panzer Army
66th Army Corps
18th Volksgrenadier Division
62nd Volksgrenadier Division
116th Panzer Division
Führer Begleit Brigade

General Hasso von Manteuffel
General der Artillerie Walther Lucht
Oberst Gunter Hoffman-Schönborn
Oberst Friedrich Kittel
Generalmajor Siegfried von Waldenberg
Oberst Otto Remer

AMERICAN FORCES

First US Army
V Corps
2nd Infantry Division
99th Infantry Division

LtGen Courtney H. Hodges
MajGen Leroy T. Gerow
MajGen Walter M. Robertson
MajGen Walter E. Lauer

VIII Corps
106th Infantry Division
CCB, 9th Armored Division

MajGen Troy H. Middleton
MajGen Alan W. Jones
BrigGen William Hoge

XVIII Airborne Corps (20 December)
82nd Airborne Division
7th Armored Division
30th Infantry Division

MajGen Matthew B. Ridgway
MajGen James M. Gavin
MajGen Robert W. Hasbrouck
MajGen Leland S. Hobbs

OPENING MOVES

Melodramatically renamed as Operation *Herbstnebel* (Autumn Mist), the Ardennes offensive began in the pre-dawn hours of Saturday, 16 December 1944. The artillery of 1st SS-Panzer Corps opened fire at 0530hrs, about two hours before dawn. The initial barrage fell on the forward lines of American trenches. The projectiles as often as not exploded in the trees overhead: a deadly pattern for exposed troops but not to the US infantry who were in log-covered trenches. Five minutes after the barrage began, the forward edge of the battlefield was illuminated by German searchlight units, which trained their lights upward against the low cloud cover, creating an eerie artificial dawn. After 15 minutes of firing, the artillery redirected their fire against secondary defensive lines and key crossroads. The fire strikes on crossroads had more effect since they often succeeded in tearing up field telephone networks. There were two more barrages, each directed further into the US defenses, finally concluding around 0700. The promised Luftwaffe support failed to materialize due to the low cloud cover. The 6th Panzer Army plan assigned five advance routes for the Panzer spearheads, labeled Rollbahn A through E.

Opening Rollbahn A and B – Battle for the Twin Villages

The northernmost element of the German attack was an attempt by the 67th Corps in the Monschau forest to push through the left wing of the 99th Division's defenses from Hofen to Wahlerscheid. This attack was

Kraas' decision to commit his Panzer regiment to the fight led to heavy tank casualties in the streets of Krinkelt. The nearest of these two Panther Ausf. G, probably that of SS-Hauptsturmführer Kurt Brodel, has been burned out and its barrel ripped off. They were knocked out in the fighting opposite the village church. (NARA)

Another view of the Panzer graveyard inside the Twin Villages, in this case another of *Hitlerjugend*'s destroyed Panther Ausf. G tanks. (MHI)

carried out by the 326th Volksgrenadier Division through forested, hilly terrain not unlike the neighboring Hürtgen forest. Without any significant armor support, the attack was stopped cold by the 395th Infantry of the 99th Division. The positions of the forward rifle platoons had been registered by the US regimental artillery, and in the cases where the German infantry reached the forward trench lines, they were pummeled mercilessly while the US infantry remained within the cover of their foxholes. This was the one sector of the front where the German offensive made no significant inroads. An attack the following day met the same results, and the division was withdrawn to its start line where it remained for the remainder of the campaign.

The most significant objective in the northern sector of the 1st SS-Panzer Corps zone was the small village of Krinkelt, which blended into the neighboring village of Rocherath. As a result, fighting for Krinkelt-Rocherath is frequently called the battle of the Twin Villages. Krinkelt sat near the junction of two roads which led towards the old Belgian army camp at Elsenborn and the ridge line in front of the Hohes Venn moor.

The initial assault was conducted by the 277th VGD through a wooded area covered by the 393rd Infantry of the 99th Division. The US regiment had only two battalions, its 2nd Battalion having been assigned to the aborted Roer dam attacks a few days before. These were initially deployed in a trench line on the eastern edge of woods along the International Highway. Their defensive focus was two forest trails, the Schwarzenbruch and Weissenstein trails that led to the open farm country in front of the villages. Two of the 277th VGD regiments took part in the first day's attack, the 989th Grenadier Regiment from Hollerath along the Schwarzenbruch trail, and the 990th Grenadier Regiment from Neuhof towards the Weissenstein trail. A plan for the third regiment to create a route to Rollbahn B through a southern trail towards Mürringen was abandoned due to the late arrival of the regiment, and instead both routes were redirected through the villages. The *Hitlerjugend* commander, SS-Oberführer Hugo Kraas, was concerned that the attack groups were not strong enough, and assembled a small battlegroup consisting of a battalion from the 25th SS-Panzergrenadier Regiment supported by Jagdpanzer IV tank destroyers to stiffen the attack if necessary.

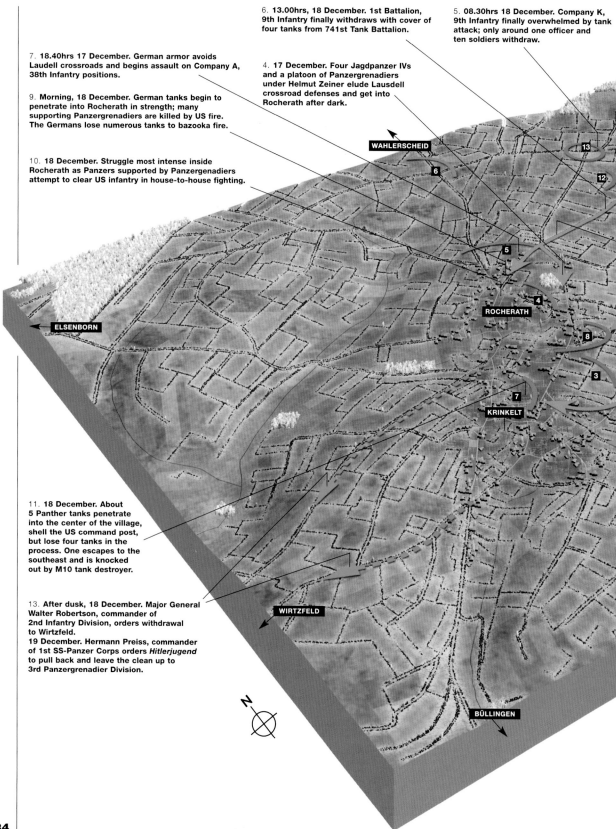

6. **13.00hrs, 18 December. 1st Battalion, 9th Infantry finally withdraws with cover of four tanks from 741st Tank Battalion.**

5. **08.30hrs 18 December. Company K, 9th Infantry finally overwhelmed by tank attack; only around one officer and ten soldiers withdraw.**

7. **18.40hrs 17 December. German armor avoids Laudell crossroads and begins assault on Company A, 38th Infantry positions.**

4. **17 December. Four Jagdpanzer IVs and a platoon of Panzergrenadiers under Helmut Zeiner elude Lausdell crossroad defenses and get into Rocherath after dark.**

9. **Morning, 18 December. German tanks begin to penetrate into Rocherath in strength; many supporting Panzergrenadiers are killed by US fire. The Germans lose numerous tanks to bazooka fire.**

10. **18 December. Struggle most intense inside Rocherath as Panzers supported by Panzergenadiers attempt to clear US infantry in house-to-house fighting.**

11. **18 December. About 5 Panther tanks penetrate into the center of the village, shell the US command post, but lose four tanks in the process. One escapes to the southeast and is knocked out by M10 tank destroyer.**

13. **After dusk, 18 December. Major General Walter Robertson, commander of 2nd Infantry Division, orders withdrawal to Wirtzfeld.
19 December. Hermann Preiss, commander of 1st SS-Panzer Corps orders *Hitlerjugend* to pull back and leave the clean up to 3rd Panzergrenadier Division.**

WAHLERSCHEID

ELSENBORN

ROCHERATH

KRINKELT

WIRTZFELD

BÜLLINGEN

N

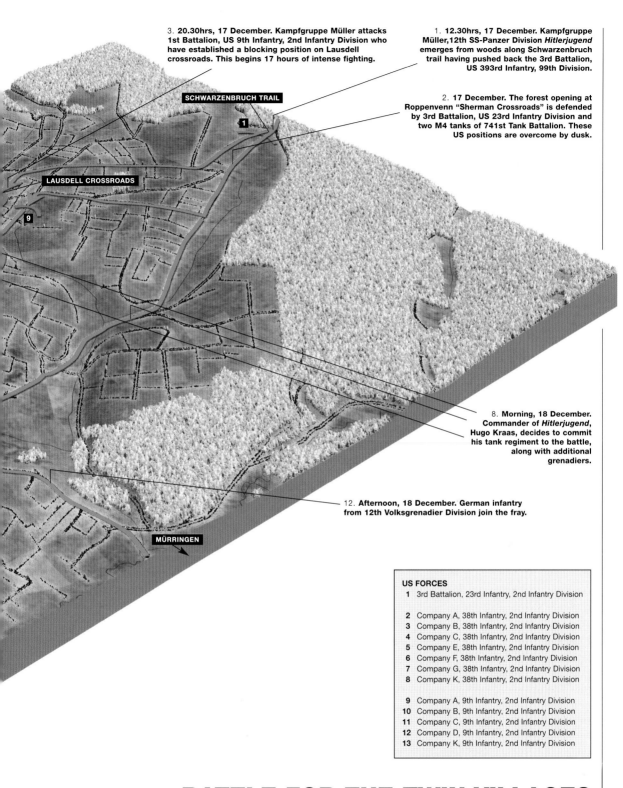

3. **20.30hrs, 17 December.** Kampfgruppe Müller attacks 1st Battalion, US 9th Infantry, 2nd Infantry Division who have established a blocking position on Lausdell crossroads. This begins 17 hours of intense fighting.

1. **12.30hrs, 17 December.** Kampfgruppe Müller, 12th SS-Panzer Division *Hitlerjugend* emerges from woods along Schwarzenbruch trail having pushed back the 3rd Battalion, US 393rd Infantry, 99th Division.

SCHWARZENBRUCH TRAIL

2. **17 December.** The forest opening at Roppenvenn "Sherman Crossroads" is defended by 3rd Battalion, US 23rd Infantry Division and two M4 tanks of 741st Tank Battalion. These US positions are overcome by dusk.

LAUSDELL CROSSROADS

8. **Morning, 18 December.** Commander of *Hitlerjugend*, Hugo Kraas, decides to commit his tank regiment to the battle, along with additional grenadiers.

12. **Afternoon, 18 December.** German infantry from 12th Volksgrenadier Division join the fray.

MÜRRINGEN

US FORCES

1	3rd Battalion, 23rd Infantry, 2nd Infantry Division
2	Company A, 38th Infantry, 2nd Infantry Division
3	Company B, 38th Infantry, 2nd Infantry Division
4	Company C, 38th Infantry, 2nd Infantry Division
5	Company E, 38th Infantry, 2nd Infantry Division
6	Company F, 38th Infantry, 2nd Infantry Division
7	Company G, 38th Infantry, 2nd Infantry Division
8	Company K, 38th Infantry, 2nd Infantry Division
9	Company A, 9th Infantry, 2nd Infantry Division
10	Company B, 9th Infantry, 2nd Infantry Division
11	Company C, 9th Infantry, 2nd Infantry Division
12	Company D, 9th Infantry, 2nd Infantry Division
13	Company K, 9th Infantry, 2nd Infantry Division

BATTLE FOR THE TWIN VILLAGES

17–18 December 1944, viewed from the south-west showing the series of costly attacks by 12th SS-Panzer Division *Hitlerjugend* on the twin villages of Krinkelt and Rocherath, defended by elements of US 38th and 9th Infantry Regiments, 2nd Infantry Division.

During the first day's fighting, the 989th Grenadiers managed to overrun a company of the 3/393rd Infantry in the first rush, and infiltrated through the woods between the two battalions, reaching the Jansbach stream about half way through the woods. Although the German attack had been halted well short of its objective, casualties in the 3/393rd Infantry amounted to nearly half its troops.

Further south, the attack of the 990th Grenadier Regiment began half an hour after the artillery barrage had lifted and the US infantry was well prepared. As the German infantry moved through the fog in the fields approaching the woods, they were hit by concentrated small arms and artillery fire. The divisional commander attempted to restart the attack by reinforcing it with some Jagdpanzer 38(t) but this attack also failed. In frustration, the divisional commander ordered the reserve regiment, the 991st Grenadier Regiment into action in the hope of outflanking the American positions. This attack was also stopped without any significant gains, but the 1/393rd Infantry suffered about 30 per cent casualties in the process. German casualties had been heavy, especially among the officers. Due to the poor training and poor quality of the new troops, the senior officers were forced to lead from the front and in three days of fighting, the 277th Volksgrenadier Division lost all its battalion commanders and 80 per cent of its company commanders, along with the majority of its NCOs, rendering the division unsuitable for any further offensive combat.

Frustrated by the delays, the corps commander, Gruppenführer Preiss ordered *Hitlerjugend* to commit its task force to assist in clearing the route the next day. On the US side, the 2nd Infantry Division was ordered to continue its attacks towards the Roer dams on the first day of the German offensive, with First Army commander Hodges believing the attack was only a spoiling action. But by afternoon, the divisional commander, MajGen Walter Robertson, realized that a major attack was underway and that it was imperative that the flank be secured. He began

to redeploy units to reinforce Elsenborn Ridge. The 3/23rd Infantry was alerted to move to Krinkelt on 16 December and arrived in the late afternoon, deploying at the edge of woods where the two main trails emerged.

In the early morning hours of 17 December, the commander of the 3/393rd Infantry ordered a counterattack down the Schwarzenbruch trail. In the meantime, the Panzer reinforcements had reached 989th Grenadier Regiment. The two attacks were launched in the early morning and careened into one another. Even though a pair of German tank destroyers were damaged by bazooka fire, the weaker American attack was halted. Under pressure, the US battalion withdrew to the western forest edge towards a roadblock covered by a newly arrived company from the 3/23rd Infantry and a pair of M4 tanks. The neighboring 1/393rd Infantry was ordered to withdraw at 1100hrs to prevent it from being cut off by Volksgrenadiers who continued to move forward through the gap between the two battalions in the woods. The continuing attack by the battalion from the 25th SS-Panzergrenadier Regiment along the Schwarzenbruch trail suffered heavy casualties on encountering the fresh 3/23rd Infantry, but the arrival of the tank destroyers settled the matter and overwhelmed the American positions. On reaching the edge of the woods, the Panzers came under fire from two M4 tanks of the 741st Tank Battalion, but both US tanks were quickly knocked out. By the end of the day, the Panzergrenadier battalion had lost so many officers in the intense fighting that "companies were being commanded by sergeants". Shortly before noon, Kraas, the 12th SS-Panzer Division commander, decided to commit a battalion of Panther tanks, the remainder of the Panzergrenadier regiment and an assault gun battalion to reinforce the attack, hoping to reinvigorate the stalled and badly delayed advance.

By dusk on 17 December, the 989th Grenadier Regiment of 277th Volksgrenadier Division had finally pushed out of the woods and the stalled 990th Grenadier Regiment was ordered to withdraw from its

Artillery played a vital role in the defense of Krinkelt-Rocherath, and as the battle reached its peak, eight US artillery battalions took part, firing nearly 30,000 rounds during the fighting. This is the 38th Field Artillery Battalion, 2nd Infantry Division on the Elsenborn Ridge on 20 December. (NARA)

PANZER GRAVEYARD – 2ND INFANTRY DIVISION VS. 12TH SS-PANZER DIVISION IN KRINKELT, 18 DECEMBER 1944
(pages 38–39)

In his impatience to get his division back on schedule, the commander of the 12th SS-Panzer Division *Hitlerjugend*, General Kraas decided to commit his Panzer regiment to help rout out the American infantry in the streets of Krinkelt. The town was shrouded in fog and icy rain, and the green GIs of the recently arrived 99th "Battlin' Babes" Division were intermixed with the hardened veterans of the 2nd Infantry Division. The twin villages of Krinkelt and Rocherath were typical of farm communities in this rural region, with sturdy buildings made of stone. They proved to be ideal defensive positions for the US infantry. Most of the German Panzergrenadiers who were supposed to accompany the tanks into the town were stripped away from the Panzers by small arms fire before they reached the village. The Panther tanks blundered down the narrow streets, nearly blind, and with no infantry support. Although it was probably the best tank of World War II, the Panther tank was not suited for urban warfare. Its sides and rear could be penetrated by the unreliable bazooka rocket launchers used by the US infantry, and the Panzers were mercilessly hunted by US anti-tank teams all day long. The bazooka gunner seen here (1) would operate as part of a team with the other infantrymen providing cover against the small number of German infantry who made it through the gauntlet of fire at the edge of town. The bazooka teams were supported by a number of US medium tanks and M10 tank destroyers, and the damage to this Panther's gun barrel suggests it was hit by a high velocity anti-tank round, not a bazooka. The tank shown here was the most modern version of the series, the Panther Ausf. G and was knocked out and burned on the street opposite the village church. It is painted in the usual German three-color camouflage scheme, which at this time was a base coat of red lead primer with a pattern of dark yellow and dark olive green. The markings on this tank are also fairly typical and include a three digit tactical number with the first digit identifying the company and the second digit the platoon. The German national insignia was not prominent. The GIs display the usual motley assortment of autumn battledress found in December 1944. The US Army was not well prepared for the winter weather, and issued the troops a variety of winter clothing. The most practical was the Model 1943 field jacket (2), which was designed to be worn with layers of sweaters and other clothing for added warmth. But this was not available in sufficient quantities, and so many GIs were issued inferior alternatives, including the outdated and cumbersome Model 1942 wool Melton overcoat (3). The overcoat was a particularly poor choice in the early December weather as it tended to absorb the cold rain common during the first days of the battle, and once wet, it offered little warmth when freezing temperatures returned in the evening. Some GIs also were issued the older Mackinaw jacket (4), but these were not as common as the overcoat. The standard infantry weapon was the M1 Garand rifle, and this was supplemented by the squad automatic weapon, the BAR (Browning Automatic Rifle).
(Howard Gerrard)

fruitless attack and fall in behind it. Frustrated by the poor performance of the infantry in breaking through the woods, Kraas ordered his SS Panzergrenadiers to continue the attack through the night.

As the remnants of the 3/23rd Infantry and 3/393rd Infantry were pulling back from the forest line, about 600 men of Lieutenant Colonel William McKinley's 1/9th Infantry, 2nd Infantry Division had been moved behind them and set up defensive positions near the Lausdell crossroads on the outskirts of Rocherath. The crossroads covered the trails leading into the northern end of Rocherath from the woods. The battalion had suffered nearly 50 per cent casualties in several days of fighting at Wahlerscheid in the Roer Dams operation, and even after Co. K, 3/9th Infantry was added, the battalion was still under-strength. McKinley, the grandson and namesake of the former US president, organized bazooka teams and had his troops lay anti-tank mines along the road.

The first German probe by four Jagdpanzer IV tank destroyers and infantry exited the woods after dark in the midst of a snow squall, and they evaded the Lausdell roadblock, reaching the town square in Krinkelt. A confused fight began with a handful of M4 medium tanks and M10 tank destroyers, and house-to-house fighting erupted between the Panzergrenadiers and GIs.

Subsequent German columns were brought under fire by American artillery, directed by McKinley's units at the crossroads. But in the dark and fog, some German units continued to infiltrate past the defenses into the villages. Confused fighting engulfed Lausdell but the US infantry disabled a number of German armored vehicles with bazookas and chains of mines pulled in front of advancing German columns. The German commander reinforced his spearhead and launched a concerted attack against the crossroads at 2230hrs. The Lausdell position was so vital to the American defense that all the available artillery, numbering some seven battalions with 112 howitzers, was directed to break up the attack even though radio communication with McKinley's battalion had been lost. After a pulverizing artillery concentration fell on all the roads leading into Lausdell, the German attacks finally bogged down around 2315hrs. McKinley's defense of the Lausdell crossroads on 17 December allowed the 2nd Infantry Division to move its 38th Infantry Regiment into Krinkelt-Rocherath to defend the approaches to the Elsenborn Ridge. It was reinforced by companies from the 741st Tank Battalion and the 644th Tank Destroyer Battalion.

To finally overcome the American roadblock, Kraas committed the remainder of his Panzer regiment to the fray in the early morning of 18 December along with another Panzergrenadier battalion. Colonel McKinley had been ordered to withdraw back to the villages before dawn, but the Germans struck first. In the early morning drizzle and fog, Panther tanks overran the forward defenses, firing point-blank into the trenches with their guns. One infantry company called in artillery fire on its own positions, which stopped the German attack but only a dozen GIs survived the barrage. McKinley's decimated battalion held its ground, and most of the German forces bypassed the crossroads to the south and charged directly into Rocherath. McKinley's force was finally extracted at 1115 when an artillery barrage was ordered to shield it from any further attacks from the woods while a local counterattack by four

M4 tanks cleared a path into Rocherath past the Panzers. Of the original 600 men, only 217 returned to US lines. Charles B. McDonald, present at the battle as a young company commander with the 23rd Infantry and later a senior US Army historian, wrote: "for all the defenses of many other American units during the German counteroffensive, probably none exceeded and few equaled McKinley's battalion in valor and sacrifice".

Besides the attack against the Lausdell crossroads, additional assaults backed by Panzers broke into the villages from north and south. During the course of the day, the assaults were reinforced by units of the 12th Volksgrenadier Division, which had come up from the south via Mürringen. Much of the German infantry was stripped away by artillery and small arms fire. With little infantry support, the Panther tanks became involved in deadly cat-and-mouse games with US bazooka teams scurrying through the stone buildings in the villages. A German tank commander later described the town as a "Panzer graveyard". House-to-house fighting continued inside the villages for most of the day, but at nightfall, Krinkelt and Rocherath were still in American hands, with pockets of German infantry and Panzers at the edge of the villages.

By the evening of 18 December, both sides were reassessing their options. Sepp Dietrich, realizing that he was badly behind schedule, suggested to Preiss, that he disengage from Krinkelt-Rocherath and move *Hitlerjugend* via the southern routes. Preiss was unwilling to do so, as Rollbahn C and D already went through Büllingen to the south. This would lead to all four columns being funneled through a very narrow corridor and his northern column needed to get on to the Elsenborn Ridge. As a compromise, Preiss agreed to pull out *Hitlerjugend* and to substitute the 3rd Panzergrenadier Division to continue the attack on to the Elsenborn Ridge once Krinkelt and Rocherath were finally cleared. At roughly the same time, MajGen Robertson had concluded that the defense of Krinkelt-Rocherath had become untenable and it was time to withdraw to the Elsenborn Ridge.

The German infantry, with tank support, resumed their attacks in the villages the following morning but were greeted with heavy fire from eight field artillery battalions. Around 1345hrs, Robertson radioed his commanders in the Twin Villages and told them that the withdrawal would begin after nightfall at 1730 with the units from the northern edge of Rocherath pulling out first, and gradually withdrawing the units from the center and the southern edge of Krinkelt. The withdrawal would be to the next largest town to the west, Wirtzfeld. The rearguard consisted of a small number of M4 tanks and M10 tank destroyers and was successfully executed in the dark.

The fighting for Krinkelt-Rocherath had effectively blocked the 12th SS-Panzer Div. *Hitlerjugend* for three entire days. Although the German plans had expected *Hitlerjugend* to reach the Meuse on the second day, they had barely reached a depth of ten kilometers. The defense of the Twin Villages enabled the V Corps to build up an impregnable defense along the Elsenborn Ridge, thereby denying the Germans the shortest route to the Meuse. A later US study concluded that *Hitlerjugend* lost 111 tanks, assault guns and other armored vehicles in the fighting, which is an exaggeration. German records are far from complete and it would appear that about 60 AFVs were knocked out of

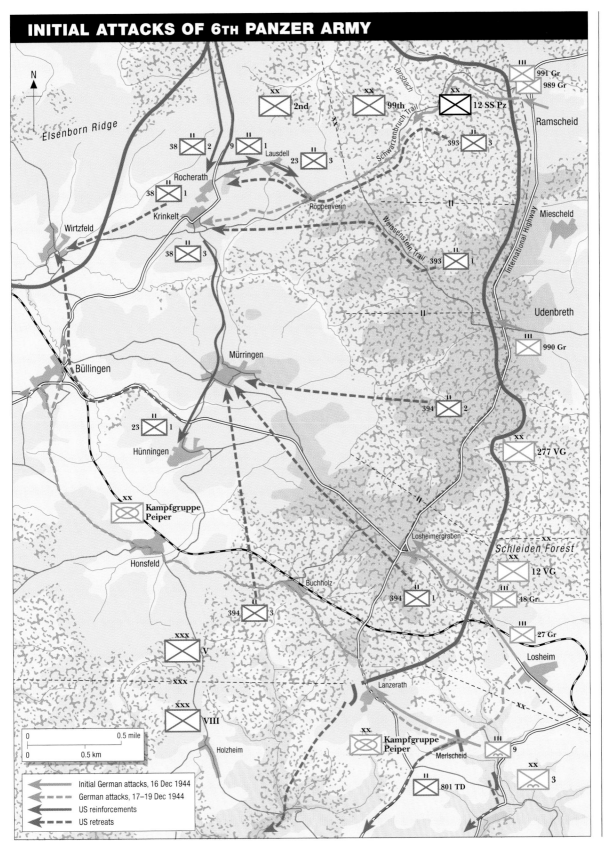

INITIAL ATTACKS OF 6TH PANZER ARMY

Elsenborn Ridge

2nd

99th

12 SS Pz

991 Gr
989 Gr

Ramscheid

38   2   9   1
Lausdell
23   3

393   3

38   1
Rocherath

Röppenverin

Miescheld

38   3
Krinkelt

Wirtzfeld

Weissenstein Trail

393   1

Udenbreth

Mürringen

990 Gr

Büllingen

394   2

23   1

Hünningen

277 VG

Kampfgruppe
Peiper

Losheimergraben

Schleiden Forest

Honsfeld

12 VG

Buchholz

48 Gr

394   1

394   3

27 Gr

Losheim

V

XXX

VIII

Lanzerath

| 0 | | 0.5 mile |
| 0 | | 0.5 km |

Holzheim

Kampfgruppe
Peiper

Merlscheid

9

3

801 TD

Initial German attacks, 16 Dec 1944
German attacks, 17–19 Dec 1944
US reinforcements
US retreats

43

which 31 tanks and assault guns and 14 light armored vehicles were total
losses. But time was far more precious than hardware, and the loss was
unredeemable.

Opening Rollbahn C and D –
Losheimergraben and Buchholz Station

Of all the road networks in the Sixth Army sector, none were more
important than those leading west out of Losheim. Originally, the plan
called for a regiment of the 277th Volksgrenadier Div. to open a route
from Udenbreth to Mürringen for *Hitlerjugend* but its late arrival
made this impossible. Instead, Losheim became the start point of both
Rollbahns C and D, and so, in theory, the start points of the heavy battle

During the fighting in Büllingen on 17 December, the spearhead of Kampfgruppe Peiper, a company of PzKpfw IV tanks led by SS-Obersturmführer Werner Sternebeck became disoriented and headed out of town north instead of west towards Witrzfeld. About a mile out of town the two lead Panzers were knocked out by some M10 3in. GMC of the 644th Tank Destroyer Battalion. (NARA)

groups of both the 1st SS-Panzer and 12th SS-Panzer Divisions. In the event, *Hitlerjugend* became bogged down in fighting at Krinkelt-Rocherath, and later at Dom Bütgenbach, and so its planned Panzer drive along Rollbahn C never materialized.

The German assault to capture this road-net was led by the 12th Volksgrenadier Division from Losheim along the International Highway where it met Losheimergraben and the route to Büllingen. The division attacked with two regiments, 27th Grenadier Regiment up the International Highway, and 48th Grenadier Regiment through the Schleiden forest. US forces in this region consisted of the 394th Infantry Regiment, 99th Division with its three battalions stretched out in a line on the eastern side of the International Highway from Weissenstein to the Buchholz railroad line, a distance of about three miles.

The attack by the 48th Grenadier Regiment went badly when one of its battalions stumbled into the opening barrages, suffering 60 per cent casualties. As a result attacks were weakest in the northern sector against 2/394th Infantry. The attack along the key route out of Losheim progressed more smoothly and by afternoon had overrun one company of the 1/394th Infantry and inflicted heavy casualties on the others. The intensity of these attacks decreased when trouble to the south forced the 27th Grenadier Regiment commander to redirect a battalion in this direction.

Buchholz rail station, the southernmost position of the 99th Division was held by the 3/394th Infantry. This company was not deployed in a trench line like its two northern neighbors, but left in an assembly area around the station to serve as a mobile reserve for the division. Shortly after the initial barrage, a battalion of 27th Grenadier Regiment attempted to use the cover of the early morning ground fog to rush the station. They were caught in the open and withdrew with serious casualties. Around 1100hrs reinforcements arrived but failed to overcome the US positions. The US battalion commander realized the precariousness of his position, and with regimental consent, withdrew his unit back towards a more defensible position near Losheimergraben after dusk, leaving two platoons behind at Buchholz station as a security force. By evening, the 27th Grenadier Regiment had patrols on the fringes of the American positions in front of Losheimergraben.

After dark, the 12th VGD officers were visited by the irate 1st SS-Panzer Corps commander who insisted that they take Losheimergraben in a dawn attack. Preceded by artillery strikes, their attacks were renewed before dawn. Intense fighting enveloped the town and surrounding woods, and though the 1/394th Infantry positions held, the battalion suffered serious casualties. By late morning, the US regimental commander decided to withdraw from the woods and set up new defensive positions on the hills east of Mürringen. The German attack failed in part because the promised support from the division's StuG III assault guns did not materialize when they got stuck in the massive traffic jam behind the lines. When the attacks on the town resumed with armored support at 1300 there was hardly any resistance except for a small rearguard. A battalion of 48th Grenadier Regiment began racing up the highway towards Mürringen but ran into elements of the 2/394th Infantry that had not yet received instructions to withdraw. The last American rearguard in the customs houses in Losheimergraben did not surrender until 1500hrs.

While the fight was going on in Losheimergraben, reinforcements in the form of the 1/23rd Infantry from the 2nd Infantry Division moved into the town of Hünningen before dawn on 17 December. They covered the afternoon withdrawal and prevented the 12th VGD from emerging from the woods. A hasty defense was set up in the neighboring village of Mürringen by the remnants of the 394th Infantry, but a night attack supported by ten StuG III assault guns captured the town around midnight. One of the routes was finally open, two days late.

Rollbahn E – Krewinkel and Lanzerath

The 3rd Fallschirmjäger Division was assigned the task of opening the southernmost corridor for the 1st SS-Panzer Corps. This should have been the easiest of the breakthroughs due to the extreme imbalance between German and US forces. The objective was the corps boundary, which was screened by nothing more than the 14th Cavalry Group. Normally, a gap this size would be assigned to an entire infantry division, not to a unit with a deployable strength roughly that of a single infantry battalion. Furthermore, the cavalry commander, Colonel Mark Devine decided to keep one of his two squadrons in reserve almost 20 miles behind the front. A defensive plan had been developed for the Losheim Gap when the 2nd Infantry Division had been responsible for the sector earlier in the month, which consisted of a withdrawal of the forward outposts to the Manderfeld ridge, pre-registered artillery strikes forward of these defenses, and a counterattack from the Schnee Eifel. When the 106th Division took over this sector on 11 December, this plan went into limbo in spite of the efforts of the cavalry. In contrast to the conditions in the V Corps sector to the north, with forests along the frontier, this sector consisted of open farmland.

The 99th Division's rifle squads built log reinforced shelters along the front line during November 1944, usually consisting of a two-man fighting trench, and a large but shallower bunker for sleeping like this one near Losheimergraben. These substantially reduced casualties from the initial artillery barrage of 16 December. (MHI)

Generalmajor Wadehn's badly depleted 3rd Fallschirmjäger Division was deployed with both available regiments up front. The 9th Fallschirmjäger Regiment was assigned to seize the small village of Lanzerath, while the 5th Fallschirmjäger Regiment was assigned the capture of Krewinkel, the nominal start point of Rollbahn E.

Defense of Lanzerath was nominally in the hands of a towed 3in. anti-tank gun platoon attached to the 14th Cavalry Group. However, once the initial barrage lifted, the platoon evacuated the village when it saw the German paratroopers marching down the road towards the town. The only other US force in the area was an understrength

The task of clearing the way into the Losheim Gap for the 1st SS-Panzer Corps was assigned to the 12th Volksgrenadier Division, commanded by Generalmajor Gerhard Engel seen here (right) conversing with the head of Army Group B, Walther Model. (MHI)

Among the most famous of the photos taken by an anonymous German military cameraman is this shot of a Waffen-SS Schwimmwagen pulled up to the road signs at the Kaiserbaracke crossroads leading towards Poteau on 18 December 1944. Often misidentified as Jochen Peiper, it is in fact a team from Fast Gruppe Knittel with SS-Unterscharführer Ochsner to the left and SS-Oberscharführer Persin behind the driver. This photo was one of those from four rolls of film later captured by the US 3rd Armored Division. (NARA)

intelligence and reconnaissance (I&R) platoon of the 1/394th Infantry under the command of Lieutenant Lyle·Bouck, that served as a screening force for the southern boundary of the 99th Division. After a brief scouting foray into the village, Bouck deployed his force, now down to a squad in size, in a trench line on the edge of the woods outside Lanzerath. To the surprise of the GIs, a paratrooper battalion emerged from the village in marching order. About 100 paratroopers deployed in a skirmish line 100m in front of their line and charged across an open field. A slaughter ensued. Through the course of the day, the Germans launched two more frontal charges with equally ghastly results. Although Bouck's men held their position, most were wounded, little ammunition remained, and their machine guns had been put out of action. In the late afternoon, the German tactics changed when a veteran NCO, infuriated by the casualties, pointedly told the commander, an inexperienced rear echelon Luftwaffe staff officer, that they should outflank the American position and not continue to attack it frontally. This time the American position was quickly overwhelmed and the survivors, including Bouck, captured. Bouck's platoon was later awarded the Presidential Unit Citation and he and his men were decorated with four Distinguished Service Crosses and five Silver Stars making it the most decorated unit of the war. An under-strength platoon had held off a regiment for an entire day, in turn blocking the advance of 1st SS-Panzer Division.

The defense of Krewinkel was more short-lived. The village was held by a platoon from C Troop, 18th Cavalry Squadron in a series of foxholes. As at Lanzerath, the 5th Fallschirmjäger Regiment attacked frontally resulting in heavy casualties. However, the American positions were so thin that German units simply continued their march westward past the defenses. The 14th Cavalry Group commander, Colonel Mark Devine, asked the 106th Division to send reinforcements as per the earlier defensive plan, but the 106th Division, largely unaware of the plan, refused. In the late morning Devine ordered his men to withdraw

An SdKfz 234/1 eight-wheel reconnaissance armored car of Kampfgruppe Knittel is seen moving forward with SS troops on its rear deck during the fighting on 18 December. (NARA)

to Manderfeld. The cavalry began withdrawing from Krewinkel at 1100, as did neighboring garrisons in Abst and Weckerath. The garrison at Roth was overrun and that in Kobsheid had to wait until dark to withdraw. Reinforcements from the 32nd Cavalry Squadron arrived near Manderfeld in the late afternoon, but by this stage, German troops were already pouring past. The surviving elements from the 18th Cavalry abandoned Manderfeld around 1600, heading for the squadron headquarters at Holzheim. For all intents and purposes, Rollbahn E and the Losheim Gap were wide open with no appreciable American defenses remaining.

The Schnee Eifel and the 106th Division

Although not in the path of the 6th Panzer Army, the fate of the 106th Division and St Vith are inextricably linked to the fate of the German Ardennes offensive in the northern sector. The 106th Division held a frontline about 15 miles wide with the 14th Cavalry Group acting as a screening force to its north. Two of its regiments, the 422nd and 423rd Infantry, were positioned in a vulnerable salient on the Schnee Eifel, a wooded ridgeline protruding off the Eifel plateau. The previous tenants, the 2nd Infantry Division felt the position was poorly situated for defense and in the event of an attack, planned to withdraw off the Schnee Eifel to a more defensible line along the Auw-Bleialf ridge, freeing up a regiment to deal with the weak cavalry defense of the Losheim Gap. Although these plans were outlined to the 106th Division commander, Major General Alan Jones, his staff had been in position for too short a period of time to appreciate their predicament. The area forward of the two regiments was very suitable for defense since it consisted of rugged forest with no significant roads. But it was flanked on either side by two good roads, from Roth to Auw, and Sellerich to Bleialf.

A Kubelwagen utility vehicle of 1st SS-Panzer Div. passes a disabled US 3in. anti-tank gun of the 820th Tank Destroyer Battalion, knocked out in the fighting for the Losheim Gap in the hamlet of Merlscheid on 18 December 1944 with the village church in the background. (NARA)

Recognizing the weakness of his infantry divisions, Manteuffel realized that 5th Panzer Army needed sound tactics to break through. Before the offensive, German patrols discovered that the inexperienced 106th Division had arrived on 10 December. Contrary to Hitler's orders, Manteuffel permitted patrols that discovered a 2km gap to the north between the weak 14th Cavalry positions in Roth and Weckerath. He decided that the American positions on the Schnee Eifel were so precarious that a single division could by-pass them, with the main thrust directed through the Losheim Gap to the north. The task was assigned to the 18th Volksgrenadier Division, which had been created from the remains of the 18th Luftwaffe Field Division destroyed in the Mons pocket in Belgium in September. While neither particularly experienced nor well trained, it had suffered few losses during its occupation duty at the front in the autumn. Its northern thrust through Roth would include two of its infantry regiments, the divisional artillery, and a supporting assault gun brigade, while its southern battlegroup had only a single infantry regiment

German Panzergrenadiers of 1st SS-Panzer Division move through Honsfeld on 17 December after Kampfgruppe Peiper captured the town. To the right is an SdKfz 251 Ausf. D, the standard German infantry half-track, while to the left is a captured example of its American counterpart, the M3 half-track. The vehicle in the background is a Mobelwagen 37mm anti-aircraft vehicle, one of two of Flak Kompanie 10/SS-Pz.Regt.1/1.SS-Pz.Div. knocked out during the fighting by a US anti-tank gun. (NARA)

supported by a self-propelled artillery battalion. The positions directly in front of the Schnee Eifel were held by only a replacement battalion since Manteuffel expected an American counterattack eastward was unlikely. The US 106th Division's third regiment, the 424th Infantry, south of the Schnee Eifel was the target of the 62nd Volksgrenadier Division.

As mentioned earlier, the tactics in the 5th Panzer Army sector for the initial assault differed significantly from those in the neighboring 6th Panzer Army sector and were based on infiltration prior to the main artillery barrage. As a result, the German infantry began moving in the dark at 0400hrs to infiltrate past the scattered defenses in the Losheim Gap. The morning was overcast with ground fog and rain that further aided this plan. Manteuffel firmly instructed his infantry officers that their

A Kingtiger drives past US prisoners, mostly from the 99th Division, captured during the fighting on 17 December. The village of Merlscheid lies in the background and the Kingtiger is on its way towards Lanzerath, the start point for Kampfgruppe Peiper. (NARA)

men were to cut all communication wire that they found to isolate the forward US positions.

The main assault force in the northern sector made it past the cavalry outposts in Roth and Weckerath without being detected, reaching the outskirts of Auw before dawn. German artillery did not begin its fire missions until 0830 against the towns held by the American cavalry, and by this time, German troops had already begun their assaults. The 14th Cavalry garrisons at Roth and Kobscheid surrendered in the late afternoon. The remnants of the 14th Cavalry further to the north were given permission by the 106th Division to withdraw to a ridgeline from Andler to Holzheim in the late afternoon. The remaining resistance in this sector came from the 592nd Field Artillery Battalion, which was subjected to a direct attack by Sturmgeschütz III assault guns. The attack was stopped by point blank howitzer fire, but by nightfall the artillery were in a precarious position.

On the right flank, the first 106th Division unit to come under heavy attack was the isolated 424th Infantry. Its foxholes on the high ground near Heckhuscheid were attacked by the 62nd VGD and Panzergrenadiers of the 116th Panzer Division. The first attack made little progress, but another attack up the Habscheid road began to isolate the 424th Infantry from the other two regiments on the Schnee Eifel. Casualties in the 424th Infantry were modest, but casualties in the inexperienced 62nd VGD had been heavy, especially amongst the officers. The neighboring regiment of the 18th VGD had similar experiences, fighting its way into Bleialf by late in the day, but at significant cost.

Manteuffel's infiltration tactics had been moderately successful. By nightfall the attack had made progress even if not as fast as hoped. The northern assault groups of the 18th VGD held positions near Auw behind the northern flank of the 106th Division as well as the Roth-Kobscheid area. On the southern side of the Schnee Eifel, the penetration was not as deep, but significant inroads had been made along the Bleialf road. Manteuffel prodded the commanders to complete their missions even if it took all night.

Peiper was infuriated by the failure of the 3rd Fallschirmjäger Division's to seize Honsfeld on 17 December 1944 and appropriated a battalion of paratroopers for his column. Some of these troops ended up riding on the engine deck of a King Tiger tank commanded by Oberscharführer Sowa of 501st schweres SS-Panzer Abteilung near Ligneuville on 18 December 1944 as seen here. (NARA)

LEFT A column of US prisoners from the 99th Division trudge towards the rear between Lanzerath and Merlscheid following the fighting on 17 December 1944. This photo was one of the series taken by a German combat cameraman accompanying Fast Group Knittel along Rollbahn D. (NARA)

RIGHT During the fighting on 18 December in the Losheim Gap, Kampfgruppe Hansen overwhelmed a column from the 14th Cavalry Group that was moving on the road between Recht and Poteau. This shows two of the M8 armored cars that were abandoned, both from C Troop, 18th Cavalry Squadron. (NARA)

The commander of Fast Group Knittel was Sturmbannführer Gustav Knittel, commander of the 1st SS-Panzer Reconnaissance Battalion. He is seen here (right) consulting a map with the chief of his headquarters company, Heinrich Goltz (left) while near La Vaux-Richard on 18 December 1944 on the approaches to La Gleize. (NARA)

Since the 106th Division had exhausted its reserves due to its overly extended front, the VIII Corps commander, MajGen Middleton, allotted Combat Command B (CCB) of the 9th Armored Division near Faymonville to the division that evening. Recognizing the gravity of the situation, Bradley in turn committed the 7th Armored Division to Middleton's beleaguered corps. That evening, Middleton telephoned Jones and the ensuing conversation was one of the most controversial of the campaign. Middleton promised to send the CCB of the 7th Armored Division to St Vith but Jones misunderstood that it would arrive by dawn on 18 December. Since it was facing a road march from the Netherlands along roads clogged with retreating troops and civilians, this was impossible. While Middleton and Jones were discussing future plans for the two regiments exposed on the Schnee Eifel, a switchboard operator accidentally disconnected the line and reconnected it moments later with unfortunate consequences. Middleton thought Jones understood that he wanted him to withdraw his two regiments off the Schnee Eifel, while Jones thought that his plans to leave the two regiments in place had been approved. As a result of all this confusion, Jones and his staff decided to deploy the CCB/9th Armored to the southern flank to reinforce the isolated 424th Infantry, and to use CCB/7th Armored Division to counterattack against the German penetration in the Losheim Gap thereby defending the two regiments on the Schnee Eifel.

After the 14th Cavalry Group column was ambushed, a German *Kriegsberichter* camera team staged a number of scenes near the burning vehicles. These are some of the only surviving images of the Battle of the Bulge from the German perspective, as the film later fell into US hands. This shows an often photographed SS-Rottenführer in a dramatic pose alongside a disabled M2A1 half-track. (NARA)

The CCB/9th Armored Division moved through St Vith around dawn with the intention of deploying near Winterspelt to block the German inroads between the 424th Infantry and the Schnee Eifel. Winterspelt was already in German hands, and first contact was made on the western bank of the Our river near Elcherath when the 14th Tank Battalion collided with the 62nd VGD. During the subsequent fighting on 17 December, the 424th Infantry became separated from the 28th Division to its south, and the intervention of CCB/9th Armored Div. was not enough to bridge the gap to the Schnee Eifel. By early evening, Jones gave the 424th Infantry permission to withdraw west and set up defensive positions along the Our river with the CCB/9th Armored Div. covering the area towards St Vith.

The situation on the Schnee Eifel had become dangerous during the night of 16/17 December as the two battle groups of the 18th VGD continued their push around the flanks of the two American regiments. On the southern flank, the town of Bleialf was hit hard at 0530hrs and was overrun shortly after dawn. This regiment, the 293rd, continued to move rapidly to the northwest against little opposition, aiming for the town of Schönberg. The US defense was further weakened by the lack of communications between Jones in St Vith and his two regimental commanders, due in no small measure to the success of the German infantry in ripping up communication wires, as well as the failure of this inexperienced unit to establish a robust radio net prior to the attack. On the northern flank, the 14th Cavalry Group's defensive efforts had evaporated by the morning of 17 December, and it began a series of uncoordinated withdrawals towards Andler and Schönberg. The northern remnants of the 14th Cavalry Group bumped into advancing columns from the 1st SS-Panzer Division. By noon, surviving elements of the 32nd Cavalry Squadron were at Wallerode on the approaches to St Vith, and the 18th Cavalry Squadron at Born, further to the northwest.

The first inkling that the two wings of the 18th VGD were about to link up behind the Schnee Eifel came in the early morning when US artillery battalions attempting to retreat near Schönberg began to run into advancing German columns. By 0900hrs the German encirclement of the two regiments of the 106th Division on the Schnee Eifel was complete, though it was by no means secure. The leading German battalions were instructed to continue to move west, and there were no efforts to establish a firm cordon around the trapped American units. The two trapped regiments set up perimeter defense and attempted to contact divisional headquarters in St Vith for further instruction. They were informed that reinforcements would attempt a breakthrough from the west on 18 December and that further supplies of ammunition would be dropped by air. Major General Jones at first believed that the imminent arrival of CCB/7th Armored Division would permit a relief of the units, and that prompt air supply would take care of their shortage of ammunition and food. As the day wore on, this seemed more and more unlikely. The call for air supply became caught up in red tape and no action was ever taken. The CCB/7th Armored Division became so entangled in traffic on its approach to St Vith that there was never any chance of it intervening on the Schnee Eifel. By the time it arrived, the fate of St Vith itself was in doubt. An order at 1445hrs to withdraw both regiments westward towards the Our river was so delayed by radio problems that it did not arrive until midnight by which time it was too late.

One of the only organized groups to escape the encirclement of the 106th Division on the Schnee Eifel was the intelligence and reconnaissance platoon of Lieutenant Ivan Long (center) from the 423rd Infantry. About 70 men from the regiment refused to surrender and reached St Vith the night of 20 December as seen here. (NARA)

Further instructions arrived at 0730 on 18 December indicating that the units should breakout towards St Vith, bypassing the heaviest German concentrations around Schönberg. The regiments destroyed non-essential equipment such as field kitchens, left the wounded with medics in regimental collection stations, and started off to the west, both regiments abreast in a column of battalions. The first contact with German forces began around 1130 when 2/423rd Infantry encountered German infantry on the main Bleialf-Schönberg road. Requesting help, two more battalions moved forward but were not able to push through. Shortly after the attacks began the divisional headquarters ordered the attack redirected towards Schönberg. During the course of the day, contact was lost between the two regiments. That night, the 423rd Infantry formed a defensive position to the southeast of Schönberg. By

Although two of the 106th Division's regiments were surrounded on the Schnee Eifel, a third, the 424th Infantry was further south and later served in the defense of St Vith. Here two soldiers of Co. C, 3/424th Infantry roll up their sleeping bags near Manhay on 28 December 1944 where the unit withdrew alongside CCB/7th Armored Division after the defense of St Vith. The "Golden Lion" divisional patch can be seen on the soldier on the right. (NARA)

this time, the unit was out of mortar ammunition, and had little rifle ammunition. The 422nd Infantry did not make contact with the German forces during the day, and when they bivouacked that evening, they mistakenly believed they were on the outskirts of their objective of Schönberg.

The German response to the American breakout attempts was made more difficult by the enormous traffic jam around Schönberg as units flowed west. As a result, the 56th Corps commander decided to counter the Americans with heavy artillery concentrations. As the 423rd Infantry formed for its attack shortly after dawn on 19 December, it was hit hard by the German artillery, followed by an infantry assault. Two rifle companies reached the outskirts of Schönberg but were pushed back by German anti-aircraft guns. By mid-afternoon, the attacks had collapsed, and the US infantrymen were down to less than a dozen rounds per rifle. With tactical control gone, the regimental commander gave the order to surrender around 1630hrs.

The 422nd Regiment moved out on the morning of 19 December across the Bleialf–Auw road near Oberlascheid but was brought under heavy small arms fire from German infantry in the woods west of the road. The 422nd had little success in advancing any further, and around 1400, the tanks of the Führer Begleit Brigade suddenly moved down the road on their way towards St Vith. This trapped a portion of the regiment between the tanks on the road and the German infantry in the woods. Some of the regiment surrendered at 1430, and most of the rest around 1600hrs. A number of groups tried to escape but most were eventually captured over the next few days. The surrender of the two regiments of the 106th Division, over 7,000 men, was the US Army's single greatest setback of the campaign in Europe.

Command Perspectives

From the perspective of Field Marshal Model of Army Group B, the breakthrough in the northern sector had finally been accomplished by 19 December, but two days behind schedule. The configuration of the breakthrough had not conformed to the plan. The anticipated break-through along the northern routes on the Elsenborn Ridge had been

stopped cold by the prolonged fighting in Krinkelt-Rocherath, stalling the assault by *Hitlerjugend*'s powerful battlegroup. The penetrations of the Losheim Gap around Büllingen were very narrow, resulting in considerable traffic congestion along these routes, which was delaying the exploitation of the breakthrough by the heavy Panzer formations. The quickest and most devastating breakthrough had not occurred in the 6th Panzer Army sector as expected, but in the 5th Panzer Army sector due to Manteuffel's more prudent tactics. While this attack appeared to be progressing well, there was the worrisome matter of St Vith. This town sat astride the main road network leading westward, and its capture would be essential to fully exploit the breakthrough in this sector. Therefore, by the third day of the offensive, the German objectives were threefold: to try to push on to the Elsenborn Ridge from points further west such as Bütgenbach; to try to exploit the breakthrough in the southern portion of the 6th Panzer Army sector by the spearhead of the 1st SS-Panzer Div., Kampfgruppe Peiper; and to develop the breakthrough in the 5th Panzer Army sector by securing the St Vith crossroads.

Hodges' First US Army headquarters, located at Spa in the Ardennes, began receiving reports of the German attacks on the morning of 16 December. Middleton's VIII Corps headquarters at Bastogne had a difficult time providing a clear picture of the unfolding events due to poor communications with its forward units. As mentioned earlier, Middleton requested that the CCB of the 9th Armored Division, located near Faymonville to support the Roer Dams operation, be returned to support VIII Corps, a request that was granted. However, Hodges refused to call off the Roer Dams offensive at 1100hrs, arguing that the activity in the Ardennes was only a spoiling attack. By early afternoon, the First Army headquarters received a copy of Rundstedt's order of the day which began

Much of the fighting in Stavelot focused on the stone bridge over the Amblève seen here – the only one still intact. To the left of the picture under a heavy coat of snow can be seen Kingtiger number 222 of 501st schweres SS-Panzer Abteilung that was knocked out while supporting Kampfgruppe Sandig's attack on 19 December. This photo was taken on 10 January 1945 after heavy snow had set in; during most of the Stavelot fighting the area was relatively free of snow. (NARA)

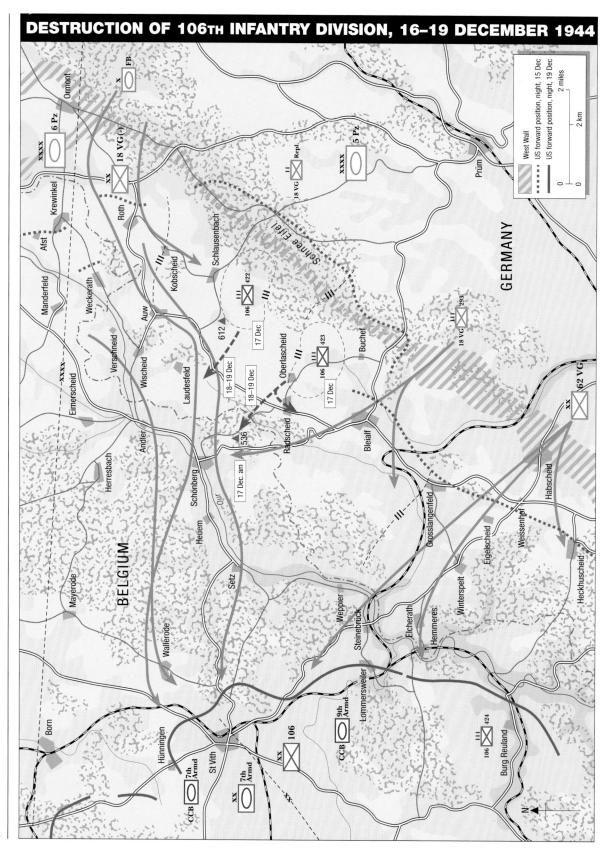

DESTRUCTION OF 106TH INFANTRY DIVISION, 16–19 DECEMBER 1944

GERMANY

BELGIUM

Schnee Eifel

Prüm

Ormont

FB

x

6 Pz

xxxx

18 VG(-)

xx

Krewinkel

Afst

Roth

Manderfeld

Weckerath

Kobscheid

Schlausenbach

Repl.

18 VG

5 Pz

xxxx

18 VG

293

III

62 VG

xx

106

422

III

III

612

17 Dec

Auw

Verscheid

Wischeid

Laudesfeld

18–19 Dec

18–19 Dec

Oberlascheid

423

III

106

17 Dec

Buchet

Elmerscheid

xxxx

Andler

Herresbach

536

Radscheid

Bleialf

17 Dec. am

Schönberg

Heuem

Our

Setz

Grosslangenfeld

III

Habscheid

Eigelscheid

Weissenhof

Heckhuscheid

Mayerode

Wallerode

Weppler

Steinebrück

Eicherath

Hemmeres

Winterspelt

Born

Hünningen

St Vith

106

xx

9th Armd

CCB

Lommersweiler

424

III

106

Burg Reuland

7th Armd

CCB

7th Armd

xx

xx

N

Key
West Wall
US forward position, night, 15 Dec
US forward position, night, 19 Dec

2 miles
2 km

58

"Your great hour has arrived … We gamble everything!" This changed the view of German intentions, but even late in the day, many in the headquarters still felt it was nothing but a diversion to discourage the two US offensives in the works – the Roer Dams operation in the north, and Patton's planned attack in the Saar to the south. Nevertheless, a regiment of the 1st Infantry Division was transferred to Gerow's V Corps, which would prove instrumental two days later in the defense of Dom Bütgenbach.

The reaction in the 12th Army Group headquarters, located in Luxembourg City, was more vigorous. Bradley was in Paris that day conferring with Eisenhower, and first word of the offensive arrived in the afternoon. Bradley knew that the 12th Army Group had minimal reserves, so he immediately telephoned Patton and told him to transfer the 10th Armored Division from his planned Saar offensive to Luxembourg. He then phoned the 12th Army Group headquarters and instructed them to transfer the 7th Armored Division from Ninth Army to the Ardennes. The only other reserves were the two airborne divisions of MajGen Matthew Ridgway's XVIII Airborne Corps, the 82nd and 101st Airborne Divisions. These were refitting around Reims after prolonged deployment, and though not ready, were ordered to move by truck to the Ardennes immediately. Bradley's prompt actions would have vital consequences over the next few days.

The debate over German intentions at the First Army headquarters ended on 17 December when the first reports emerged of German

During the fighting in Stavelot, this Kingtiger of sSS-PzAbt.501 stalled while climbing the hill on Rue Haut-Rivage, and then rolled back down the hill into this house where it became stuck. A couple of GIs from the 30th Division look it over after the town was retaken. (NARA)

Although desperate for fuel, Kampfgruppe Peiper was unaware of the US fuel dump on the Francorchamps road above Stavelot. Fearing it might fall into German hands, US troops set all 124,000 gallons on fire. It was the only major fuel dump not evacuated by the US Army. (NARA)

Kampfgruppe Peiper left Stavelot on its way north-west, and was followed later on 18 December by Kampfgruppe Knittel, which fought a losing battle against the 30th Infantry Division for the town later in the day. This SdKfz 251/9 75mm assault gun half-track was knocked out by a rifle grenade in the fighting. (NARA)

Panzers racing through the Losheim Gap. It was finally recognized that this was no spoiling attack. The Roer Dams attack was called off, and Gerow was given a free hand to organize a defense of Elsenborn Ridge. By 0930, the first reports began to arrive that two regiments of the 106th Division had been surrounded. The rest of the day was spent attempting to secure additional reinforcements. Within First Army, the remainder of 1st Infantry Division, and a regiment of the 9th Infantry Division were transferred to Gerow's embattled V Corps. General William Simpson of the Ninth Army telephoned and offered the 30th Infantry Division and the 2nd Armored Division. The 30th Infantry Division was the first of the two units to begin moving. By midnight 17/18 December, 80,000 troops and 10,000 vehicles were on their way to the Ardennes, a much prompter response than the Germans had anticipated. The CCB/9th Armored Division, and 7th Armored Division were committed to Middleton's VIII Corps, originally with plans to help rescue the two trapped regiments of the 106th Division. The 1st Infantry Division was used to buttress the defenses on the Elsenborn Ridge. The 30th Infantry Division was dispatched to the Malmédy area and the 82nd Airborne Division to Werbomont to seal off the Losheim Gap.

When a copy of the German operational plan was captured late on 16 December, First Army headquarters learned that the German offensive would eventually depend on captured fuel. As a result, on 17 December an effort began to remove the several large fuel dumps in the Ardennes especially the truck-head at Bütgenbach and the network of dumps south of Malmédy. Most of these were withdrawn except for 124,000 gallons near Stavelot which were burned to prevent them from falling into German hands.

On the afternoon of 18 December word arrived that a spearhead from Kampfgruppe Peiper had reached to within six miles of the First Army headquarters in Spa, a rumor that proved untrue. Nonetheless, the proximity of the German forces down the road in La Gleize convinced them to evacuate the headquarters at 2200hrs to Chaudfontaine in the suburbs of Liège. The haste with which this was done left a bad impression, especially among subordinate commands who found themselves temporarily cut off from instructions or support. Even though the move helped improve the headquarters security from immediate German attack, it posed another threat as the new site was in the flight path of V-1 buzz bombs being launched at Liège and Antwerp. The G-4 traffic headquarters was hit en route by a V-1.

One of the most effective efforts by the headquarters was the unconventional activity of the section chiefs. Colonel William Carter, the engineer chief, mobilized his units to prepare roadblocks, lay minefields, demolish bridges, and construct barrier zones in the northern sector of the front. These were mostly rear area service units, normally assigned to construction and road building, but trained for secondary combat roles. The Germans would soon curse the "damned engineers" for harassing the Panzer spearheads and blowing key bridges. The 49th Antiaircraft Brigade responsible for defense against V-1 flying bombs moved a number of its units of 90mm anti-aircraft guns to defend the approaches to key locations including Huy, Liège, and Spa. Even the armor section got in on the act, taking the crews of the newly arrived 740th Tank Battalion and outfitting them with a motley selection of British Shermans, tank destroyers, DD tanks and whatever else was available, and dispatching them to the front. This unit would later serve as the cork in the bottle when Kampfgruppe Peiper was trapped at La Gleize.

On 19 December Eisenhower met with the senior commanders including Patton, Bradley and Devers at Verdun to discuss ways to deal with the German attack. The two basic options were to establish a secure defensive line to make a stand, or to begin counterattacking as soon as forces were available. Eisenhower made it clear he desired the second option, and wanted the initial attack to come from the south. Eisenhower was surprised by Patton's eagerness to shift a corps of three divisions in only three days, but this was possible due to the preparation of these units for the abortive Saar offensive. In addition Patton had shown foresight in

Riflemen of the 117th Infantry, 30th Division prepare to break down a door during street fighting in Stavelot on 21 December 1944. The two riflemen nearest the door have rifle-grenades fixed on their M1 Garand rifles, while the soldier to the left is armed with a M1 carbine. (NARA)

ATTACK IN THE ARDENNES – KAMPFGRUPPE PEIPER,
17 DECEMBER 1944 (pages 62–63)

Probably the most vivid image to have emerged from the Battle of the Bulge was the sight of the massive Kingtiger tanks advancing through the snowy pine forests of the Belgian border, immortalized by a series of photographs taken by a German combat cameraman on the morning of 17 December near the German/Belgian border. In many accounts of the battle, these images have symbolized the armored spearhead of Kampfgruppe Peiper as it steamrolled through American defenses at the start of the Ardennes offensive. In reality, the image highlights the underlying problems of the German offensive. The Kingtigers (1) of s.SS-Pz. Abt. 501 were not in the vanguard of the German attack, but brought up the rear of Kampfgruppe Peiper due to the difficulties of moving such awkward and accident-prone tanks on the narrow country roads of Belgium. Peiper's spearheads were the old, reliable, and more fleet-footed PzKpfw IV medium tanks. The troops on the Kingtiger wear the distinctive camouflage smocks of the elite *Fallschirmjäger* paratroopers (2), long respected by the US Army as the best of the German light infantry. Troops of this unit, the 3.Fallschirmjäger Division, had fought against the US Army in Normandy where they earned their fearsome reputation. By December 1944, however, they were a pale reflection of their former glory. Decimated in the summer

1944 fighting, the division was reconstructed using surplus Luftwaffe ground personnel and other recruits who would have been rejected in years past by such an elite formation. But the division's real problem was its leadership, with many of its units led by inexperienced Luftwaffe staff officers, not combat-hardened veterans. The declining effectiveness of the paratroopers was made embarrassingly clear on 16 December when a paratrooper regiment was held up all day at Lanzerath by a US infantry platoon, delaying the start of Kampfgruppe Peiper's advance by 24 hours. Infuriated by such incompetence, Peiper commandeered a battalion of paratroopers to reinforce his own force. Since the paratroopers could not keep up with his columns on foot, he had them ride on the backs of the Kingtiger tanks. The smoldering M4 tank (3) by the roadside is a victim of the earlier passage of Kampfgruppe Peiper; the Kingtigers saw very little combat during the opening phase of the offensive. Only a handful of Kingtiger tanks made it past Stoumont and on to La Gleize where Kampfgruppe Peiper was finally trapped. The illustration here is based on the famous photos taken on 17 December. The Kingtigers are finished in the typical camouflage pattern from the fall of 1944, called the ambush pattern, with a pattern of small dots over the usual three-color camouflage finish. The paratroopers are in their distinctive jump smocks and the unique helmets with the reduced rims. (Howard Gerrard)

As can be seen in this aerial view of La Gleize, the town was heavily shelled. This view looks towards the northwest with the road to the left upper corner heading towards Stoumont and the road to the right center heading to Trois Ponts. (MHI)

planning for such an eventuality some days previously based on the assessments of his G-2 of the likelihood of a German attack in the Ardennes.

On the evening of 19 December Bradley received a telephone call from Eisenhower's chief of staff, Lieutenant General Walter Bedell Smith, suggesting that Eisenhower wanted to turn over control of the US First and Ninth Armies on the northern shoulder of the Bulge to Montgomery since this would avoid problems if communications were cut by the German advance. The main repeater station at Jemelle was located in the path of Manteuffel's advancing Panzers between Bastogne and Dinant. Bradley was concerned that the switch would discredit the American command at a very sensitive moment, and reluctantly agreed in the hopes that the British would commit their reserves to the campaign. He also received assurances that the reorganization would only be temporary. Bradley was deeply suspicious of this change as a result of Montgomery's interminable campaign to be appointed the main Allied ground commander.

The handover took place on 20 December and Montgomery strode into Hodges' HQ at Chaudfontaine later in the day like "Christ come to cleanse the temple". Though Montgomery's theatrics and arrogance infuriated the American officers, his energy and tactical skills helped to stabilize the command situation on the northern shoulder. He began to move the reserve XXX Corps to the Meuse to make certain that no German units would penetrate into central Belgium, and he dispatched liaison officers from the Phantom service[2] to coordinate the defensive actions along the front. American tactical commanders such as Hasbrouck and Clarke of the 7th Armored Division were later effusive in their praise of his role in restoring control. Never one to let modesty stand in the way, Montgomery's tactless remarks to the press several weeks later led to a crisis in the Allied high command that nearly resulted in Eisenhower relieving him of command.

---

2 Montgomery's personal liaison service to communicate with his sub-units. It also included a signals intelligence unit that monitored Allied radio traffic to keep track of his subordinate units.

EXPLOITING THE BREAKTHROUGH

KAMPFGRUPPE PEIPER

The first attempt to exploit the breakthrough took place on the southern wing of the 6th Panzer Army by the 1st SS-Panzer Division. The delays in opening up the main approach avenue through Losheimergraben on 16 December prompted Hermann Preiss, the 1st SS-Panzer Corps commander, to re-arrange the route allotments and direct Jochen Peiper to move his Kampfgruppe (KG) through Lanzerath to the rail station at Buchholz, leaving the direct road to Losheimergraben open for the stalled *Hitlerjugend*.

The spearhead of Peiper's formation began moving towards Buchholz at 0330, and quickly overran the two hapless platoons from 3/394th Infantry who had been left behind when the rest of the battalion had pulled back. As the column cleared the woods approaching Honsfeld, the only opposition was the scattered elements of the 14th Cavalry Group and its attached 801st Tank Destroyer Battalion. The town itself had been used as a rear area rest camp for the 99th Division and stragglers had drifted in the previous day. There were also a dozen towed 3-in. anti-tank guns, some still limbered for travel. KG Peiper's column moved past a pair of 3in. anti-tank guns in the dark that were then overrun by infantry, and encountered small arms fire on reaching the town. Resistance quickly evaporated, and about 250 GIs were captured. While being marched back to Lanzerath a number of

This aerial view of Stoumont is centered on the Sanatorium where much of the heaviest fighting took place. This view looks towards the east, and the road to La Gleize is to the right and to Targnon to the lower left. (MHI)

A column of M36 90mm tank destroyers move forward in support of the 82nd Airborne Division's attempt to halt the advance of Kampfgruppe Peiper near Werbomont, Belgium on 20 December 1944. These were the only US Army vehicle capable of handling the Panther or Tiger tank in a frontal engagement. (NARA)

American prisoners of war and Belgian civilians were randomly killed, the beginning of the 1st SS-Panzer Division's loathsome record of atrocities during the campaign.

Peiper pushed his column forward to Büllingen, and there was little organized defense of the town except for the 254th Engineer Battalion, which hastily deployed a company along each of the main roads leading into town. Peiper's column reached the town before dawn and there was sporadic fighting between the engineers and the lead Panzers. Bazooka teams and 3in. anti-tank guns knocked out a few German tanks. Peiper's column also overran two airfields used by divisional spotting aircraft, but those from the 2nd Infantry Division mostly managed to escape. The engineers withdrew to a manor farm along the Bütgenbach road dubbed "Dom Bütgenbach" that would later figure in the fighting, but which for now was ignored by the German advance. There are two roads out of Büllingen, one towards Elsenborn Ridge via Bütgenbach (currently called N632), and the other, N692 to the southwest. Peiper moved to the southwest, as the other route to the northwest was allotted to the neighboring *Hitlerjugend* which was still entangled in the Krinkelt-Rocherath fighting.

The spearhead of Peiper's columns moved through open farm country from Moderscheid to Thirimont. To save time, some tanks and half-tracks tried to go across the farm fields, only to find the ground so muddy that they became stalled. The columns, which stretched all the way back to the German border, were subjected to at least three strafing attacks by US P-47 fighters during the morning, but with little damage.

During this advance, Peiper captured some US military police and was told there was a major American headquarters in the village of Ligneuville. Peiper decided to investigate, and ordered a company to take a short-cut along minor farm roads but they became trapped in the mud. As a result, Peiper ordered his armored spearhead under Werner Sternebeck to go the long way around via Waimes, and the Baugnez crossroads. While approaching the crossroads, they ran into a column of trucks from B/285th Field Artillery Observation Battalion, one of the elements of the 7th Armored Division moving to St Vith. As the columns met around 1300hrs, the lead German PzKpfw IV tanks fired on the trucks, bringing them to a halt. Sternebeck's men quickly captured the lightly armed Americans and about 90 men were herded together in a field near the crossroads, joined later by additional prisoners when more American trucks stumbled into the ambush. After most of Peiper's column had passed the crossroads, a massacre took place of the prisoners, the details of which remain controversial to this day. It would appear that the massacre started around 1500hrs when a tank crew assigned to guard the prisoners began taking random pot shots at the prisoners, a vile amusement repeated from earlier in the day at Honsfeld. This was followed by machine gun fire from the two tanks. For a while, troops from passing vehicles continued to fire randomly at the wounded and the dead, and finally troops from the SS-Pioneer Company were sent into the field to finish off any survivors. In total, some 113 bodies were found in the field in January when the US Army recaptured the crossroads. The incident has become infamous as the Malmédy massacre and a post-war trial was conducted of Peiper and many of his surviving officers and men.

In fact there was no major US headquarters in Ligneuville and at the time the village had been abandoned by the service elements of CCB/9th Armored Division, which had set off earlier in the day towards St Vith. The lead Panther of the column was knocked out by an M4 dozer tank under repair, but the town was taken with little fighting. Through dusk Peiper's columns snaked their way through the foothills of the Amblève valley without encountering any opposition. On the approaches to the town of Stavelot around 1800hrs, they encountered a small engineer roadblock and came under small arms fire. Surprisingly, Peiper decided against a night attack into the town. The exhaustion of his troops after two days with little sleep was probably a more important factor than the feeble resistance encountered. At the time, the town was held only by a single engineer company. Peiper's delay in attacking Stavelot gave the US defenders time to prepare. A small task force from the 526th Armored

Skorzeny's Panzer Brigade 150 was committed to the attack on Malmédy on 21 December. The Panther tanks kept their disguise as American M10 tank destroyers, and this one was knocked out with a bazooka by Private F. Currey of the 120th Infantry who was later decorated with the Medal of Honor for his actions that day. (MHI)

Infantry Battalion arrived after dark, and with so little knowledge of the layout of the town, the defense was poorly prepared and the key Amblève bridge weakly defended and not prepared for demolition.

Kampfgruppe Peiper resumed their attack at 0400 on 18 December by deploying Panzergrenadiers in the southern fringes of the town opposite the bridge. As the newly arrived GIs attempted to set up roadblocks with anti-tank guns at 0600, they were brought under fire. A Panzergrenadier platoon made its way over the bridge but was quickly forced back to the southern side. In the meantime, German engineers determined that the bridge was not prepared for demolition. After receiving reinforcements, another attack was made at dawn but control of the north side was in question until the first Panther tanks arrived. The first Panzer was hit by a 57mm anti-tank gun positioned up the street, which failed to penetrate, and the tank drove over the gun. The German troops advanced rapidly through the town, losing one Panzer to a 3in. anti-tank gun, but by 1000 the town was in their hands. The remnants of the US task force retreated north to a large fuel dump on a side road outside the town. To prevent the Germans from capturing it, 124,000 gallons of gasoline were poured into a gully and ignited. Peiper, in a rush to seize the critical bridges at Trois Ponts, had not realized it was there.

The three bridges in Trois Ponts for which the town received its name, had all been prepared for demolition by US engineers. A lone 57mm anti-tank gun guarded the road from Stavelot and managed to knock out the lead German tank when it approached around 1145hrs. Although the gun was quickly destroyed and the small roadblock overwhelmed, the delay gave the engineers time to blow up both the Amblève bridge and one of the two bridges over the Salm river. Prevented from using the main route to Werbomont and having left his tactical bridging behind, Peiper redirected his columns along the more circuitous route up the Amblève valley through La Gleize. A small bridge on a poor secondary road was found near Cheneux, but in the late afternoon the weather cleared and the column was hit by US fighter-bombers. Two tanks and several half-tracks were damaged, blocking the road. As importantly, US observation aircraft slipped through the cloud cover and were able to pass back detailed information on the size and direction of Peiper's force for most of the rest of the afternoon.

By the time that the damaged vehicles at Cheneux were moved aside it was dusk. A bridge was found over the Lienne stream, but it was blown by US engineers as the German spearhead approached. After dark a small group of half-tracks and tank destroyers attempted to use small side roads to reach the road junction at Werbomont, but were ambushed by an advance patrol from the US 30th Infantry Division. As Peiper had been moving through the Amblève valley, newly arrived American reinforcements began to block the main exits towards Liège. Instead of facing small rearguards made up of engineers and scratch defense forces, Peiper would now begin to face more substantial opposition.

A new threat began to emerge behind him. He had expected that the bulk of the 3rd Fallschirmjäger Division would close up behind his columns and occupy Stavelot. But a battalion from the US 30th Division joined the remnants of the task force that had fought for Stavelot earlier in the day and launched an attack on the town in the late afternoon. A Panzer column returning from Trois Ponts through Stavelot became

A bazooka team from Co. C, 325th Glider Infantry, 82nd Airborne Division guard a road near Werbomont on 20 December after a probe from Kampfgruppe Peiper reached as far as Habiemont, four kilometers to the east. This was the furthest point west reached by Peiper, and his forces pulled back to Stoumont later in the day due to increasing US attacks. (NARA)

Besides the five Panther tanks converted to resemble M10 tank destroyers, Panzer Brigade 150 also had five Sturmgeschütz III assault guns, painted in American markings, with an ineffective disguise. This one from Kampfgruppe Y was abandoned between Baugnez and Geromont. (NARA)

mixed up in the battle, as did a few Kingtiger heavy tanks. The fighting continued through the night and the next day Stavelot was back in US hands. The US control was still patchy so that some German forces were still able to infiltrate past to reinforce Peiper. Nevertheless, the recapture of Stavelot cut Peiper off from the rest of his division.

With his rear now under attack, Peiper frantically tried to find other routes to the west. Since the road out of La Gleize to the southwest was blocked, Peiper decided to try the better road towards Stoumont, even though there were already reports it was held in force by US troops. In fact, the lead elements of the 119th Infantry, 30th Division arrived in Stoumont after dark, shortly after the spearhead of Kampfgruppe Peiper had bivouacked outside the town.

By the morning of 19 December Peiper's force in La Gleize had dwindled to a paltry 19 Panthers, 6 PzKpfw IVs and 6 Kingtigers, the remaining 86 Panzers having broken down, been knocked out, bogged down, or become lost during the previous days' odyssey. With thick fog covering the area, Peiper decided to strike Stoumont before the Americans could prepare their defenses. The US forces in Stoumont consisted of the 3/119th Infantry supported by eight towed 3in. anti-tank guns and a 90mm anti-aircraft gun. The attack began at 0800 with the Panzers going straight down the road, and the Panzergrenadiers advancing through the fog on foot. The 3in. anti-tank guns were quickly overrun and in the ensuing two-hour battle, one US infantry company was surrounded and forced to surrender, and the other two pushed out of town. The US regimental commander dispatched a reserve infantry company to the scene, and in conjunction with ten M4 tanks of the 743rd Tank Battalion, executed a fighting retreat along the road past Targnon with Panzers on their heels.

While attempting to exploit their success the Panzer spearhead ran into a 90mm anti-aircraft gun situated on a bend to the west of the town, and were temporarily halted. A few Panzers reached the village of Targnon where a bridge led to the southwest and the Werbomont road junction. Peiper was hesitant to push his force in this direction, as by late afternoon, his armored vehicles were running very low on fuel. To reinforce the Targnon roadblock, the First Army cobbled together

some tank support. The 740th Tank Battalion had recently arrived in Belgium without tanks and some of its officers were dispatched to a depot and told to requisition whatever tanks were available. This totaled 14 British M4 tanks, five M4A1 duplex-drive amphibious tanks, and a M36 90mm tank destroyer. A platoon from this unit arrived to the west of Stoumont at 1530 and was thrown into the fray to support an infantry attack on the Stoumont railroad station west of Targnon. Three Panthers were knocked out in the ensuing encounter and Peiper pulled his forces back into Stoumont. Whether he realized it at the time or not, this was his battlegroup's high-water mark.

The German offensive was going badly awry. By late on 19 December additional forces were closing in on Peiper from the north and west. The 82nd Airborne Division had already arrived at Werbomont and was moving towards the Amblève valley from the west. A combat command of the 3rd Armored Division was dispatched down the road from Liège and its three task forces approached La Gleize down three separate roads to prevent Peiper from moving towards the First Army headquarters in Spa. By the end of 19 December Kampfgruppe Peiper was low on fuel and trapped in the Amblève valley around La Gleize, 45km from Liège, and 65km from its initial objective on the Meuse River at Huy that Peiper had hoped to reach on the first day of the offensive.

The southern arm of 1st SS-Panzer Division had advanced with far less opposition. Kampfgruppe Hansen had cleared the border area near Krewinkel, and after a short delay in minefields along the front line, they began a rapid advance with the Jagdpanzer IV tank destroyers in the lead. Their route was through the Losheim Gap, weakly defended by retreating elements of the hapless 14th Cavalry Group. By late on 17 December Hansen's battlegroup was only a short distance behind Peiper's and had encountered no serious opposition. The following day a small task force of the 18th Cavalry Squadron and some towed 3in. anti-tank guns were ambushed by a group of Hansen's Panzergrenadiers bivouacked in a woods astride the road from Poteau

to Recht. The column was quickly overcome. While this small encounter hardly figures in the larger picture of combat actions in the sector, the aftermath of the skirmish was caught by a German photographer whose film was later captured by the US 3rd Armored Division. These four rolls of film constitute most of the surviving images of the German Ardennes offensive, and are among the most famous of the battle. Kampfgruppe Hansen advanced no further as at 1400, he was ordered to withdraw his force to Recht with an aim to keep open this route for the planned advance of the 9th SS-Panzer Division, the lead element of the 2nd SS-Panzer Corps. Hansen was furious at the order, as the route to the Salm River crossing at Viesalm was weakly protected and his troops could have arrived there later in the day. Instead, the lead elements of the US 7th Armored Division arrived in Poteau late in the day – the opening phase of the battle for St Vith. Hansen's troops remained idle through 19 December, awaiting the 9th SS-Panzer Division.

On 20 December US forces were again pressuring Kampfgruppe Peiper's defenses. The main US concern was the threat posed to Spa, but Peiper was oblivious to the US headquarters there. Task Force McGeorge was sent down the road from Spa but was stopped before reaching La Gleize. Two companies of the 504th PIR, 82nd Airborne Division attempted to secure Cheneux, but two attacks during the afternoon and evening left them with barely a toehold in the town.

Of more immediate consequence to Peiper, US actions at Stavelot were ending any hope of reinforcement. Task Force Lovelady from the CCB/3rd Armored Division seized control of the road from La Gleize to Stavelot on 20 December and engaged Kampfgruppe Knittel near Trois Ponts which controlled the only remaining access to La Gleize from the German side. Knittel made another attempt to wrest control of Stavelot from the 117th Infantry, but by the end of the day, the Americans were in firm control of the west bank of the Amblève. The following day, the 1st SS-Panzer Div. commander, Wilhelm Mohnke, ordered Kampfgruppe Hansen to reinforce Knittel for another try against Stavelot. The 1st SS-Panzergrenadier Regiment crossed the Amblève east of Trois Ponts but a Jagdpanzer IV following the grenadiers collapsed the bridge and left them isolated on the western bank without support. Attempts to bridge the Amblève were a failure. TF Lovelady

linked up with the Stavelot defenders and was reinforced by two more companies from the 30th Division. After another hard day of fighting, the third German attempt to regain Stavelot was foiled.

Peiper's defenses were driven in by attacks on 21 December. After failing to clear out the paratroopers in the outskirts of Cheneux in the morning, another battalion from the 82nd Airborne Div. outflanked the town that afternoon, forcing Peiper to withdraw his infantry back to La Gleize. American attacks against the more heavily defended positions in Stoumont were frustrated by the heavy fog and Panther tanks. The road behind Stoumont was temporarily captured by US infantry, but a quick counterattack restored the situation in the afternoon. Although Kampfgruppe Peiper had managed to hold the village for another day, Peiper had too little infantry to defend the town and withdrew his forces back to La Gleize after dark.

The renewed attempts to relieve Peiper from the Stavelot area on 22 December were again frustrated by Task Force Lovelady. A counterattack near Biester in the late afternoon almost cut the task force in two, but instead resulted in heavy casualties for Kampfgruppe Hansen.

After consolidating in La Gleize, KG Peiper had been reduced to less than a third of its starting strength – some 1,500 troops – and a fifth of its original Panzers: 13 Panther tanks, 6 PzKpfw IVs, and 6 Kingtigers as well as an assortment of other vehicles. Fuel and ammunition were low. The day's fighting proved frustrating for both sides as they ineffectively probed each other's defenses. Late on 22 December Mohnke contacted Peiper and let him know that the attempt to reach him earlier in the day had failed again. Peiper consulted with his senior officers and asked Mohnke permission to attempt a breakout. This was refused but the corps commander, Hermann Preiss, asked Dietrich for permission to divert the 9th SS-Panzer Division from its advance to clear out Stavelot and open up an escape route. Dietrich refused, and an attempt to airlift supplies to La Gleize that night proved ineffective as only about a tenth of the material parachuted from three Ju-52 aircraft landed within the German perimeter.

US forces began a major effort to clear the remaining German forces from the western side of the Amblève on 23 December but didn't manage to do so until the following day. Kampfgruppe Knittel withdrew its last forces before dawn on Christmas day and by Christmas the Stavelot area was in US hands. This ended any plans to rescue Kampfgruppe Peiper.

Peiper was surrounded by about three battalions of infantry and four tank companies with US units probing eastward from Stoumont, and and westward from the other side of La Gleize. These attacks were frustrated by Panzer fire from La Gleize, but Peiper's troops were on the receiving end of a punishing artillery bombardment. One of the most effective weapons was a single M12 155mm self-propelled gun that fired almost 200 rounds into the town from the outskirts at practically point-blank range. Although Dietrich had refused permission for Peiper to break out the day before, the grim situation around Stavelot led him to pass the buck down the chain of command to the divisional commander, Wilhelm Mohnke. Peiper was given permission to breakout at 1400hrs on 23 December and began planning to escape that night. About 800 men were deemed fit enough for the attempt, and all the

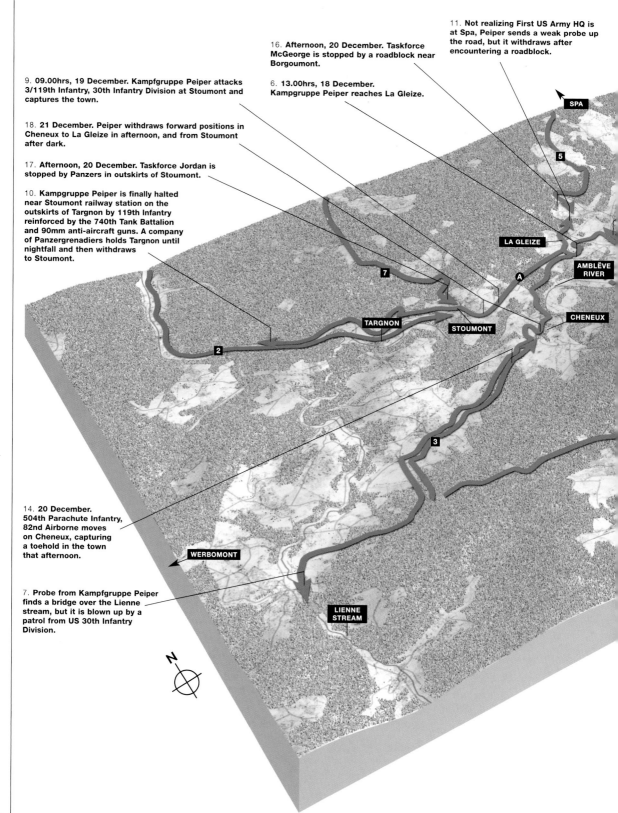

11. **Not realizing First US Army HQ is at Spa, Peiper sends a weak probe up the road, but it withdraws after encountering a roadblock.**

16. **Afternoon, 20 December. Taskforce McGeorge is stopped by a roadblock near Borgoumont.**

6. **13.00hrs, 18 December. Kampgruppe Peiper reaches La Gleize.**

9. **09.00hrs, 19 December. Kampfgruppe Peiper attacks 3/119th Infantry, 30th Infantry Division at Stoumont and captures the town.**

18. **21 December. Peiper withdraws forward positions in Cheneux to La Gleize in afternoon, and from Stoumont after dark.**

17. **Afternoon, 20 December. Taskforce Jordan is stopped by Panzers in outskirts of Stoumont.**

10. **Kampgruppe Peiper is finally halted near Stoumont railway station on the outskirts of Targnon by 119th Infantry reinforced by the 740th Tank Battalion and 90mm anti-aircraft guns. A company of Panzergrenadiers holds Targnon until nightfall and then withdraws to Stoumont.**

14. **20 December. 504th Parachute Infantry, 82nd Airborne moves on Cheneux, capturing a toehold in the town that afternoon.**

7. **Probe from Kampfgruppe Peiper finds a bridge over the Lienne stream, but it is blown up by a patrol from US 30th Infantry Division.**

SPA

5

LA GLEIZE

AMBLÈVE RIVER

A

7

CHENEUX

TARGNON

STOUMONT

2

3

WERBOMONT

LIENNE STREAM

N

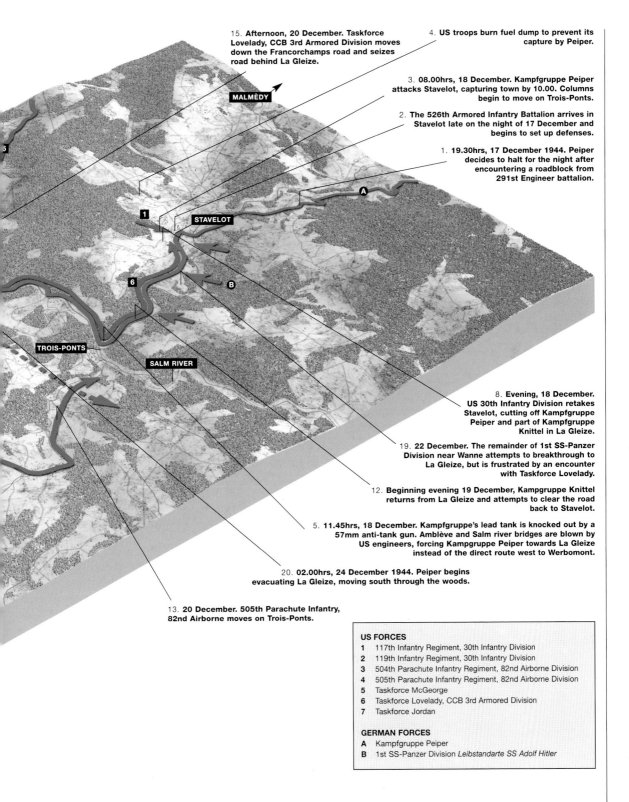

15. **Afternoon, 20 December.** Taskforce Lovelady, CCB 3rd Armored Division moves down the Francorchamps road and seizes road behind La Gleize.

4. **US troops burn fuel dump to prevent its capture by Peiper.**

3. **08.00hrs, 18 December. Kampfgruppe Peiper attacks Stavelot, capturing town by 10.00. Columns begin to move on Trois-Ponts.**

2. **The 526th Armored Infantry Battalion arrives in Stavelot late on the night of 17 December and begins to set up defenses.**

1. **19.30hrs, 17 December 1944. Peiper decides to halt for the night after encountering a roadblock from 291st Engineer battalion.**

MALMÈDY

A

1 STAVELOT

6 B

TROIS-PONTS

SALM RIVER

8. **Evening, 18 December. US 30th Infantry Division retakes Stavelot, cutting off Kampfgruppe Peiper and part of Kampfgruppe Knittel in La Gleize.**

19. **22 December. The remainder of 1st SS-Panzer Division near Wanne attempts to breakthrough to La Gleize, but is frustrated by an encounter with Taskforce Lovelady.**

12. **Beginning evening 19 December, Kampfgruppe Knittel returns from La Gleize and attempts to clear the road back to Stavelot.**

5. **11.45hrs, 18 December. Kampfgruppe's lead tank is knocked out by a 57mm anti-tank gun. Amblève and Salm river bridges are blown by US engineers, forcing Kampfgruppe Peiper towards La Gleize instead of the direct route west to Werbomont.**

20. **02.00hrs, 24 December 1944. Peiper begins evacuating La Gleize, moving south through the woods.**

13. **20 December. 505th Parachute Infantry, 82nd Airborne moves on Trois-Ponts.**

US FORCES
1   117th Infantry Regiment, 30th Infantry Division
2   119th Infantry Regiment, 30th Infantry Division
3   504th Parachute Infantry Regiment, 82nd Airborne Division
4   505th Parachute Infantry Regiment, 82nd Airborne Division
5   Taskforce McGeorge
6   Taskforce Lovelady, CCB 3rd Armored Division
7   Taskforce Jordan

GERMAN FORCES
A   Kampfgruppe Peiper
B   1st SS-Panzer Division *Leibstandarte SS Adolf Hitler*

KAMPFGRUPPE PEIPER 18–23 DECEMBER 1944
Viewed from the south-west, showing the increasingly desperate attempts by the battlegroup to open a viable route west towards the Meuse as the cordon of US units tightens around it.

wounded were left behind. The walking wounded were given the task of setting fire to or disabling the surviving equipment after the evacuation had taken place. The retreat out of La Gleize began around 0200hrs on 24 December through the woods to the immediate south of the town. About 770 survivors reached German lines 20km away about 36 hours later, having had only brief encounters with paratroopers from the 82nd Airborne Division. US troops occupied La Gleize in the early morning hours of 24 December after brushing past some rearguards and were surprised to find the town abandoned except for the German wounded and 107 captured GIs.

The 1st SS-Panzer Div. had failed in its mission and had suffered heavy casualties. Personnel casualties through Christmas were about 2,000 men of which more than 300 were prisoners. Equipment losses through Christmas were far heavier and included 11 Kingtigers, 27 Panthers, 20 PzKpfw IV, 12 JagdPz IV or about 65 per cent of the division's initial tank and tank destroyer strength with a significant fraction of the remainder broken down or trapped in the mud.

SPECIAL OPS: OPERATION *GRIEF* AND *STÖSSER*

The German special operations associated with the Ardennes offensive proved complete non-events, yet had consequences far beyond their meager accomplishments. Skorzeny's formation, Panzer Brigade 150, had been formed in November 1944 in an attempt to recruit soldiers with a knowledge of English who could pass as American troops. Less than a dozen with colloquial American English were found, along with another 400 who spoke the language with less proficiency. As a result the size of the unit was scaled back to two battalions and the best speakers were segregated into a commando unit – the Steinhau team. Attempts to collect captured American equipment were not particularly successful as few German frontline units wanted to part with their much-prized jeeps, and the tanks and armored cars that were rounded up were in poor mechanical condition. Five Panther tanks were modified to look like M10 tank destroyers, and five Sturmgeschütz III assault guns were modified to hide their identity. The brigade was assigned two separate missions. The Steinhau team totaling 44 soldiers was broken up into six groups, usually consisting of a few men in a jeep, with four groups to infiltrate behind US lines for reconnaissance and two groups to conduct diversionary tasks such as destroying bridges, misdirecting traffic and cutting communications. The main body of Panzer Brigade 150 was positioned to the rear of 1st SS-Panzer Corps, and once the Hohes Venn was reached beyond the Elsenborn Ridge, the unit would be injected in front of the advancing German force, pretending to be fleeing US troops, and race to capture at least two bridges over the Meuse at Amay, Huy or Andenne.

The Steinhau teams departed during the first two days of the offensive. At least 8 commandos were captured, although American records suggest that a total of 18 were caught. The actual effect of the teams is difficult to calculate since they have become shrouded in myth and legend. While no major reconnaissance discovery or major demolition operation was carried out by the Steinhau teams, the capture of several of the groups caused chaos in American rear areas. The 106th Division captured a document outlining the general scheme of Operation Grief the first morning of the fighting, and several of the captured German commandos revealed their mission. One spread the rumor, entirely false, that a team was on its way to assassinate General Eisenhower, which led to his virtual imprisonment at his headquarters for a few days. A young American counter-intelligence officer, Earl Browning, came up with the idea of asking suspicious characters trivia questions about sports or Hollywood that would only be known by someone living in the United States. The security precautions caused far more trouble than the Steinhau teams themselves.

After the 1st SS-Panzer Corps failed to make a significant dent in American defenses in the Elsenborn region, Skorzeny realized that there was little chance that his unit would actually be used as intended. On the evening of 17 December, he was given permission for it to serve with the 1st SS-Panzer Division in an attempt to capture the key crossroads town of Malmédy, which had been by-passed by Kampfgruppe Peiper earlier in the day.

Malmédy was initially held by the 291st Engineer Battalion. Curiously enough it was then reinforced by a US unit specifically assigned to deal with rear area threats. In November 1944 the First US Army had formed a Security Command around the 23rd Tank Destroyer Group to counter German guerilla groups and saboteurs. Two of its units, the 99th (Norwegian) Infantry Battalion and "T Force" consisting of an armored infantry battalion with a supporting tank destroyer company, were dispatched to the Malmédy-Stavelot depot area to guard the junction until the 30th Division arrived. The 120th Infantry, 30th Division arrived in Malmédy before Peiper's attack began on 21 December.

Peiper's force attacked before dawn along the two main roads into the town. In the early morning darkness, the columns were stopped by concentrated rifle and bazooka fire, reinforced with artillery. As dawn broke and the fog lifted, American artillery spotters were able to work over the German forces stalled near one of the bridges leading into town. By the afternoon both German battlegroups were forced to withdraw having lost many of their strange Panzers. Another attack was launched before dawn on 22 December but was quickly beaten back. Rather than risk any further German advances, the US engineers blew several of the key bridges later in the afternoon. One of the most tragic episodes of the Malmédy fighting occurred the next day when US bombers, mistakenly informed that Malmédy was in German hands, bombed the town, killing over 200 civilians as well as some US troops. Panzer Brigade 150 remained in the lines until late December and was later returned to Germany and disbanded.

The German paratroop mission, Operation *Stösser*, was an even clumsier mess than Operation *Grief*. After having been delayed a day due to a lack of trucks to transport Colonel von der Heydte's paratroopers to the airbases, it finally set off at 0300hrs on 17 December. One rifle company was dumped 50km behind German lines near Bonn and the signal platoon ended up immediately in front of German lines along the stalemated Monschau front in the north. The drop was hindered

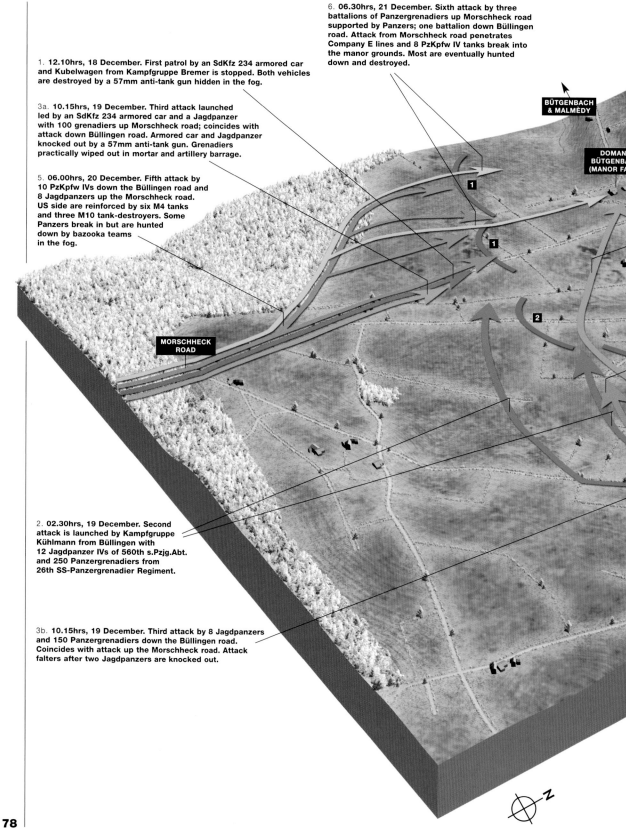

1. **12.10hrs, 18 December.** First patrol by an SdKfz 234 armored car and Kubelwagen from Kampfgruppe Bremer is stopped. Both vehicles are destroyed by a 57mm anti-tank gun hidden in the fog.

3a. **10.15hrs, 19 December.** Third attack launched led by an SdKfz 234 armored car and a Jagdpanzer with 100 grenadiers up Morschheck road; coincides with attack down Büllingen road. Armored car and Jagdpanzer knocked out by a 57mm anti-tank gun. Grenadiers practically wiped out in mortar and artillery barrage.

5. **06.00hrs, 20 December.** Fifth attack by 10 PzKpfw IVs down the Büllingen road and 8 Jagdpanzers up the Morschheck road. US side are reinforced by six M4 tanks and three M10 tank-destroyers. Some Panzers break in but are hunted down by bazooka teams in the fog.

6. **06.30hrs, 21 December.** Sixth attack by three battalions of Panzergrenadiers up Morschheck road supported by Panzers; one battalion down Büllingen road. Attack from Morschheck road penetrates Company E lines and 8 PzKpfw IV tanks break into the manor grounds. Most are eventually hunted down and destroyed.

BÜTGENBACH & MALMÉDY

DOMAN BÜTGENBA (MANOR FA

MORSCHHECK ROAD

2. **02.30hrs, 19 December.** Second attack is launched by Kampfgruppe Kühlmann from Büllingen with 12 Jagdpanzer IVs of 560th s.Pzjg.Abt. and 250 Panzergrenadiers from 26th SS-Panzergrenadier Regiment.

3b. **10.15hrs, 19 December.** Third attack by 8 Jagdpanzers and 150 Panzergrenadiers down the Büllingen road. Coincides with attack up the Morschheck road. Attack falters after two Jagdpanzers are knocked out.

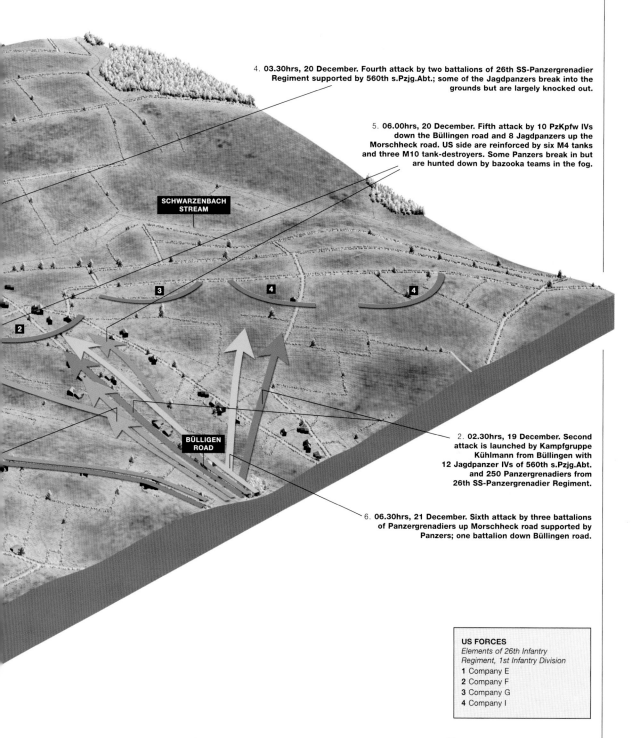

4. 03.30hrs, 20 December. Fourth attack by two battalions of 26th SS-Panzergrenadier Regiment supported by 560th s.Pzjg.Abt.; some of the Jagdpanzers break into the grounds but are largely knocked out.

5. 06.00hrs, 20 December. Fifth attack by 10 PzKpfw IVs down the Büllingen road and 8 Jagdpanzers up the Morschheck road. US side are reinforced by six M4 tanks and three M10 tank-destroyers. Some Panzers break in but are hunted down by bazooka teams in the fog.

SCHWARZENBACH STREAM

BÜLLIGEN ROAD

2. 02.30hrs, 19 December. Second attack is launched by Kampfgruppe Kühlmann from Büllingen with 12 Jagdpanzer IVs of 560th s.Pzjg.Abt. and 250 Panzergrenadiers from 26th SS-Panzergrenadier Regiment.

6. 06.30hrs, 21 December. Sixth attack by three battalions of Panzergrenadiers up Morschheck road supported by Panzers; one battalion down Büllingen road.

US FORCES
Elements of 26th Infantry Regiment, 1st Infantry Division
1 Company E
2 Company F
3 Company G
4 Company I

HITLERJUGEND HALTED AT DOM BÜTGENBACH

18–21 December, viewed from the south-east, showing the series of attack against the manor farm held by elements of US 26th Infantry Regiment. 12th SS-Panzer Division *Hitlerjugend* are subsequently withdrawn from this sector.

by severe crosswinds as well as poor navigation, and only about 60 paratroopers landed with von der Heydte himself in the Hohe Venn moors. This was too small a group to carry out the planned capture of Meuse bridges since such a small force could certainly not hold on to any bridge. Over the next few days, the paratroopers performed reconnaissance, conducted nuisance raids, and gathered another 300 paratroopers scattered over the Belgian countryside. With 1st SS-Panzer Corps nowhere near the Meuse River and not even on Elsenborn Ridge, the mission of the paratroopers was pointless. Late on 21 December they were ordered to cross back to German lines near Monschau.

Hitlerjugend Halted

On the evening of 18 December, after its costly attack on Krinkelt-Rocherath, the 12th SS-Panzer Division *Hitlerjugend* was ordered by the corps commander, Hermann Preiss, to shift the main direction of its attack towards Bütgenbach. Movement was slow due to the traffic jams in the Eifel and the wretched state of the roads through Losheimergraben after the past days' heavy traffic. The forest roads were not designed for this level of use, and in some areas, the constant travel of heavy tracked vehicles had worn down the road into muddy trenches with the road banks level with the Panzers' engine decks.

The 26th Infantry of "Big Red One" – the 1st Infantry Division – held the Bütgenbach approaches. The regiment was in rough shape after having fought along the fringes of the Hürtgen forest earlier in the month. It was deployed east of Bütgenbach, with its lead battalion, the 2/26th Infantry on a hill overlooking the manor farm of Domane Bütgenbach, better known to the Americans as Dom Bütgenbach. The first element of *Hitlerjugend* to arrive in the area around noon of 18 December was Kampfgruppe Bremer, based around a reconnaissance battalion. A patrol consisting of an SdKfz 234 armored car and a Kubelwagen moved up the road towards Dom Bütgenbach and both vehicles were destroyed by a 57mm anti-tank gun hidden in the fog. The two trucks that followed disgorged their infantry into the woods to the south of the farm and they were decimated by an artillery barrage.

The main elements of *Hitlerjugend* reached Büllingen on the night of 18/19 December in three battlegroups. The first attack was launched around 0230hrs by Kampfgruppe Kühlmann consisting of 12 Jagdpanzer IV tank destroyers from schweres Panzerjäger Abteilung 560 and two companies of Panzergrenadiers of 26th SS-Panzergrenadier Regiment. With the armor in the vanguard and the grenadiers behind, the attack formed up 700 yards in front of the American positions, cloaked in the dark and thick fog. The 26th Infantry began firing illumination rounds from their mortars and then called in artillery. The potent combination of artillery and small arms fire stopped the Panzergrenadiers, and several of the tank destroyers became bogged in the muddy ground in front of the American positions. Three tank destroyers broke through into the manor itself, but they turned back when confronted with a 155mm artillery barrage. Two of the three were knocked out while trying to escape. The attack petered out after an hour leaving about 100 dead, and three burning Jagdpanzers.

The American positions were pounded by German artillery until around 1015hrs. An attack from the south along the Morschheck road was spearheaded by an SdKfz 234 armored car and a tank destroyer. Both were knocked out at close range by a 57mm anti-tank gun and the Panzergrenadier company was almost wiped out in the ensuing artillery and mortar barrage. A second attack was launched shortly after from Büllingen but after two Jagdpanzers were knocked out the attack faltered. By this stage, the forward elements of *Hitlerjugend* were suffering from ammunition shortages, and further attacks were postponed until more supplies could be brought forward along the congested roads. *Hitlerjugend*'s commander, Hugo Kraas, reinforced Kampfgruppe Kühlmann with the remainder of his available tanks and Jagdpanzers. The reinforced German battlegroup set off around midnight and was immediately subjected to US artillery fire even while forming up. The main thrust came from Büllingen with a supporting thrust from Morschheck. Once again spearheaded by tank destroyers from the 560th schweres Panzerjäger Abteilung, the attack again encountered very stiff resistance and heavy artillery fire. At least five Jagdpanzers broke through the infantry trench line and advanced into the manor farm itself. Without infantry support, two were destroyed by bazooka teams and two more withdrew. Several of the German tank destroyers became stuck in the mud and the fighting finally ended around 05.30 as both sides licked their wounds. The American infantry had held, but there were serious shortages in bazooka rockets and anti-tank mines. Casualties on both sides had been high, and about 12 Jagdpanzers had been knocked out or bogged down in the fourth attack on Dom Bütgenbach.

Rather than give the Americans time to recover and reorganize their defense, Kraas sent other elements from Kampfgruppe Kühlmann to attack the manor around 0600hrs. This included eight surviving Jagdpanzers from Morschheck, and about ten PzKpfw IVs and Panthers from Büllingen. The Jagdpanzers crunched into the American trench line, running over at least one 57mm anti-tank gun. As in the previous attacks, American artillery and small arms fire kept the Panzergrenadiers away from the American trench line, and when the German Panzers reached the forward defenses, they were hunted down in the fog by bazooka teams. The attack finally collapsed around dawn. It was the last major attack on 20 December, though smaller infantry attacks continued through the day to little effect. The sPzJgAbt.560, which had been the backbone of the attacks on the manor, was reduced in strength to three Jagdpanthers and ten JagdPz IVs, from an initial strength of 12 Jagdpanthers and 25 JagdPz IVs.

In desperation Kraas decided to make one last assault with all his Panzergrenadier battalions and surviving armor. All four artillery battalions supported the attack with their remaining ammunition. The heavy artillery barrage hit the American positions around 0300 on 21 December, causing severe casualties. The Americans responded by calling in their own artillery on suspected assembly points. The attack was postponed when a Panzergrenadier battalion became lost in the dark. It was finally located and the attack began around 0625, three hours behind schedule. The attack began badly when the lead Panther tank and a Jagdpanther following it were destroyed by 57mm anti-tank gunfire. Nevertheless, the Panzers managed to knock out every surviving 57mm anti-tank gun defending the southern positions facing the Morschheck road. The attack continued until dawn, with eight PzKpfw IV tanks fighting their way into the manor itself. Two M4 tanks and two PzKpfw IV tanks were destroyed in a point-blank duel. The remaining six began moving through the farm buildings, followed by a half-dozen Panzergrenadiers, the only German infantry to make it into the manor. They were quickly killed by headquarters staff from the regimental command post, and the PzKpfw IV tanks used the cover of the stone farm buildings to try to avoid being hit by tank fire from a pair of M4 tanks on a neighboring hill.

The pre-dawn attack had ripped open a gap in the American defenses along the southern side, but continual artillery fire prevented the German infantry from exploiting it. A renewed Panzer attack around 1000 from the south side was stopped cold when an M10 tank destroyer knocked out several tanks in quick succession. The fighting continued intermittently through the late morning, with reinforcements finally arriving in the early afternoon on the American side in the form of four M36 90mm tank destroyers of the 613th TD Battalion. These were assigned to hunt down the surviving PzKpfw IV tanks lurking in the farm itself. They began firing their guns through the wooden walls of the barn, convincing the Panzer crews to retreat. Two of the three tanks were hit while withdrawing and only one escaped.

This last attack convinced Kraas that it would be impossible to open Rollbahn C towards Liège. The *Hitlerjugend* Division was subsequently pulled out of this sector and sent into the southern sector, later becoming involved in an equally futile attack against Bastogne. Casualties in the attack on the Dom Bütgenbach manor were over 1,200 of which there were 782 dead. During the five days of fighting at Krinkelt-Rocherath and Dom Bütgenbach, *Hitlerjugend* lost 32 of its 41 Panthers, 12 of its 33 PzKpfw IV tanks, three of its 14 Jagdpanthers, and 18 of its 26 Jagdpanzer IV tank destroyers – almost 60 per cent of its initial armored strength.

The losses in the 23rd Infantry had been heavy as well, including 500 killed, wounded or captured out of an initial strength of about 2,500 men. Equipment losses were heavy including five 57mm anti-tank guns, three M4 tanks and three M10 3in. tank destroyers. But the 23rd Infantry had

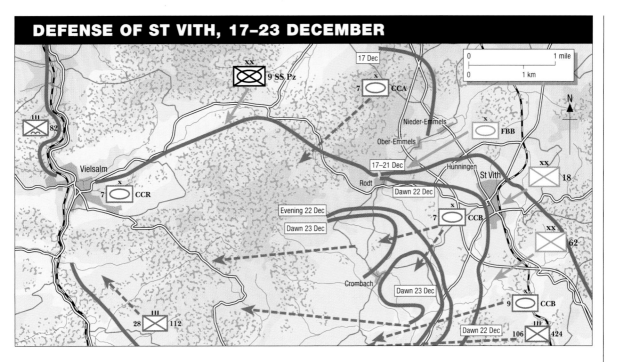

held the Bütgenbach manor and prevented a German breakthrough along the northern route. Divisional artillery, and supporting artillery from neighboring units on the Elsenborn Ridge had been essential in the defense, and during the fighting, about 10,000 artillery rounds were fired in support of the 23rd Infantry.

The Lost Gamble

The failure of the 1st SS-Panzer Corps along the northern shoulder of the Ardennes salient doomed Hitler's plans. The reasons for their failures are many, ignoring for the moment the basic strategic problems with the plan. Dietrich had no "finger-feel" for the battlefield, underestimating the problems posed by the US infantry defenses in the wooded area along the forward edge of battle. The preliminary artillery barrage was a mistake since it caused few US casualties yet ensured that US defenses were alerted when the first wave of German infantry advanced into the forest. The lead infantry units were not given sufficient armored support to overcome the American defenses, as a result of which they faltered in the face of well-entrenched troops. The attacks were channeled down the handful of roads suitable for vehicle traffic instead of making use of the many smaller forest trails which would have allowed the use of more infantry units to infiltrate past the sparsely scattered US defenses and envelope them from the rear. Once out of the woods, the 12th SS-Panzer Division became entangled in the defenses at Krinkelt-Rocherath. Skeptical of the fighting quality of the Volksgrenadier divisions after their failures in the forest fighting, *Hitlerjugend* failed to use them in overcoming the American defenses in the Twin Villages or later at Dom Bütgenbach. The use of isolated tanks in the built-up towns without sufficient infantry support led to a "Panzer graveyard".

Peiper was much more successful in sticking to the mission plan since he faced such paltry opposition in the opening days of the attack.

The farmyard of Dom Bütgenbach was littered with knocked out equipment including this PzKpfw IV, one of the handful to reach the manor itself during the final skirmishes. In the foreground is a M36 90mm gun motor carriage of 613th Tank Destroyer Battalion. (NARA)

Yet the delays of the first few days, first at Lanzerath, and then on the outskirts of Stavelot, proved fatal. The configuration of his force was ill-suited to a contested advance, being encumbered by fuel-guzzling tanks, especially the Kingtigers, and bereft of bridging equipment or adequate infantry and artillery support. Although fuel shortages would help trap his group in La Gleize, German tactical intelligence was so poor that Peiper had no information on the location of significant US fuel dumps that were within his grasp.

THE DEFENSE OF ST VITH

Of the three German armies that staged the Ardennes operation, the only one to gain a significant breakthrough was Manteuffel's 5th Panzer Army in the center. With the disintegration of the 106th Division on the Schnee Eifel, a substantial rupture was created in the American line. This rupture assisted the southern elements of the 6th Panzer Army, notably Kampfgruppe Peiper, and led to rapid advances by units of the 5th Panzer Army, especially the drive of the 116th Panzer Division on Houfallize. However, the full exploitation of this sector was hampered by an extended salient around the key road junction of St Vith that acted as "a thumb down the German throat".

St Vith had been the headquarters of the hapless 106th Division. By 17 December William Hoge's CCB/9th Armored Division had begun to arrive and was in the process of reinforcing the isolated 424th Infantry. The commander of CCB/ 7th Armored Division, BrigGen Bruce Clarke, arrived in St Vith at 1030hrs. Major General Alan Jones explained that he had lost contact with his two regiments on the Schnee Eifel, and that he wanted Clarke to attack towards the Losheim Gap to relieve them. With his armored columns having a difficult time moving from the Netherlands due to the congested roads, Clarke suggested that they contact both regiments and agree on a common meeting point. Clarke was disturbed to learn that the division had no firm radio communications with either regiment as all the field telephone lines had been cut and the division had not set up a proper radio net prior to the attack. During this discussion, Colonel Devine of the 14th Cavalry Group burst in, following the rout of his command along the Poteau-Recht road, in a state of near collapse. The divisional headquarters was in turmoil and paralyzed by confusion, yet at 1330 when MajGen Middleton called Jones, he was told that "Clarke is here, he has troops coming. We are going to be all right." Clarke was disturbed that Jones would provide such a deceptive picture of the actual situation to the corps commander, but Jones remarked that "Middleton has enough problems already". By 1430 German troops were beginning to approach St Vith from the east, and small arms fire could be heard on the approaches to the town. Jones turned to Clarke and said "You take command, I'll give you all I have". Although inferior in rank to Jones and several of his divisional staff, Clarke was the only officer at the headquarters with any combat experience, and so took command of the rapidly disintegrating defense. The only organized force in the town was the divisional engineer battalion and an attached corps engineer battalion. Clarke ordered the division engineer, Lieutenant Colonel Tom Riggs, to take the troops along with the headquarters security platoon and to advance down the road to the east of the town, dig in and stop any advancing German forces. There were a few bright spots. Lieutenant Colonel Roy Clay, commander of the 275th Armored Field Artillery Battalion, attached to the shattered 14th Cavalry Group, showed up at the headquarters and asked Clarke if he wanted any fire support. His unit provided the only artillery support of the St Vith defense until the 7th Armored Division arrived and remained a vital element of the defense.

Command of the St Vith sector fell to BrigGen Bruce Clarke of CCB/7th Armored Division after the 106th Division's headquarters departed. Clarke had commanded the CCA/4th Armored Division in September 1944 when it repulsed an earlier German counter-offensive during the Lorraine campaign. (MHI)

By the afternoon some 7th Armored Division units began to arrive led by Troop B, 87th Cavalry Recon Squadron. They were hastily dispatched to create a defensive line north and east of the town. German attacks were uncoordinated due to the rush to move westward. Elements of Kampfgruppe Hansen bumped into the western defenses near Poteau, while infantry forces from the 18th VGD probed along the eastern edges of the town. The bitterest fighting on 18 December took place around Poteau as CCA/7th Armored Div. attempted to seize the town which was essential to keep open supply lines to the rear.

Manteuffel had expected his units to capture St Vith on the first day of the offensive. The town posed a variety of problems, not the least of which was that it split the 5th Panzer Army in two. Furthermore, it controlled the best roads through the area between 6th Panzer Army and 5th Panzer Army, including the only decent east–west rail line, vital to resupply the offensive once the Meuse was reached. On the night of 17/18 December, Manteuffel discussed the problem with Model, who suggested that the Führer Begleit Brigade (FBB) be committed to destroying the St Vith pocket. This brigade was one of the best in 5th Panzer Army, its cadres having been taken from the *Grossdeutschland* Division. It was in army reserve, with an aim to use it as the main exploitation force after one of the Panzer corps succeeded in making a breakthrough. As a result reassigning it to deal with St Vith meant giving up the opportunity to use it in the central role in the later phase of the campaign. This reassignment indicates how seriously both Model and Manteuffel viewed the threat posed by St Vith. Manteuffel hoped that the injection of this unit into the St Vith battle would result in a quick

THE FORTIFIED GOOSE EGG – REARGUARD DEFENSE IN
ST VITH, 21 DECEMBER 1944 (pages 86–87)

General Bruce Clarke's approach to defending St Vith was to use the mobility and firepower of his tank units to keep the Wehrmacht at bay as long as possible. US armored divisions were weak in infantry with only three battalions per division, and while they could be used for defense, the type of linear defense in depth practiced by infantry units was out of the question. So the tanks and other supporting troops held positions as long as possible, and then fell back to more defensible positions. Here we see a pair of M4 medium tanks conducting a rearguard action in the outskirts of St Vith shortly before Clarke was forced to abandon the town. The M4 medium tank was a durable, reliable design but by the winter of 1944, it was out-classed when facing the newer German Panzers such as the PzKpfw V Panther tank. Like most of the campaigns of 1944–45, the St Vith fighting saw very few tank-vs.-tank encounters and the M4 usually fought against German infantry. In such a mission, many tankers preferred the older version of the M4 armed with the 75mm gun as seen here (1), rather than the newer version introduced in the summer of 1944 with the long-barreled 76mm gun. Although the 76mm gun was more effective against Panzers, it fired a mediocre high explosive projectile compared to the older 75mm projectile, which contained almost twice the amount of high explosive. More than three-quarters of the tank gun projectiles fired in 1944–45 were high explosive, so the preference for the older gun was not as crazy as it sounds. A significant problem with the M4 medium tank was its mediocre armor, which

had not been increased since its debut in 1942. While some tank units had begun to add sandbags or other forms of improvised armor to their Sherman tanks, this was not yet a common practice in the 7th Armored Division during the Ardennes fighting. Actually, the division had used sandbags during the summer and fall, but when Clarke took over the CCB, he ordered all the sandbags and camouflage netting removed. Clarke, like many veterans of the Patton's Third Army, felt that sandbags were ineffective and adversely affected the tank's automotive performance. The tank in the background has been hit and the crew can be seen baling out (2). One of the most common causes of US tank losses in the late 1944 fighting was the German *Panzerfaust*, a small disposable rocket launcher that fired a shaped-charge grenade. This was capable of penetrating the armor of the M4, but it was not particularly accurate, and had to be fired from close range, rendering its user very vulnerable to return fire. If it did hit the M4, it stood a good chance of setting off an internal ammunition fire. It is largely a myth that the Sherman burned due to its use of a gasoline engine. Operational studies concluded that most were lost after their ammunition caught fire. Usually the ammunition propellant caught fire when its brass casing was penetrated by a hot shard of metal from the anti-tank projectile. It took about 30 seconds before the propellant fire spread to neighboring ammunition, and once this occurred, the inside of the tank became a blast furnace with the fire often lasting a day or more. Sherman crews soon learned that once their tank was hit, it was a good idea to bale out as soon as possible. (Howard Gerrard)

decision, permitting the brigade to revert back to its original mission. Moving the brigade through the congested area behind the Schnee Eifel proved to be a major problem and even though the brigade was underway on the morning of 17 December, it was still tied up in the traffic jams around Schönberg late the following night. The plan called for the FBB to attack the town from the north, the 18th VGD from the east, and the 62nd VGD from the south. Although the initial attack was scheduled for 19 December, the continued delays in moving the FBB into position made this impossible.

The southern sector held by CCB/9th Armored Div. and the 424th Infantry was precarious, so late in the day, Hoge's combat command withdrew over the Our river. Hoge drove to St Vith that night expecting to meet with Gen Jones, but encountered Bruce Clarke instead. Although nominally under the command of the 106th Division, Hoge agreed to remain in the salient with Clarke to protect the southern flank. Other units also gravitated to the St Vith pocket including the 112th Infantry, separated from its 28th Division.

The first serious attack against St Vith developed around midnight on 19/20 December when the FBB deployed the first units to arrive in the sector, an infantry battalion and two assault gun companies. This attack was quickly repulsed, but later in the day, the lightly defended outposts in Ober- and Nieder-Emmels were taken. The attacks substantially intensified on 21 December as more of the FBB arrived. One battalion from the brigade managed to temporarily seize control of a portion of the road westward from St Vith to Viesalm, but this force was pushed back by CCB/7th Armored Division. One of the most significant changes from the previous days' fighting was the more extensive use of German artillery, which had finally escaped from the traffic jams. An intense barrage of the town began at 1100hrs. Most of the German attacks were preceded by intense artillery fire, and the grenadiers attacked with little respite. The positions of the 38th Armored Infantry Battalion on the eastern side, which included the remnants of Col Riggs' original engineer defense force, was hardest hit in five attacks that afternoon. More intense attacks followed with three more in the late afternoon and early evening, the first along the Schönberg road, then down the Malmédy road, and finally up the Prum road. The defensive line of the CCB/7th Armored Division was penetrated in at least three places by evening, with few replacements available. By 2200hrs Gen Clarke realized that the current positions were not tenable and decided to pull his forces out of the town, to the high ground southwest of the town. The town was occupied by the 18th VGD the night of 21/22 December. Clarke estimated that he had lost almost half his strength in the day's fighting.

The American resistance in the St Vith salient was substantially delaying the German advance westward since it prevented the 6th Panzer Army from supporting the rapid advance of the 5th Panzer Army further south. Model ordered the pocket crushed and directed Dietrich to commit elements of the 2nd SS-Panzer Corps to assist in the task. The early morning fighting of 22 December took place in the midst of a heavy snowfall, and began at 0200hrs with a major attack of the FBB against Rodt, to the west of St Vith. This saw the heaviest use of Panzers in this sector to date, amounting to three companies with about 25 tanks. The FBB had great difficulty operating tanks due to the extremely muddy

The CCB of 9th Armored Division was the first reinforcement to reach St Vith, and was commanded by BrigGen William Hoge. He commanded the Engineer Special Brigade at Normandy, and when posted to the 9th Armored Division, the commander complained, arguing that he should have been given a divisional command. (NARA)

conditions in the area, and several Panzers became stuck in the mud before reaching the town. The fighting in Rodt was savage with M4 tanks blasting away at Panzergrenadiers ensconced in the town's stone houses, but by late morning, the US defenders were forced to withdraw. The fighting lasted for nine hours and action separated Clarke's CCB from the rest of the 7th Armored Division. The 62nd VGD also succeeded in pushing back the CCB/9th Armored Division, further compressing the St Vith pocket.

There had been a re-organization of the command structure in the sector that day, with the 7th Armored Division now falling under the XVIII Airborne Command, and the northern elements of the First US Army coming under the overall command of the British 21st Army Group and Field Marshal Bernard Montgomery. During the fighting Clarke was visited by his divisional commander, MajGen Robert Hasbrouck ,who had brought along the new plan for the sector from Gen Matthew Ridgway of the XVIII Airborne Corps. Ridgway proposed that 7th Armored Division remain in place, even though surrounded, in several "fortified goose-eggs" that would be supplied by air. Clarke remarked that it looked more like "Custer's last stand" and both officers were disturbed by the concept, which they thought reflected Ridgway's paratrooper mentality, inexperience with armored units, and lack of understanding of the precarious state of the units in the salient. Ridgway wanted Clarke to hold on to St Vith and planned to eventually push forward with the 82nd Airborne Division. The British liaison officer at Hasbrouck's command post caught wind of the argument and informed Montgomery. Montgomery visited the 7th Armored Division to gain his own impressions, and later left for Ridgway's headquarters. After a heated discussion with Hodges at First US Army headquarters, Montgomery sent a message to the 7th Armored Division commander, Robert Hasbrouck, "You have accomplished your mission – a mission well-done – It is time to withdraw", having rejected Ridgway's unrealistic plan. The 82nd Airborne pushed forward to Vielsalm to create an escape corridor for the forces inside the St Vith salient.

By the evening of 22 December, CCB/7th Armored Div. had been pushed back about a kilometer along a ridge line stretching from the village of Hinderhausen to Neubruck, with CCB/9th Armored Div. being pushed in behind it from the south. By this stage, the 82nd Airborne Division held the west bank of the Salm river near Vielsalm, but intense pressure from the 6th Panzer Army was making this defense increasingly difficult. The plan was to withdraw the CCB/9th Armored Div. first but this proved impossible due to the intensity of the contact with the 62nd VGD and the muddy condition of the roads. Hoge was seriously concerned that they would have to abandon all their vehicles and retreat on foot as the mud was so deep. Hasbrouck radioed Clarke and Hoge that "if you don't join them [the 82nd Airborne] soon, the opportunity will be gone". The withdrawal time was reset for 0600hrs on the morning of 23 December. That evening Clarke instructed rear area troops to chop branches from pine trees along the escape route to provide some firm footing along the muddy road. Much to his relief, the temperature dropped abruptly on the night of 22/23 December, freezing the ground rock hard along the one road out of the salient. The withdrawal was successfully executed, with German forces close on the heels of the retreating US forces. During the morning fighting, two FBB Panzers were knocked out, and a few of the US tanks were lost as well. The cost of the defense of St Vith was 3,400 casualties, 59 M4 tanks, 29 M5A1 light tanks and 25 armored cars.

AFTERMATH

The successful defense of the St Vith salient for six days had several significant effects on German operations. It tied down forces of 5th Panzer Army intended for other missions, especially the Führer Begleit Brigade. Its proximity to the main advance routes of the 6th Panzer Army seriously delayed the commitment of the 2nd SS-Panzer Corps until the second week of the fighting. After the war Manteuffel wrote to Clarke that "the outstanding delaying actions around St Vith were decisive for the drive of my troops and for the 6.SS-Panzer Army too! In that respect, the battle of St Vith was of greatest consequence for the two armies – and the whole German offensive. In the end, St Vith fell, but the momentum of the 58th Panzer Corps in the south had been destroyed and that influenced the southern [47th Panzer] corps too!" The defense of St Vith influenced other sectors as well, preventing the 6th Panzer Army from using alternate routes to relieve Kampfgruppe Peiper, trapped at the time in La Gleize.

While the Battle of the Bulge was far from over on 23 December 1944, Hitler's plans had been foiled. The main stroke, the 6th Panzer Army attack towards Liège, had been decisively stopped by the defeat of the 12th SS-Panzer Division at Krinkelt-Rocherath and Dom Bütgenbach, and the destruction of the spearhead of the 1st SS-Panzer Division at La Gleize. When the road junctions around St Vith were finally opened on 23 December, it permitted a belated surge of German Panzer units forward towards the Meuse – so badly delayed it was a charge to nowhere. The 2nd Panzer Division came near to reaching the Meuse at Dinant on Christmas Day, but ran out of fuel. By this time British armored units had taken up positions on the western bank of the Meuse, and there were no significant strategic objectives in this sector. Units of the 2nd SS-Panzer Corps raced west only to find the approaches blocked by fresh American reinforcements. There would be fierce battles along the front for the next few days, but the German advance had reached its high water mark by Christmas far short of its objectives. The delay caused by the defense of St Vith had given the 12th Army Group time to shift additional forces into the Ardennes, including the 2nd and 3rd Armored Divisions. These reinforcements halted the Panzers during a series of sharp battles around Christmas. On 26 December the spearheads of the 5th Panzer Army began retreating. Furthermore, the spearhead of Patton's Third Army, the 4th Armored Division, was on the outskirts of Bastogne, and the siege of that other vital road junction would end shortly.

PART 2
BASTOGNE

The German counter-offensive in the Ardennes in December 1944 was the decisive campaign of the war in North-West Europe. Hitler's desperate gamble to reverse the course of the war in the West failed within a fortnight. The earlier volume in this series covered the opening stages of this campaign, focusing on the critical German failures on the northern shoulder along the Elsenborn Ridge and near St Vith.[1] The German attack was heavily weighted towards its right wing, the attack by the 6th Panzer Army towards the Meuse River near Liege. When this assault failed to win a breakthrough, its smaller neighbor, the 5th Panzer Army succeeded in overwhelming the green 106th Infantry Division, opening up a gap in the American lines. During the second week of the Ardennes counter-offensive, Hitler attempted to redeem his failing offensive by exploiting the success of the 5th Panzer Army. Panzer divisions formerly assigned to 6th Panzer Army were shifted towards the rupture in the center. Although the Panzer spearheads managed to penetrate deep behind the American lines, precious time had been lost and American armored reinforcements arrived in the days before Christmas. In a series of hard-fought battles before the Meuse in the final days of the year, the Panzer divisions were decimated and the attack decisively halted. Nevertheless, with the onset of harsh winter weather, it would take a month to finally erase the bulge.

THE STRATEGIC SITUATION

The German Ardennes offensive was conducted by three armies along a 37-mile (60km) front, aimed at splitting the Allied armies by driving all the way to Antwerp. Most senior Wehrmacht commanders doubted that such an ambitious objective could be achieved. A number of commanders proposed an operation with the more limited and practical objective of reaching the Meuse, but this was not formally proposed to Hitler because the chief of the Wehrmacht operations staff recognized that Hitler would reject it out of hand. Borrowing from bridge terms, the German officers called the two options "Little Slam" and "Grand Slam". The "Little Slam" objectives help to explain why the German commanders continued to push their forces forward after Christmas, long after it was clear that Hitler's "Grand Slam" objectives could never be reached.

The attack force was not spread evenly along the front, but weighted very heavily towards the right flank and the 6th Panzer Army. The reasons for this were both the geography of the Ardennes and the timing of the operation. The most direct route across the Meuse River was on the

---

1 Campaign 115 *Battle of the Bulge 1944 (1) St Vith and the Northern Shoulder* (2003)

northern side of the attack, using the road network stretching from the German border to Liege. In the center of the attack zone, there were also routes leading to Liege, but they were more circuitous and stretched for a greater distance. In the southern sector emanating out of Luxembourg, the terrain was too mountainous for rapid mobile operations. Time was a critical element, since the plan assumed that the Allies would begin shifting forces into the Ardennes once the attack began. So the shortest route was inevitably the most attractive route. To succeed, the plan required that the Meuse be reached and crossed within four days. Any longer, and the Allies could bring up enough forces to halt the attack.

The heaviest Panzer forces were allocated to the 6th Panzer Army, including two Waffen-SS Panzer corps and about 60 percent of the armored strength of the entire offensive. The 5th Panzer Army in the center had most of the remainder of the armored force in the form of two weaker Panzer corps. The mission of this force was to protect the left flank of 6th Panzer Army, as well as to seize control of the longer, but still valuable, routes to the Meuse in this sector. The final element of the attack, the 7th Army, had practically no armor at all and was an infantry force better suited to the mountainous terrain in Luxembourg. Given its lack of mobility, there were few expectations that it would play a major role in the breakthrough. Instead of pushing to the northwest like the other two armies, once it overcame the initial border defenses it was to wheel to its left, creating a defensive line against American reinforcements coming from the south.

As has been detailed in Part 1, the initial attacks in the northern sector failed. The stereotyped tactics used to punch through the forested border area caused needless delays, and permitted the US Army to conduct a slow, deliberate retreat while bringing in significant infantry reinforcements. The attacks of 1st SS-Panzer Corps failed to make a breakthrough of the US infantry defenses and suffered heavy casualties in the process. The right wing of the 5th Panzer Army used more appropriate infiltration tactics to penetrate the initial American defensive line and managed to trap two of the regiments of the 106th Infantry Division, leading to the largest mass surrender of US troops in Europe in World War II. Having created a massive gap in the American lines, the 5th Panzer Army inserted two of its Panzer divisions to exploit the success. The main problem in this sector was that the breach had not been complete. US forces still held the vital road and rail junction at St Vith, which impeded the full exploitation of the gap since it made it difficult to reinforce the spearhead units. The American troops in the salient at St Vith finally withdrew on 23 December. Having covered these operations in the previous volume in this series, the focus here will be on the operations in the southern and central sectors, primarily the operations of the 5th Panzer Army in the center and the 7th Army in Luxembourg.

CHRONOLOGY

11 October First draft of Ardennes plan, codenamed *Wacht am Rhein*, submitted to Hitler.

04.00, 16 December Infantry in 5th Panzer Army sector begin infiltration over Our River.

05.30, 16 December Operation *Herbstnebel* (Autumn Mist) begins with opening barrages against forward US positions in Ardennes.

06.00, 16 December German preparatory artillery ends, infantry begins advancing.

Afternoon-evening, 16 December Bradley orders 10th Armored Division to Bastogne; Eisenhower agrees to shift XVIII Airborne Corps to Ardennes.

17 December 110th Infantry Regiment HQ overwhelmed in Clerf, gap in American lines is open after nightfall.

Midnight, 17 December Middleton deploys CCR, 9th Armored Division, to block approaches to Bastogne.

Nightfall, 18 December First elements of 101st Airborne arrive in Bastogne.

08.00, 19 December First probes by German reconnaissance units into US defenses on outskirts of Bastogne.

Nightfall, 19 December US defenses in Wiltz overwhelmed by end of day; another road to Bastogne is open.

19 December Eisenhower meets with senior US commanders to plan further responses to German attack.

20 December Eisenhower shifts control of US First and Ninth Army units, except for Middleton's VIII Corps, from Bradley's 12th Army Group to Montgomery's 21st Army Group.

Noon, 20 December Model redeploys the II SS-Panzer Corps from the failed 6th Panzer Army attack to the center.

Morning, 21 December III Corps of Patton's Third Army begins attack to relieve Bastogne.

Afternoon, 21 December 116th Panzer Division reaches Hotton but cannot secure town. Battles for the road junctions on the Tailles plateau begin.

11.30, 22 December German emissaries demand Bastogne's surrender; General McAuliffe replies "Nuts".

Evening, 22 December Bastogne is surrounded when Panzer Lehr Division begins moving towards the Ourthe River.

Night 22/23 December High-pressure front moves into Ardennes bringing clear skies and freezing temperatures.

06.00, 23 December US forces begin withdrawal from St Vith salient.

Late morning, 23 December II SS Panzer Corps begins moving towards Tailles plateau with 2nd SS Panzer Division in the lead.

Evening, 23 December 2nd Panzer Division reports it has reached within 6miles (9km) of Meuse River near Dinant.

Late evening, 23 December 2nd SS Panzer Division *Das Reich* overruns US defenses and seizes Manhay road junction.

25 December Clear weather permits intense Allied air activity.

Morning, 25 December US 2nd Armored Division begins surrounding and destroying advance guard of the 2nd Panzer Division on the approaches to Dinant.

Late afternoon, 26 December Task force from 4th Armored Division punches through German defenses, beginning the relief of Bastogne.

Dawn, 27 December 2nd SS Panzer Division pushed out of Grandmenil and Manhay; 6th Panzer Army ordered over to the defensive.

30 December Germans and Americans plan attacks in Bastogne area; German attacks fail to make headway.

3 January Manteuffel attempts a final attack on Bastogne that fails; last major German attack of the Ardennes campaign. US First Army begins attack towards Houfallize to meet up with Patton's Third Army.

16 January US First Army and US Third Army link up at Houfallize.

28 January The last of the territory lost to the German attack is retaken by US troops.

OPPOSING PLANS

THE GERMAN PLAN

The 5th Panzer Army attack was three corps wide, with the 66th Infantry Corps on the right (northern) wing, the 58th Panzer Corps in the center and the 47th Panzer Corps on the left (southern) wing. The task of the 66th Infantry Corps was to capture the key road junction and town of St Vith, and although the corps succeeded in overwhelming the US 106th Infantry Division, it was unable to seize the town, frustrating its intended mission of closing on the Meuse. The task of the 58th Panzer Corps, consisting of the 116th Panzer Division and the 560th Volksgrenadier Division, was to penetrate the border area and move on the Meuse via Houfallize. The 47th Panzer Corps, consisting of the 2nd Panzer Division and the 26th Volksgrenadier Division, had Bastogne as its target. After taking this vital road center, the corps was to proceed to the Meuse and cross in the area south of the heavily fortified city of Namur. Supporting these three corps was a Panzer reserve consisting of the Panzer Lehr Division and the Führer Begleit Brigade, which would be committed once one of the corps secured a major breakthrough. In the event, the problems in overcoming American resistance at St Vith forced the 5th Panzer Army commander, General Hasso von Manteuffel, to commit the Führer Begleit Brigade prematurely.

Given the limited forces at his disposal, Manteuffel realized that he would have to cut corners to accomplish the mission. If the objective was indeed to lunge past the Meuse, then the objectives stated in the plan could not be taken literally. The attack force was spread too thin to actually seize and hold several of the larger towns and cities such as Bastogne, Houfallize, La Roche and St Vith. Accordingly, Manteuffel made it clear to his subordinates that if stiff resistance was encountered, the Panzer forces were to bypass the towns and leave them for the infantry formations following behind to deal with. While this tactic made sense given the strategic objective of the offensive, in the event it would come back to haunt Manteuffel after the main objective of the Meuse River proved to be out of reach, since it left a major obstruction, Bastogne, as a center of resistance in his rear.

Manteuffel's deployment plan was different from that of the neighboring 6th Panzer Army under SS-Obergruppenführer Sepp Dietrich, which was echeloned in depth along very narrow attack corridors. Manteuffel believed that such an approach was foolhardy in view of the lack of adequate roads in the Ardennes, and much as he predicted, the SS-Panzer divisions quickly became bogged down in traffic jams once the attack began. His approach was to deploy his units more broadly on the basis that "if we knocked on ten doors, we would find several open". In the event, his tactics proved far more successful than Dietrich's.

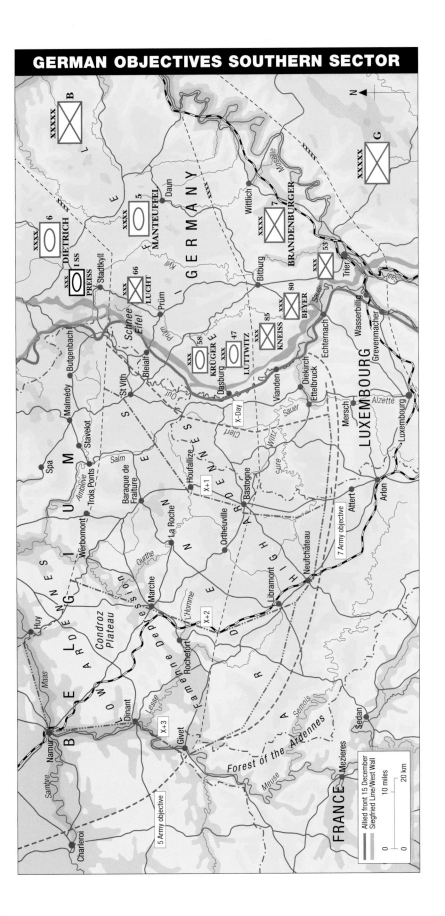

The 7th Army attack was conducted on a narrow axis two corps wide due to the mountainous terrain in Luxembourg. The 85th Infantry Corps on the right was to push through the area around Vianden and, once the US defenses were overcome, swing to the south. The 80th Infantry Corps on the left wing was not expected to push as far through US defenses, but would then swing to the left and establish defensive positions. As in the case of the 5th Panzer Army, the plans contained ambiguous and contradictory elements. Although the emphasis of the plan was for both corps to establish a firm defensive line stretching roughly from Mersch to Gedinne, it also spoke of the need to send out mobile patrols further south along the Semois River to prevent US crossing operations. Yet given the lack of mobility of the divisions under its control, such a task could not be easily accomplished since at many points the Semois was more than 6 miles (10km) further south from the German defensive line.

Hitler ordered a significant shift in Luftwaffe resources to support the Ardennes operation by transferring a large number of fighters from strategic air defense over the Reich to tactical fighter missions over the battlefield. As a result, Luftwaffe Command West's fighter component increased from only 300 single-engine fighters in October 1944 to 1,770 at the time of the offensive. This did not provide much solace for the Wehrmacht however, since there were only 155 ground-attack aircraft available. The majority of fighter pilots were poorly trained compared to their Allied adversaries, and what training they had received focused on ground-controlled intercepts of heavy bombers, not the rough-and-tumble of dogfights and ground strafing. The air operations were supposed to begin with a massive attack on forward Allied airfields codenamed Operation Bodenplatte (baseplate). In the event, the poor weather in the first week of the offensive severely limited Luftwaffe operations and forced the postponement of Bodenplatte until New Year's Day, by which time it was irrelevant. The Ardennes offensive also saw the use of a number of German "wonder weapons", including the bomber version of the Me-262 jet fighter, the first use of the Arado Ar-234 jet bomber, and extensive use of the V-1 guided missile.

The weather in the Ardennes in mid-December was slightly above freezing in the daytime with frequent rain and fog, and sometimes slipping below freezing at night especially in the wooded and hilly areas shaded from the sun. From the German perspective, the frequent overcast and ground fog provided a welcome relief from Allied airpower, and helped to shield the build-up of German forces in the Eifel region. But the weather was a double-edged sword, and the Wehrmacht would pay a price once the offensive began. The wet autumn and frequent cold drizzle left the farm fields in the Ardennes sodden and muddy. This complicated any movement off the roads, and turned every little hamlet and road junction into a bottleneck that had to be overcome before the advance could proceed. For a campaign dependent on speed, the weather was far from ideal.

AMERICAN PLANS

In December 1944, Lieutenant General Omar Bradley's 12th Army Group consisted of three armies. From north to south these were LtGen William H. Simpson's Ninth Army, LtGen Courtney Hodges' First Army and LtGen George S. Patton's Third Army, and they stretched across a front from the Netherlands, along the German–Belgian border to Luxembourg and then to the German frontier along the Saar where they met LtGen Jacob Dever's 6th Army Group. The focus of operations in late November and early December had been on either extreme of the front line, with the central area in the Ardennes quiet due to the difficulty of operating in the hilly and forested terrain. In the northern First and Ninth Armies' zones, the main emphasis had been on the campaign to reach the Roer River, as a preliminary stage to reaching and crossing the Rhine River. By early December, the First Army was in the concluding phase of a bloody struggle to push through the Hürtgen forest to reach the crucial Roer River dams.

The "ghost front" in the Ardennes was held by MajGen Troy Middleton's VIII Corps. The high Ardennes was widely viewed by the US Army as unsuitable for winter operations, so the front was thinly held by four to five divisions. The two northern divisions, the 99th and 106th Divisions, were both green units that had only recently arrived in Europe and were deployed in the quiet Ardennes to gain some experience. The sector further south from St Vith towards Bastogne was held by two veteran divisions, the 28th and 4th Divisions, which had been decimated in the bloody Hürtgen forest fighting. They were in the Ardennes to recuperate and to rebuild their strength. Parts of another new division, the 9th Armored Division, were also present.

Further to the south was Patton's Third Army stretching from Luxembourg into France and posted opposite the Siegfried Line and the Saar region of Germany. Patton's forces had spent November and early December in a series of frustrating battles along the muddy French–German frontier, pushing first through the old Maginot Line then colliding with the Siegfried Line. By mid-December, the Third Army units had secured footholds in the Siegfried Line, and were preparing for a major offensive operation aimed at breaking through the German defensive fortifications and pushing on towards Frankfurt. Codenamed Operation Tink, the attack was planned to be the largest US Army operation of December 1944. Originally scheduled for 19 December, it was finally rescheduled for 21 December.

On 7 December 1944, Eisenhower met with his two senior army group commanders, Bradley and Montgomery in Maastricht to discuss the course of future operations. Montgomery again repeated his view that the 1945 offensive into Germany should be focused on a single thrust spearhead by his 21st Army Group into the northern German plains towards the Ruhr. Eisenhower again disagreed with this strategic option, continuing to favor the broad front approach epitomized by Patton's planned assault towards Frankfurt later in the month. This meeting did not set any specific dates for future offensive operations, since the Allied armies still needed to gain secure footholds for the upcoming Rhine campaign. Little attention was paid to Patton's forthcoming Operation Tink, and it can be surmised that many of the participants felt that it had little more chance of success than the November breakout attempt in the First Army sector, Operation Queen. The presence of the 6th Panzer Army was noted in these discussions, but the general impression was that it was in position near Cologne in preparation for a counter-stroke against any Allied operation over the Rhine.

While most senior Allied leaders failed to anticipate the German offensive in the Ardennes, there were exceptions. One of the most vocal was the G-2 (intelligence) of Patton's Third Army, Colonel Oscar Koch. During a 7 December briefing to Patton in preparation for Operation Tink, Koch detailed the formidable build-up opposite the First Army in the Ardennes, and the potential threat it posed to Third Army operations in the Saar. What worried Patton was the proverbial "dog that did not bark". In spite of some significant advances by Third Army along the Saar in early December, it was not subjected to the usual German counterattack, in spite of the availability of forces along the German frontier. This strongly suggested to him that the Wehrmacht was holding back these units for a specific mission. Patton passed on this assessment to the G-2 section of Eisenhower's headquarters, but when Ike's G-2, General Kenneth Strong, raised this issue with Bradley's intelligence section, they received the standard response. Bradley and his First Army staff were convinced that an offensive in the Ardennes in the winter would be foolhardy, and therefore the force build-up was not for a pre-emptive strike, but rather was intended for a reactive counter-stroke to any major Allied breakthrough towards the Rhine in early 1945.

OPPOSING COMMANDERS

General der Panzertruppen Erich Brandenberger, commander of the 7th Army in the Ardennes.

GERMAN COMMANDERS

The commander of German forces in the west was **Generalfeldmarschall Gerd von Rundstedt**, and the Ardennes sector was the responsibility of Army Group B under **Generalfeldmarschall Walter Model**. Additional details on these senior commanders are contained in the previous volume in this series.[2] The two senior commanders in the southern sector of the Ardennes attack were the two army commanders, Hasso von Manteuffel of 5th Panzer Army and Erich Brandenberger of 7th Army. **General der Panzertruppen Hasso von Manteuffel** was the most talented of the army commanders involved in the Ardennes operation. He was a dynamic, intelligent officer, sometimes nicknamed "Kleiner" by his close friends due to his short stature of only five foot two inches. He was wounded in combat in 1916 while fighting on the Western Front, and had been a youthful advocate of the Panzer force in the 1930s while serving under Heinz Guderian. After a distinguished performance as a regimental commander in North Africa, he was elevated to command the *Grossdeutschland* Division on the Russian Front. He attracted Hitler's personal attention and leapfrogged from divisional commander to 5th Panzer Army commander due to Hitler's favor and his obvious command skills. He was not a political crony like the neighboring 6th Panzer Army commander, Sepp Dietrich, but had received Hitler's recognition as a result of his battlefield accomplishments.

Commander of the 5th Panzer Army, General Hasso von Manteuffel on the left confers with the Army Group B commander, General Walter Model (right) and the inspector of the Panzer force on the Western Front, Generalleutnant Horst Stumpf (center). (MHI)

General der Panzertruppen Erich Brandenberger was a highly capable officer, but his leadership style did not earn him the favor of either Hitler or Model. The Army Group B commander preferred the flashy brilliance of Manteuffel, to the steady, scholarly approach of Brandenberger whom he derided as "a typical product of the general staff system". Yet Brandenberger had a fine combat record, leading the 8th Panzer Division during the invasion of Russia in 1941. He commanded the 29th Army Corps in Russia for a year before the Ardennes offensive when he was given command of the 7th Army.

Manteuffel's corps commanders were, without exception, seasoned Russian Front veterans. They had all started the war as young battalion or regimental commanders and worked their way up through divisional command in Russia. **General der Artillerie Walther Lucht** had begun the war in 1939 as an artillery regiment commander in Poland, and by the time of the France campaign in 1940 he had been elevated to corps artillery command. During the Russian campaign, he was first promoted to army artillery commander, then in February 1942 to command of the 87th Infantry Division, and in March of the 336th Infantry Division, which took part in the efforts to relieve the encircled forces in Stalingrad. He was the area commander for the Kerch Straits in the summer and autumn of 1943 before being posted to 66th Corps command in November 1943 when the formation was on occupation duty in southern France.

General der Panzertruppen Walter Krüger began the war as an infantry regimental commander, was a brigade commander in the 1st Panzer Division during the France campaign in 1940, and was promoted to command the division in July 1941 during the invasion of Russia. He served as the 1st Panzer Division commander in Russia for most of the war, until he was appointed to command the 58th Panzer Corps in February 1944, taking part in the 1944 fighting in France.

General der Panzertruppen Heinrich von Lüttwitz resembled the Hollywood caricature of a German general: fat, monocled, and arrogant.

General der Panzertruppen Heinrich von Lüttwitz, commander of 47th Panzer Corps. (MHI)

Obergruppenführer Willi Bittrich, commander of the II SS-Panzer Corps

Model is seen here consulting with Generalmajor Siegfried von Waldenburg, commander of the 116th Panzer Division in the Ardennes. (MHI)

Generalleutnant Fritz Bayerlein, Rommel's former aide in North Africa, and the commander of Panzer Lehr Division in the Ardennes. (MHI)

Yet he was a seasoned, dynamic Panzer commander. He started the war commanding a motorcycle battalion and became a regimental commander after the France campaign. He first assumed divisional command with the 20th Panzer Division in October 1942, seeing heavy fighting in Russia, and was transferred to the 2nd Panzer Division in February 1944, serving as its commander in the summer fighting in France until the end of August when he was promoted to corps command. The 2nd Panzer Division was the spearhead of his corps during the Ardennes campaign, and he paid it special attention both due to his past connection to the division as well as his doubts about the capabilities of its current commander, Oberst Meinrad von Lauchert who took command only a day before the offensive began.

The corps commanders in Brandenberger's 7th Army were also seasoned Eastern Front veterans, two of them survivors of the summer 1944 debacles in the east. **General der Infanterie Baptist Kneiss** began the war as commander of the 215th Infantry Division, leading it through the early campaigns in France and northern Russia. In November 1942 he was promoted to command the 66th Corps, which was on occupation duty in southern France, and the 85th Corps in July 1944, also in southern France.

General der Infanterie Franz Beyer began the war as an infantry regiment commander, and was promoted to lead the 331st Infantry Division at the end of 1941 during its training in Austria. He remained in command of the division during its assignment to the Russian Front. In March 1943 he was transferred to command the 44th Infantry Division, which was being re-formed in Austria after the original division was lost at Stalingrad and subsequently the unit was deployed to Italy. He was given corps command in late April 1944 on the Eastern Front, serving for short periods with four different corps in the summer battles, finally in the disastrous Crimean campaign in July–August 1944. He was appointed to the 80th Army Corps in early August 1944.

AMERICAN COMMANDERS

The Ardennes sector was part of the front controlled by **Lieutenant General Omar Bradley's** 12th Army Group. The First US Army, commanded by **Lieutenant General Courtney H. Hodges**, covered the broadest area of any Allied army at the time from the Hürtgen forest in the north to the French–Luxembourg border in the south. Hodges was older than Bradley and Patton, and had risen through the ranks of the army after dropping out of the US Military Academy at West Point in 1904 for academic reasons. He saw combat in the Mexican punitive expedition, and again in France in 1918 with the 6th Regiment where he won the Distinguished Service Cross. He was Chief of the Infantry in 1941, and served as deputy commander of the First US Army under Bradley in Normandy in 1944. When the US forces in France expanded in August, Hodges took over command of the First Army when Bradley became 12th Army Group commander. Hodges was the polar opposite to his neighbor to the south, George S. Patton. Dour, reticent, and unassuming, he remained in Bradley's shadow for most of the autumn 1944 campaign. Both Bradley and Eisenhower considered him highly competent, though

ABOVE, LEFT **Major General Troy H. Middleton commanded the VIII Corps in the Bastogne sector and is seen here talking with General Dwight Eisenhower at St Vith in the autumn of 1944. (NARA)**

LEFT **Ike talks with Major General Norman Cota, hero of Omaha Beach, and later commander of the 28th "Keystone" Division during the fighting in the Hürtgen forest and the Ardennes. (NARA)**

ABOVE **George S. Patton awards the Distinguished Service Cross to Brigadier General Anthony McAuliffe on 29 December in Bastogne. McAuliffe was in temporary command of the division during the Battle of the Bulge as Major General Maxwell Taylor was in Washington at the time. (NARA)**

other American commanders felt he was not assertive enough and that he might be overly influenced by his dynamic chief of staff, Major General William Kean. Hodges' performance during the first few days of the campaign remains something of a mystery. Although active in the planning on 16 December when the Germans first attacked, on 17 December he was not widely seen around the headquarters for much of the day. Kean said he was bed-ridden with viral pneumonia for two days. One aide has suggested it was due to nervous exhaustion, and in the event, Kean took over until he recovered.

When command of the US First Army units northwest of Bastogne passed to Montgomery's command, he took control of the counterattack force of VII Corps commanded by Major General J. Lawton Collins to the left and XVIII Airborne Corps led by Major General Matthew Ridgway to the right, seen here at the VII Corps HQ on 26 December. (NARA)

Commander of the US 2nd Armored Division was Major General Ernest Harmon, a classmate of the VII Corps commander, "Lightning Joe" Collins. (NARA)

Although overshadowed by the 101st Airborne Division, the Combat Command B of the 10th Armored Division played a critical role in the initial defense of Bastogne. Here, its commander Colonel W. L. Roberts, is seen after receiving the Silver Star from General Maxwell Taylor in Bastogne after the siege. (MHI)

The southern wing of the Ardennes sector was controlled by VIII Corps, commanded by **Major General Troy H. Middleton**. He was a decade older than many of his German counterparts and had commanded infantry regiments in combat in World War I. The later army chief of staff George Marshall wrote in his file that "this man was the outstanding infantry regimental commander on the battlefield in France." He retired from the Army in 1939 and served as an administrator at Louisiana State University. He returned to the army after war broke out and led the 45th Division in combat on Sicily and during the Italian campaign. He was nearly forced out of the army during the Italian campaign due to knee problems, but his talents were so widely admired that Eisenhower joked that "I'll take him into battle on a litter if we have to." He led the VIII Corps in combat in France in the summer of 1944. At the time of the German attack on 16 December 1944, VIII Corps controlled the sector from St Vith south through Luxembourg, linking with Patton's Third Army near the junction of the French, German, and Luxembourg frontiers.

OPPOSING FORCES

GERMAN UNITS

T he Wehrmacht was an emaciated shadow of the force that had conquered most of Europe in 1939–41. The war on the Eastern Front had bled the army white, yet it remained a formidable fighting force and particularly tenacious in its defense of German soil. Its weaknesses became more evident in an offensive operation such as the Ardennes campaign where its lack of motorization, weak logistics, shortage of fuel, and lack of offensive air power severely hampered its striking power.

The fighting power of German infantry divisions had become increasingly illusory as the war progressed due to Hitler's insistence on maintaining a large order of battle. The nominal strength of these units however does not adequately explain their combat potential. The severe personnel shortage in the wake of the 1944 summer debacles forced the Wehrmacht to scrape the bottom of the barrel to recreate the new infantry divisions. Older men, under-age recruits, troops from other services such as the Luftwaffe and navy, and men who had previously been excluded due to medical problems were all put into infantry units, usually with incomplete training. Heavy equipment such as artillery was often an agglomeration of captured foreign types mixed with standard German types. To make matters worse, some of the divisions allotted to the Ardennes offensive had been involved in the furious fighting in the autumn of 1944, and were withdrawn only days or weeks before the start of the offensive without adequate time for rebuilding.

German Panzer regiments in the Ardennes were of mixed composition, including the PzKpfw IV as seen here in the center, and the later Panther Ausf. G seen above and to the right. In the foreground is a SdKfz 251/9 (7.5cm), an assault gun version of the standard German armored half-track used to provide fire support in Panzergrenadier units. (USAOM-APG)

The workhorse of the German field artillery was the 105mm field howitzer like these that were captured by the 35th Division near Lutrebois on 17 January 1945. This is the improved leFH 18/40, which used the lighter carriage of the PaK 40 anti-tank gun. (NARA)

When planning the campaign, Gen Brandenberger of the 7th Army had asked for a Panzer or Panzergrenadier division to spearhead the thrust along 7th Army's right flank plus six infantry divisions. He instead received only four infantry divisions due to the relatively low priority given to this sector. The main effort on the right flank was assigned to the 5th Fallschirmjäger Division, which had been recently rebuilt using only partially trained, surplus Luftwaffe personnel. Brandenburger glumly noted that "In training and in the quality of its officers, both junior and senior, the division displayed notable deficiencies." To make matters worse, many of the senior paratrooper officers were contemptuous and sometimes insubordinate to the new divisional commander. But it was the largest of the divisions in his army, and the best equipped in heavy weapons including an assault gun battalion, so it was given the main mission. The 352nd Volksgrenadier Division was a reconstituted replacement for the division that had fought the US Army so well at Omaha and in Normandy. But it had been badly beaten up in the autumn fighting along the Siegfried Line. It was close to full strength at the start of the offensive, though lacking about a quarter of its authorized NCOs. The 212th Volksgrenadier Division was a reconstruction of a division shattered in Lithuania in the summer of 1944, and rebuilt in Bavaria before the Ardennes campaign. It was closer to authorized strength than the other Volksgrenadier divisions and Brandenberger felt it was his best division. The 276th Volksgrenadier Division was a recreation of a division destroyed in the Falaise pocket in August 1944.

Manteuffel's 5th Panzer Army was significantly larger and with a far better assortment of units due to its more important assignment. The 18th Volksgrenadier Division was created in September 1944 in Denmark using remnants of the 18th Luftwaffe Field Division, surplus navy personnel, and army troops from units shattered on the Eastern Front. It was committed to action near Trier in November, and against the US V Corps during the Roer fighting in early December. It was pulled out of the line shortly before the offensive and brought up to strength. The 62nd Volksgrenadier Division was reconstituted after the disastrous summer 1944 fighting in the east, using inexperienced recruits from the 583rd Volksgrenadier Division.

Heavy firepower for German artillery was provided by the schwere Feldhaubitze 18 15cm. These served in a heavy artillery battalion in German infantry divisions. (MHI)

It was nearly at authorized strength at the start of the offensive but Manteuffel did not consider it suitable for offensive operations.

The 58th Panzer Corps was the weaker of the two Panzer corps in 5th Panzer Army. The 560th Volksgrenadier Division was a new division formed in August 1944 from Luftwaffe personnel in Norway and Denmark and initially deployed in southern Norway. It was near full strength at the start of the offensive, though completely inexperienced. The 116th Panzer Division had been fighting on the Western Front since the summer and had been repeatedly decimated and rebuilt. After taking part in the initial defense of Aachen, the division was withdrawn in the early autumn and rebuilt. Although it was close to authorized strength in personnel at the start of the offensive, it was short of tanks with only 26 PzKpfw IV, 43 PzKpfw V Panthers, and 13 Jagdpanzer IV tank destroyers. At the time, a Panzer division had an authorized strength of 32 PzKpfw IV, 60 PzKpfw V Panthers, and 51 StuG III assault guns. Manteuffel considered all three of his Panzer divisions to be "very suitable for attack" in mid-December even if they were not fully up to strength in armored vehicles.

Lüttwitz's 47th Panzer Corps was the strongest element of Manteuffel's 5th Panzer Army. The 26th Volksgrenadier Division was recreated in October 1944 after its namesake division was decimated by the Red Army along the Baranow front in Poland in September 1944. It was rebuilt with troops from the 582nd VG Division, fleshed out with surplus navy and Luftwaffe troops. The 2nd Panzer Division had been destroyed in the Falaise pocket, and was rebuilt in the Eifel region in the autumn of 1944. It was only slightly better equipped than the 116th Panzer Division, with 26 PzKpfw IV, 49 PzKpfw V Panthers, and 45 StuG III assault guns. The Panzer Lehr Division was destroyed in Normandy during the US breakout

near St Lô, rebuilt again, and sent into action against Patton's Third Army in the Saar. It was pulled out of the front lines at the last moment and deployed to the Ardennes. At the start of the offensive it was close to authorized strength in personnel, but the weakest of Manteuffel's three Panzer divisions in tanks with only 30 PzKpfw IV, 23 PzKpfw V Panthers, and 14 Jagdpanzer IV tank destroyers. The army reserve was the Führer Begleit Brigade, which was relatively well equipped with 23 PzKpfw IV tanks, 20 StuG III assault guns, and a near full complement of troops.

German artillery in the Ardennes was adequate in number, but with feeble motorization and sparse ammunition supplies. In November 1944, the Wehrmacht had only half of the 105mm howitzer ammunition and a third of the 150mm stocks they possessed when attacking Poland in September 1939. After the first few days of the offensive, about half of the towed artillery was left behind by the advancing corps due to lack of motorization and road congestion.

AMERICAN UNITS

One young officer described the Ardennes sector as the US Army's "kindergarten and old-age home" – the sector where the newest and most battle-weary divisions were deployed. The VIII Corps had three infantry divisions and two of the three combat commands of the 9th Armored Division. Its northernmost unit, the 106th Division, was covered in detail in the earlier volume. The 28th Division was deployed along an extended front that largely coincided with the attack sector of the 5th Panzer Army from near the junction of the Belgian–Luxembourg–German borders, south along the Luxembourg frontier. The division was based around a Pennsylvania National Guard division, and was commanded by the hero of Omaha Beach, General Norman Cota. The division had been shattered by the fighting in the Hürtgen forest in early November and had suffered 6,184 casualties in two weeks of fighting, one of the most ferocious blood-

Supplementing the 105mm howitzer in the divisional artillery was the 155mm howitzer. These are from Battery C, 108th Field Artillery Battalion, 28th Division on 11 January near Arsdorf.

The M1 155mm gun was one of the most effective pieces of US field artillery, and was usually deployed in corps-level battalions. This battery is seen in action east of Bastogne on 17 January while supporting Patton's drive to link up with the First Army near Houfallize. (NARA)

lettings suffered by any US Army division in World War II. The division had been sent for rebuilding to the Ardennes front and by mid-December, was back near authorized strength. All three infantry regiments were in the line with the 112th Infantry in the north, the 110th in the center and the 109th in the southern sector. The front was grossly overextended: for example, the 110th held ten miles of front with only two battalions with the third in divisional reserve. Under such circumstances, the best the units could do was to create a thin defensive screen. So typically, the infantry battalions strung out their companies in a few villages a mile or so behind the front on Skyline Drive, the road that ran along the ridgeline that paralleled the frontier. Each company had a few outposts closer to the front that were manned only during daylight hours. With so few forces to cover such a broad front, the regiment was concentrated to bar access to the best routes westward. The heavily forested and hilly front line was in reality a no man's land, and both sides sent out small patrols at night to take prisoners and harass their opponents. Combat Command A of the 9th Armored Division held the area south of the 28th Division. The 9th Armored Division was divided into its three combat commands, with CCA fighting in the south between the 28th and 4th Infantry Divisions, the CCB fighting in the defense of St Vith, and the CCR positioned in reserve. The CCA, 9th Armored Division had a relatively narrow sector about two miles wide along the Our River. Due to its defensive mission, the 60th Armored Infantry Battalion held the front line with the 19th Tank Battalion and 89th Reconnaissance Squadron behind it. The division arrived in Europe in September 1944, but was not committed to action as a whole until the Ardennes fighting.

The 12th Infantry Regiment of the 4th Infantry Division held the southernmost area of the German attack zone. The regiment was spread along a sector about nine miles wide, with the neighboring sector to the south being held by the division's 8th Infantry Regiment. The 4th Infantry Division had landed at Utah Beach on D-Day, and had fought in the brutal hedgerow battles in Normandy through the summer, suffering 100 percent casualties in its infantry companies. The division had recuperated in the early autumn, only to be subjected to the horrific fighting in the Hürtgen forest in November 1944. In two weeks of fighting in late November, the division suffered 6,000 casualties, leaving it a hollow shell. It was deployed on the "ghost front" to recuperate and rebuild. Many of its rifle companies were at half strength, and the attached 70th Tank Battalion had only 11 of its allotted 54 M4 medium tanks. The 12th Infantry, which would bear the brunt of the fighting, had been rated as "a badly decimated and weary regiment" in the days before the German offensive.

ORDER OF BATTLE – SOUTHERN SECTOR, 16 DECEMBER 1944

GERMAN FORCES

5th Panzer Army	***General der Panzertruppen Hasso von Manteuffel***
66th Army Corps	*General der Artillerie Walther Lucht*
18th Volksgrenadier Division	Oberst Günther Hoffmann-Schönborn
62nd Volksgrenadier Division	Oberst Friedrich Kittel
58th Panzer Corps	*General der Panzertruppen Walter Krüger*
560th Volksgrenadier Division	Oberst Rudolf Langhäuser
116th Panzer Division	Generalmajor Siegfried von Waldenburg
47th Panzer Corps	*General der Panzertruppen Heinrich von Lüttwitz*
2nd Panzer Division	Oberst Meinrad von Lauchert
Panzer Lehr Division	Generalleutnant Fritz Bayerlein
26th Volks Grenadier Division	Oberst Heinz Kokott
Reserve	
Führer Begleit Brigade	Oberst Otto Remer
7th Army	***General der Panzertruppen Erich Brandenberger***
85th Army Corps	*General der Infanterie Baptist Kneiss*
5th Fallschirmjäger Division	Generalmajor Ludwig Heilmann
352nd Volksgrenadier Division	Oberst Erich Schmidt

80th Army Corps	*General der Infanterie Franz Beyer*
212th Volksgrenadier Division	Generalleutnant Franz Sensfuss
276th Volksgrenadier Division	Generalmajor Kurt Möhring

AMERICAN FORCES

First US Army	***LtGen Courtney Hodges***
VIII Corps	*MajGen Troy Middleton*
106th Infantry Division	MajGen Alan Jones
28th Infantry Division	MajGen Norman Cota
4th Infantry Division	MajGen Raymond Barton
9th Armored Div. (minus CCB)	MajGen John Leonard

BATTLE OF THE BULGE – SOUTHERN SECTOR

5TH PANZER ARMY VERSUS 28TH DIVISION

The German attack began in the dark, at 05.30hrs on Saturday, 16 December 1944 with a brief 20-minute barrage, 40 rounds per tube, intending to disrupt communication and transport. The barrage succeeded in downing many telephone lines, but could not interfere with radio communication. It was followed by a "fire waltz", a rolling barrage against deeper targets with 60 rounds per tube. The barrage was a mixed blessing for the advancing German infantry, as in many sectors, it did not hit the forward US troop dispositions and merely alerted them to the start of the German attack.

In the pre-dawn hours, shock companies of the German infantry regiments had already begun moving over the front lines in the hopes of infiltrating past the forward American strongpoints before the initial artillery salvoes. These tactics had mixed results. The 116th Panzer Division pushed the shock companies of its two Panzergrenadier regiments forward. One was nearly wiped out by flanking fire from US infantry. The other managed to make its way past the command post of the 1/112th Infantry by dawn but once the sun rose, found itself out in the open and most of its troops were captured. The initial advance of 60th Panzer Regiment went little better, even after some flamethrower tanks were used

A 105mm howitzer of Battery B, 229th Field Artillery Battalion of the 28th Division near Welchenheusen shortly before the start of the Ardennes offensive. (MHI)

to soften up the US infantry machine-gun nests. The only real success on the first day for the 116th Panzer Division occurred at the boundary between the 112th and 110th Infantry when 112th Panzergrenadier Regiment managed to seize a bridge over the Our River near Heiner-scheid. Attempts to seize bridges near Ouren were repeatedly rebuffed by stiff US resistance. The 116th Panzer Division responded the next morning by dispatching 13 Panther tanks to reinforce the Panzergrenadiers. The Panthers advanced right up to the dug-in infantry foxholes, firing point blank. After a frantic radio call, a platoon of M18 76mm gun-motor carriages of the 811th Tank Destroyer Battalion arrived, and managed to knock out four Panzers at a cost of three of their four vehicles. Artillery support from the 229th Field Artillery Battalion proved instrumental in weakening the German attack. One of its forward batteries was brought under direct tank attack, but the accompanying Panzergrenadiers were cut down by a company of M16 anti-aircraft half-tracks, each mounting quadruple .50cal machine-guns. By the afternoon of 17 December, the 116th Panzer Division had committed most of its armor to the fight for Ouren, gradually pushing back the US infantry. By late afternoon, the 112th Infantry was given permission to withdraw to the ridgeline behind Ouren after dark. The 1/112th Infantry, which had been surrounded for most of the day, managed to make their way out by a ruse. On approaching a bridge manned by a few German infantry, the battalion officers lined up the troops in "German formation" and shouting orders in German, marched them across the bridge. The vigorous defense of Ouren forced the 116th Panzer Division to turn their attention south. The 112th Infantry was gradually forced northward, eventually merging its efforts with the defenders of St Vith. In conjunction with the 560th Volksgrenadier Division, the bridgehead at Heinerscheid was reinforced and expanded through 17/18 December, exploiting the gap between the 112th and 110th Infantry.

The hardest hit of the 28th Division's regiments was Colonel Hurley Fuller's 110th Infantry. At a reduced strength of only two battalions, the 110th Infantry was hit by elements of three Panzer divisions and two infantry divisions, roughly 2,000 Americans against 31,000 German troops. The 110th Infantry attempted to hold a string of small villages against the onslaught of the 2nd Panzer Division and Kokott's 26th Volksgrenadier Division on 16 December. Kokott wanted to start the offensive with his forces over the Our River, so he moved two entire regiments over the river prior to the start of the attack. The defenses of the 110th Infantry were so thinly held that this premature deployment was hardly noticed. The west bank of the Our River was soon swarming with Kokott's infantry and Panzergrenadiers from the 2nd Panzer Division. The 110th Infantry clung tenaciously to their village defenses, forcing the Germans to use battalions against single companies, and in some cases, battalions against platoons. The use of Panzers in this sector was delayed by the need to erect a heavy bridge near Dasburg. By late afternoon, the situation in this sector had become so precarious that Cota committed his reserve, the 707th Tank Battalion, in an effort to clear away German infantry who had infiltrated up to the Skyline Drive. The tanks were instrumental in bolstering the infantry defenses and assisting in local counterattacks. By the end of the first day, the situation facing the two forward deployed battalions of the 110th Infantry was grim. They were running low on ammunition, and as darkness

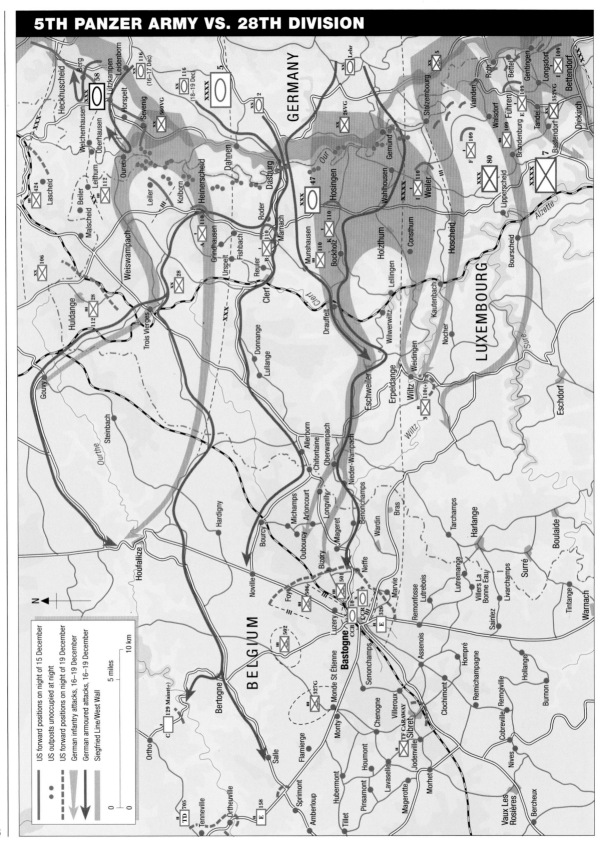

5TH PANZER ARMY VS. 28TH DIVISION

GERMANY

LUXEMBOURG

BELGIUM

Heckhuscheid
Berg
Lützkampen
Leidenborn
Welchenhausen
Horspelt
Sevenig
Oberhausen
Leithum
Beiler
Ouren
Kolborn
Heinerscheid
Dahnen
Dasburg
Leiler
Roder
Lascheid
Malscheid
Weiswampach
Grindhausen
Urspelt
Fishbach
Reuler
Warnach
Clerf
Munshausen
Bockholz
Huldange
Drauffelt
Holzthum
Consthum
Hoscheid
Trois Vierges
Donnange
Lullange
Wilwerwiltz
Weidingen
Eschweiler
Erpeldange
Wiltz
Gouvy
Steinbach
Nocher
Kautenbach
Allerborn
Chifontaine
Oberwampach
Nieder-Wampach
Houffalize
Hardigny
Michamps
Arloncourt
Longvilly
Mageret
Benonchamps
Bras
Bourcy
Oubourcy
Bizory
Neffe
Wardin
Tarchamps
Noville
Foy
Luzery
Marvie
Harlange
Bastogne
Remonfosse
Lutrebois
Lutremange
Villers La Bonne Eau
Livarchamps
Surré
Bertogne
Monde St Étienne
Senonchamps
Assenois
Hompré
Remichampagne
Boulaide
Salle
Monty
Chenogne
Villeroux
Clochimont
Cobreville
Remoiville
Burnon
Flamierge
Houmont
Lavaselle
Jodenville
Sibret
Morhet
Nives
Bercheux
Sprimont
Hubermont
Pinsamont
Tillet
Magerotte
Morhet
Vaux Les Rosières
Ortho
Amberloup
Tenneville
Ortheuville

Eschdorf

Vianden
Walsdorf
Führen
Brandenburg
Tandel
Bettendorf
Diekirch
Bettel
Gentingen
Longsdorf

Wahlhausen
Gemünd
Hosingen
Weiler
Lipperscheid
Bourscheid

N

US forward positions on night of 15 December
US outposts unoccupied at night
US forward positions on night of 19 December
German infantry attacks, 16–19 December
German armoured attacks, 16–19 December
Siegfried Line/West Wall

0   5 miles
0   10 km

116

The town of Clerf remains littered with destroyed vehicles in the aftermath of the fighting. To the left is an M4 of the 707th Tank Battalion, which was supporting the 110th Infantry, and to the right is a knocked-out German StuG III assault gun. (NARA)

fell, the German infantry was flowing past them in increasing numbers. Several companies called in artillery on their own positions as they were overrun in the darkness. Two heavy bridges at Dasburg were finished at twilight, and Panzers began moving forward after dark. Although the 48th Panzer Corps had failed to reach its first day objective of the Clerf river, American resistance was obviously weakening as the 110th Infantry was being overwhelmed by forces many times their size. General Cota radioed to the 110th Infantry that they were to hold "at all costs", knowing full well that the regiment guarded the only hard-surface road to Bastogne, the route through Clerf (Clervaux). Cota still had a very modest reserve on hand, 110th Infantry's 2nd Battalion and the light tank company of the 707th Tank Battalion. Before midnight, he ordered the battalion forward to reinforce the Marnach sector in hope of keeping the key road through Clerf blocked to the Panzers.

By dawn on 17 December, German forces were nearing Fuller's headquarters in Clerf. The attempted counterattack by the 2/110th Infantry on the morning of 17 December had hardly set off when it was brought under heavy fire by German infantry supported by Panzers and assault guns. By this stage, the regiment's artillery battalion was down to a single battery, and this unit was driven from its position that morning, losing half its howitzers in the process. The attack by D/707th Tank Battalion went awry when eight of its M5A1 light tanks were picked off by German anti-tank guns, and three more succumbed to anti-tank rockets. A company of infantry made its way into Marnach, only to find that the town had already been abandoned.

With defense of Marnach now impossible, the 110th Regiment attempted to halt the German advance at Clerf. The town was located in a narrow valley with access roads entering down a wooded, winding road. A spearhead from the 2nd Panzer Division consisting of about a dozen PzKpfw IV tanks followed by 30 SdKfz 251 half-tracks full of Panzergrenadiers, approached the town around 09.30hrs. A platoon of M4 tanks from A/707th Tank Battalion clanked out of town to meet them, and in the ensuing skirmish, the Germans lost four tanks and the American

A pair of survivors of the 110th Infantry, 28th Division on 19 December after the regiment had been shattered by the German assault.

platoon lost three. Diverted from the main road, the German column attempted to enter the town via an alternate road, but this approach was blocked when the lead Panzer was hit. In the meantime, further US reinforcements had arrived in the shape of B/2nd Tank Battalion from 9th Armored Division's CCR. This was not enough to stem the advance, and by nightfall, Clerf was swarming with German tanks and Panzergrenadiers. Around 18.25hrs, Fuller was forced to abandon his headquarters when a German tank stuck its barrel through a window into the command post. Fuller and his headquarters attempted to join up with Company G but were captured. Most of the remnants of the 110th in Clerf withdrew in the darkness, but some US infantry continued to hold out in the stone chateau in the town, sniping at German columns through 18 December as the Panzer columns raced on towards Bastogne.

The 3/110th Infantry had been gradually pushed back out of the border villages by the advance of the 26th Volksgrenadier Division, with the last remnants of the battalion finally congregating in the village of Consthum on 18 December. An afternoon attack, supported by assault guns, penetrated into the town, but fog permitted the American survivors to withdraw out of town, with some 40mm Bofors guns providing a rearguard. The following day, the remnants of the battalion were ordered to withdraw to the divisional headquarters at Wiltz. By the second day of combat, the 110th Infantry had been overwhelmed in their unequal struggle. But their two-day battle had cost the Germans precious time. Middleton later wrote to Fuller, after he was released from a PoW camp, that "had not your boys done the job they did, the 101st Airborne could not have reached Bastogne in time."

The 28th Division's third regiment, the 109th Infantry, was in the attack sector of the German 7th Army. The 5th Fallschirmjäger Division assaulted its northernmost companies on 17 December. The inexperienced Luftwaffe troops did not advance as quickly as their neighbors from 5th Panzer

Army to the north, but by 18 December, were on their way through the American defenses and approaching the divisional headquarters at Wiltz. By this time, the lead elements of the Panzer Lehr Division had gained access to the roads, and headed towards Wiltz along the northern route. On the morning of 19 December, General Cota transferred the headquarters of the 28th Division from Wiltz to Sibret, leaving behind a provisional battalion formed from the headquarters staff and divisional support personnel, and later reinforced by the 200 survivors of 3/110th Infantry. The commander of the 5th Fallschirmjäger Division, Oberst Heilmann, had planned to bypass Wiltz, but had lost control of his units in the field. In the event, an uncoordinated attack began against Wiltz as the town was near the boundary between the 5th Panzer and 7th Army. Units from the 26th Volksgrenadier Division began an attack from the north on the afternoon of 19 December, while the 15th Parachute Regiment from 5th Fallschirmjäger Division began attacking the town from the south, even though Heilmann had ordered it to attack Sibret. By nightfall, the US defenses had been compressed into the center of the town. The US commander, Colonel Daniel Strickler, decided to retreat, but the withdrawal was confused. The provisional battalion ran a gauntlet of German formations on the way to Bastogne, losing many troops in the process. But some troops did manage to reach Bastogne. The 687th Field Artillery Battalion was surrounded to the south of town, and had to fight off numerous German attacks before a small portion of the unit could withdraw. The 44th Combat Engineers served as the rearguard in Wiltz itself and was decimated in the process.

By 20 December, the 5th Panzer Army had finally overcome the principal centers of resistance held by the 28th Division, and the roads were open towards Houfallize and Bastogne. But the determined defense by the badly outnumbered 28th Division had cost precious time, and by the time that Wiltz was finally taken, Bastogne had already been reinforced. It is worth comparing the performance of the veteran 28th Division against that of the inexperienced regiments of the neighboring 106th Division. While the 106th Division was quickly surrounded and forced to surrender, the battered but experienced regiments of the 28th Division were able to hold off much larger German forces for two days before finally being overwhelmed in desperate combat.

7TH ARMY ATTACKS

Brandenberger's 7th Army had the least ambitious objectives of the three attacking armies, but also had the most modest resources with which to achieve them, and some of the most difficult terrain. The initial artillery barrage that started the offensive was not particularly effective as the 7th Army had poor intelligence on US dispositions. The shock companies leading the attack were generally successful in infiltrating past the forward US outposts due to the huge gaps in the US lines. In Vianden, the 2/109th Infantry outposts in the ruins of the chateau were overrun, but many other outposts were simply bypassed in the early morning fog. Other German assault companies managed to get across the Our River without opposition in rubber boats. The mountainous terrain and the porous defenses permitted the initial German assault battalions to slip through the positions of the 109th Infantry for most of the morning with only sporadic contact with US platoons in the villages. The GR.915 of the 352nd Volksgrenadier Division was able to move most of its forces between the 2nd and 3rd battalions, 109th Infantry, via the deep ravines in the 2,000yd (1,829m) gap between the two battalions. By noon, the 352nd VG Division had scouts well behind the forward US positions, with assault companies not far behind. In contrast, the GR.916 had few terrain advantages, and were quickly pinned down along the Our River by two US artillery battalions that had observers with the 3/109th Infantry on the heights above. By nightfall, the 109th Infantry commander, Colonel James Rudder, thought his situation was reasonably secure except for an encircled company at Führen, not realizing that his positions had been thoroughly penetrated. Around 02.40hrs on 17 December, Rudder was ordered by General Cota to use his reserve to stop an unexpected German penetration. The 14th Parachute Regiment had managed to move some StuG III assault guns and other vehicles across a weir near Vianden, and was motoring down Skyline Drive deep behind American lines from Hosheid towards Ettelbruck. The US garrison in Hosheid was finally forced to withdraw, but their defense held up the paratrooper regiment.

On 17 December, the two German divisions on the right wing of the 7th Army attack continued to move units over the Our River, but their advance was frequently frustrated by small US garrisons, and by accurate artillery fire delivered against their columns from forward observers on the hills above. US attempts to relieve the surrounded company in Führen were frustrated. By late in the day, the vital artillery positions were coming under direct attack as small groups of German troops infiltrated deep behind the forward US positions. Several artillery batteries had to deploy their personnel as riflemen to fight off German infantry. German prospects improved dramatically after nightfall on 17 December when a

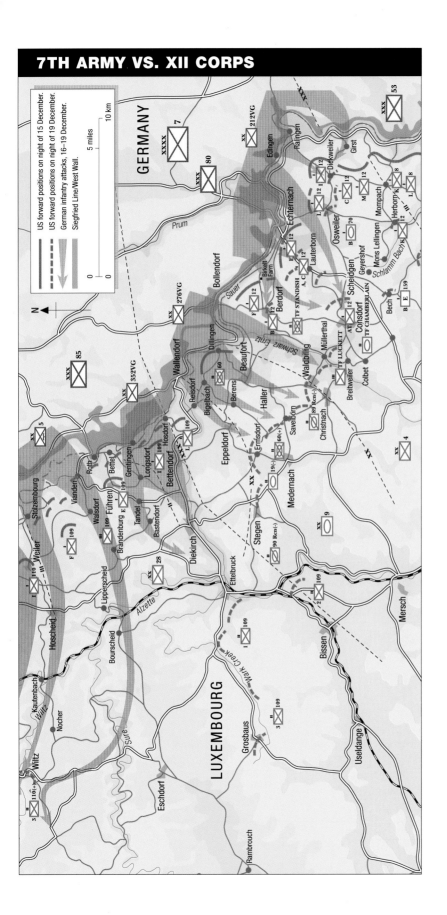

7TH ARMY VS. XII CORPS

US forward positions on night of 15 December.
US forward positions on night of 19 December.
German infantry attacks, 16–19 December.
Siegfried Line/West Wall.

5 miles

10 km

N

GERMANY

LUXEMBOURG

long-delayed bridge over the Our was finally completed, permitting the transit of the corps' only armor unit, the 11th Assault Gun Brigade, plus the vehicles and divisional artillery of the 5th Fallschirmjäger Division. The 352nd Volksgrenadier Division's bridge at Gentingen was slow being completed, but by 18 December enough artillery and heavy arms had been moved over the Our that their attack against the 3/109th Infantry intensified considerably. The renewed vigor of the reinforced German attacks on 18 December undermined the 109th Infantry defenses. In the early afternoon, Colonel Rudder received permission to withdraw the regiment back towards the high ground around Diekirch. The 352nd VG Division reached the 109th Infantry defenses around Diekirch on the afternoon of 19 December. The 352nd VG Division had lost so many of its experienced officers and NCOs that in the afternoon the attack was led by the divisional commander, Oberst Erich Schmidt, who was wounded in the process. By the morning of 20 December, the 109th Infantry withdrew to Ettelbruck, destroyed the bridges there, and established defensive positions in the hills west of the town.

A platoon of Co. B, 630th Tank Destroyer Battalion in newly dug foxholes outside Wiltz on the road to Bastogne on 20 December. By this stage, the company had lost all of its 3in. towed anti-tank guns and was assigned by Middleton to defend the approaches to Bastogne. (NARA)

Further to the south, the 7th Army attacks had not progressed as well. The 276th Volksgrenadier Division had crossed the Sauer River opposite the defenses of the 60th Armored Infantry Battalion (AIB) of CCA, 9th Armored Division. Although the division was able to gain a foothold all along the western bank of the river, the three regiments had been unable to overcome the US positions on the high ground. On 17 December, the German infantry managed to infiltrate into the 60th AIB's positions via a deep, wooded gorge. However, the CCA managed to fend off many of the attacks by counterattacking with armored cars of the reconnaissance squadron. After dark, the 1/GR.988 managed to infiltrate behind the 60th AIB and capture the town of Beaufort in spite of a determined stand by a cavalry troop. General Brandenberger was extremely unhappy with the poor performance of the division, and he relieved the commander, even though many of its problems could be traced to the success of American artillery in preventing the construction of a bridge over the Sauer at Wallendorf.

The 60th AIB attempted to rout out the main German incursion by launching a counterattack with the remaining light armored vehicles of the reconnaissance squadron. But when the attack was launched at dawn on 18 December, it stumbled into a battalion of GR.986 that had been reinforced with an anti-tank company with several dozen Panzerschreck and Panzerfaust anti-tank rockets intended for a planned attack towards Medernach. Seven M5A1 light tanks were quickly put out of action, and the cavalry force did not have enough riflemen to contest the German defenses. By the end of the day, the 276th Volksgrenadier Division had made so many penetrations past the forward defenses of CCA, 9th Armored Division, that a new defensive line was established away from the Sauer River. However, the three line companies of the 60th AIB were cut off, and it took three days to extricate the survivors. German attacks slackened on 19 December as the new 276th VG Division commander,

Oberst Dempwolff, attempted to reorganize his demoralized troops, and put off any further attacks until the delayed assault guns finally arrived. When three or four Jagdpanzer 38 finally appeared in the afternoon of 20 December, the GR.988 at Haller launched an attack against a forward US outpost near Waldbillig. The attack failed, but after dark, the GR.987 advanced through a gorge on the other side of Waldbillig forcing the US tank destroyer and cavalry detachments to retreat. Although not apparent at the time, this represented the high-water mark for the division.

The attacks further south by the 212th Volksgrenadier Division against the 12th Infantry, 4th Division, were even less successful. German intelligence in this sector was better and most of the 12th Infantry positions had been accurately spotted. The terrain in this sector was very rugged, the area being known as "Little Switzerland". Two regiments led the German attack over the Sauer River using rubber boats. The main opposition to the crossing proved to be the river itself. Attempts to land the GR.320 near the main objective of Echternach failed due to the swift current, and the regiment had to be landed three miles downstream, delaying the attack. Although radio warnings went out to the widely dispersed 12th Infantry outposts in the early morning, many US units did not receive them, and were unaware of the German attack until German patrols appeared in mid-morning. US artillery was less effective in this sector than further north, even though an artillery observation plane reported that the "area was as full of targets as a pinball machine". Most of the forward US outposts pulled back to the company positions in the forward villages along the frontier, but by late in the day, some of these had been isolated by German infiltration. The 12th Infantry headquarters responded by sending small task groups down the road consisting of a few tanks from the badly under-strength 70th Tank Battalion carrying a small number of infantry reinforcements.

The 5th Fallschirmjäger Division captured six M4 tanks intact in Wiltz, and put them back into service after painting them prominently with German crosses. This one is seen abandoned a few weeks later in the center of Esch-sur-Sûre. (NARA)

By 17 December, the 212th Volksgrenadier Division had managed to reinforce its forward regiments even though its new supply bridge had been knocked down before being completed. While the Germans had significantly more infantry than the 12th Infantry in this sector, the Americans held an advantage in tanks, which was further reinforced on 17 December with a company from the 19th Tank Battalion, 9th Armored Division. In addition, the US forces still had markedly better artillery support since the absence of a bridge had prevented the Germans from bringing any significant artillery across the Sauer. The GR.987 made a deep penetration along the Schwarz Erntz Gorge, but were unable to fight their way out of the gorge after a pummeling by American artillery. Task Force Luckett was formed from some tanks and tank destroyers, and sent towards the gorge to prevent further penetration. The GR.320 had more success by circling around Echternach, thereby penetrating between two rifle companies, but none of these was serious enough to threaten the US defense line.

Breakthrough Achieved

By the morning of 18 December, or X+2 according to the German schedule, the roads to Bastogne were open. The 5th Panzer Army had managed to blast a massive gap in the American lines by overwhelming the 110th Infantry Regiment and pushing back the other regiments of the 28th Division on either side. However, due to the stubborn defense of the 110th Infantry, Hitler's timetable was badly slipping. The plans had called for 5th Panzer Army to take Bastogne on X+1 and reach the Meuse by X+3. The 7th Army's attacks had proceeded less well, particularly in the southernmost area. There were two principal road nets towards the Meuse available to Manteuffel's forces, so the 116th Panzer Division set out via Houfalize while the bulk of the 5th Panzer Army and some elements of the 7th Army headed towards Bastogne.

The delaying actions by the 28th Division gave Middleton some breathing space to prepare the defense of Bastogne. On the afternoon of 16 December, Bradley began to commit his reserves to bolster the badly overextended Ardennes sector. The only reserves available to the 12th Army Group were the 82nd and 101st Airborne Divisions that were refitting near Reims after two months of hard fighting in Holland. The 82nd was directed towards the northern sector around St Vith, and the 101st to the southern sector around Bastogne. With no other reserves on hand, Bradley was forced to pilfer resources from the neighboring armies. Patton's Third Army had the 10th Armored Division in reserve for Operation Tink and Bradley ordered it be sent to Middleton. Patton complained, but when it became evident that the Ardennes attack was no mere spoiling attack, Patton told his staff to reinvigorate plans to reinforce the First Army in the Ardennes.

While waiting for these reinforcements to arrive, Middleton began to deploy the modest reserves he had on hand. Since Bastogne was the most vital initial objective in the corps' area, he was determined to hold it at all costs. Shortly before midnight on 17 December, Middleton learned that Clerf had fallen, giving the 5th Panzer Army access to a good hard road into Bastogne. He planned to block the road using the CCR of the 9th Armored Division. This was reorganized into combined arms teams with mixed companies of infantry and tanks. The weaker of

When the VIII Corps headquarters was ordered to evacuate Bastogne, many corps support units withdrew. This is a column from the 54th Signal Battalion on the road between Bastogne and Marche on 19 December 1944. (MHI)

the two forces, Task Force Rose, was assigned to block the road from Clerf, using a company of tanks and a company of infantry. Task Force Harper was placed behind them near Allerborn, and included less than two companies of tanks and an infantry company. The M7 self-propelled howitzers of the 73rd Armored Field Artillery Battalion (AFAB), near Buret, covered the two task forces. To defend Bastogne itself, Middleton ordered the three engineer battalions of the 1128th Engineer Group to draw weapons and revert to an infantry role, forming a semi-circular defense of Bastogne from Foy in the northeast to Marvie in the south.

The first contact between the advancing 5th Panzer Army and the Bastogne defenders occurred at 08.30hrs, when reconnaissance elements of the 2nd Panzer Division encountered Task Force Rose at the Lullange roadblock. The remainder of the division was delayed due to continued sniper fire from Americans still holding out in Clerf. After inconclusive skirmishing early in the morning, the lead Kampfgruppe laid smoke in front of the American positions, and moved two companies of Panzers forward under its cover. When the smoke lifted around 11.00hrs, tank fighting ensued at ranges of around 800 yards (732m) with both sides losing three tanks. The Kampfgruppe deployed forces on all three sides of the roadblock and gradually whittled it away. Permission was requested to pull back TF Rose or reinforce it from TF Harper, but Middleton refused both requests. The situation deteriorated in the early afternoon when elements of the advancing 116th Panzer Division brushed up against the 73rd AFAB in Buret, forcing them to redeploy. In the early evening, TF Rose was given permission to pull back a few miles to Wincrange, in part to deal with Panzers that had been leaking past the Lullange roadblock. By the time it had pulled back, it was completely surrounded by advancing elements of the 2nd Panzer Division and cut off from TF Harper.

The TF Harper roadblock at Allerborn was hit by artillery around 20.00hrs followed closely by a Panzer attack. The 9th Armored Division accounts claim that the attack was so successful due to the use of infrared.

night-fighting equipment on the Panthers but there is no evidence that this was actually the case. By midnight, TF Harper had been shattered. The commander and assault gun platoon escaped northward towards Houfallize, and the other battalion vehicles southward towards Tintigny. This left only some token headquarters units, two self-propelled artillery battalions, and a platoon of light tanks along the road into Bastogne. With its forces destroyed or surrounded, the headquarters elements of the CCR, 9th Armored Division, began pulling back to Bastogne shortly after midnight.

Combat Command B, 10th Armored Division, drove from Arlon to Bastogne on 18 December and was instructed by Middleton to divide into three teams to cover Longvilly, Wardin, and Noville. Team Cherry arrived in Longvilly on the night of 18 December, but was instructed to advance no further in spite of the predicament of TF Harper. The plans to use CCB, 10th Armored Division, to defend this corridor quickly went awry.

The unit assigned to take Bastogne was Bayerlein's Panzer Lehr Division. On 18 December, it was split into two Kampfgruppen based around its two Panzergrenadier regiments, Kampfgruppe Poschinger (Panzergrenadier Regt.902) on the road behind the southern wing of 2nd Panzer Division heading towards Oberwampach, and Kampfgruppe Hauser (Panzergrenadier Regt.901), still engaged with the 3/110th Infantry at Consthum. With Panzer Lehr in action east of Bastogne, the 2nd Panzer Div. Kampfgruppe that had attacked TF Cherry and TF Harper veered off northward towards Noville in an effort to reach the Meuse river. Delayed by the muddy road conditions, KG Poschinger reached Oberwampach around 18.30hrs on the evening of 18 December, and penetrated into Mageret after midnight. But the Panzers were without infantry support since the Panzergrenadiers and their Steyr trucks were stuck in the muddy roads leading to the town. There, Bayerlein encountered a Belgian civilian who told him, erroneously, that at least 40 American tanks and many more vehicles, led by an American two-star general had passed through Mageret that evening. At the time, Bayerlein had less than a dozen of his tanks with him, and was concerned that he had stumbled into a US armored division. He ordered a defensive deployment on the northeast side of Mageret and decided to wait until morning to launch his attack towards Bastogne.

The lead elements of the 101st Airborne Division arrived in Bastogne by truck on the night of 18 December. The division was led by Brigadier General Anthony McAuliffe, the divisional artillery officer, as its commander, Maxwell Taylor was back in the US. The division had little time to prepare for the move, and the troops left without adequate cold weather uniforms or ammunition. In view of the increasingly precarious situation around Bastogne, Bradley ordered Middleton to pull his corps headquarters out of the city on 19 December and leave command of Bastogne to McAuliffe. Julian Ewell's 501st Parachute Infantry Regiment (PIR) was the first into Bastogne, and deployed a combat team from 3rd Bn, 501st PIR to try to determine the situation along the road to Mageret.

Increasingly skittish due to the sudden appearance of more and more new American units, Bayerlein ordered his advance guard, Kampfgruppe Fallois, to push through Neffe in the hope that a fast raid might gain a foothold in the outskirts of Bastogne. Neffe was held by the headquarters

A view near Wardin along the
main road into Bastogne from
the south, with a knocked out
M4 medium tank of Task Force
O'Hara, 10th Armored Division to
the right. (MHI)

of Team Cherry and a few tanks. Although KG Fallois was able to push
into Neffe by 08.00hrs, they had not thoroughly cleared the town of
American troops, and had overlooked American infantry in the stone
chateau. On reaching the edge of the town and peering towards Bastogne
they saw columns of American infantry advancing forward, a glimpse of
Ewell's combat team. The paratroopers were supported by an air-portable
105mm light howitzer, the sound of which Bayerlein misinterpreted as
tank fire. Instead of raiding into Bastogne, Bayerlein ordered his forces
in this sector to prepare to repulse what he thought was a major American
counterattack and not merely a local probe. The pugnacious sally by the
paratroopers derailed Bayerlein's long delayed attack into Bastogne.
Furthermore, Panzergrenadiers marching through Neffe were dispersed
by sniper fire from US troops still in the castle, and even tank gun fire
could not get them to budge.

Even though Team Cherry was surrounded in Longvilly, it posed a
threat to the planned attack of the 26th VG Division towards Bizory, so
Bayerlein decided to clean it out once and for all. In the meantime, the
division's second Kampfgruppe had been freed of its assignment near
Consthum, and lead elements including the divisional tank destroyer
battalion, Panzerjäger Lehr Abteilung 130, arrived that morning. The
attack on Longvilly began hours late, in the early afternoon. As the tank
destroyers crested the ridge of Hill 490, they encountered an enormous
traffic jam of US vehicles consisting of advancing elements of CCB, 10th
Armored Div., retreating elements of CCR, 9th Armored Div., and various
and sundry other US units. Besides the Panzer Lehr Kampfgruppe, the
26th VG Division was also closing in on this area, and the 2nd Panzer
Division had sent six 88mm tank destroyers to deal with 9th Armored
Division self-propelled howitzers that had been shelling their troops.
Elements of these three German divisions began to descend on the
trapped American column, systematically destroying it. Team Cherry tried
to get off the road and defend the area, but lost all 14 of its medium and

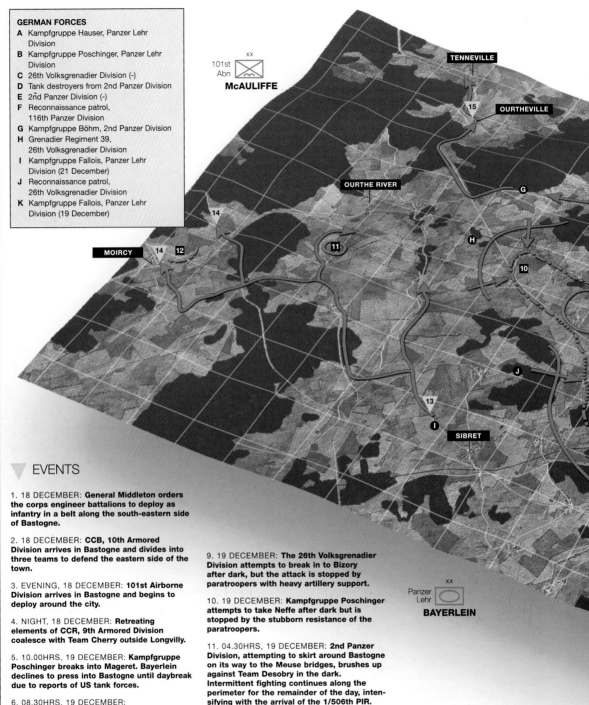

GERMAN FORCES
- **A** Kampfgruppe Hauser, Panzer Lehr Division
- **B** Kampfgruppe Poschinger, Panzer Lehr Division
- **C** 26th Volksgrenadier Division (-)
- **D** Tank destroyers from 2nd Panzer Division
- **E** 2nd Panzer Division (-)
- **F** Reconnaissance patrol, 116th Panzer Division
- **G** Kampfgruppe Böhm, 2nd Panzer Division
- **H** Grenadier Regiment 39, 26th Volksgrenadier Division
- **I** Kampfgruppe Fallois, Panzer Lehr Division (21 December)
- **J** Reconnaissance patrol, 26th Volksgrenadier Division
- **K** Kampfgruppe Fallois, Panzer Lehr Division (19 December)

101st Abn **McAULIFFE**

TENNEVILLE

OURTHEVILLE

OURTHE RIVER

MOIRCY

SIBRET

Panzer Lehr **BAYERLEIN**

▼ EVENTS

1. 18 DECEMBER: **General Middleton orders the corps engineer battalions to deploy as infantry in a belt along the south-eastern side of Bastogne.**

2. 18 DECEMBER: **CCB, 10th Armored Division arrives in Bastogne and divides into three teams to defend the eastern side of the town.**

3. EVENING, 18 DECEMBER: **101st Airborne Division arrives in Bastogne and begins to deploy around the city.**

4. NIGHT, 18 DECEMBER: **Retreating elements of CCR, 9th Armored Division coalesce with Team Cherry outside Longvilly.**

5. 10.00HRS, 19 DECEMBER: **Kampfgruppe Poschinger breaks into Mageret. Bayerlein declines to press into Bastogne until daybreak due to reports of US tank forces.**

6. 08.30HRS, 19 DECEMBER: **Kampfgruppe Fallois pushes into Neffe, but spots an approaching patrol from the 3/501st Parachute Infantry Regiment.**

7. EARLY AFTERNOON, 19 DECEMBER: **A trapped column consisting of elements of the CCR, 9th Armored Division and Team Cherry, 10th Armored Division are attacked and destroyed by elements from three German divisions.**

8. Team O-Hara is attacked by Kampfgruppe Fallois, Panzer Lehr Division, which pushes them out of Wardin and back towards Marvie.

9. 19 DECEMBER: **The 26th Volksgrenadier Division attempts to break in to Bizory after dark, but the attack is stopped by paratroopers with heavy artillery support.**

10. 19 DECEMBER: **Kampfgruppe Poschinger attempts to take Neffe after dark but is stopped by the stubborn resistance of the paratroopers.**

11. 04.30HRS, 19 DECEMBER: **2nd Panzer Division, attempting to skirt around Bastogne on its way to the Meuse bridges, brushes up against Team Desobry in the dark. Intermittent fighting continues along the perimeter for the remainder of the day, intensifying with the arrival of the 1/506th PIR.**

12. 05.30HRS, 20 DECEMBER: **Starting with a pre-dawn attack, 2nd Panzer Division pushes Team Desobry back from Noville and breaks into the paratrooper defenses in Foy.**

13. 21 DECEMBER: **As it becomes evident that the defense of Bastogne has hardened, Luttwitz gives Bayerlein permission to move the Panzer Lehr Division around the south side of Bastogne to continue its race for the Meuse bridges. With Kampfgruppe Fallois in the lead, this move will cut off Bastogne from the south and west.**

14. 21 DECEMBER: **Late in the day Kampfgruppe Fallois reaches the Ourthe river crossings.**

15. 20 DECEMBER: **Kampfgruppe Böhm, the reconnaissance element of the 2nd Panzer Division, seizes a bridge over the Ourthe river at Ortheuville. Kampfgruppe Cochenhausen follows, but the division is unable to quickly exploit the breakthrough due to a lack of fuel.**

BASTOGNE ENCIRCLED

19–23 December 1944, viewed from the southeast. Spearheads of the 5th Panzer Army reach the outskirts of Bastogne in the pre-dawn hours of 19 December. They are thwarted in their attempts to capture the city on the run by the sacrifice of several armored task forces on the approach roads to the city, and by the timely arrival of the 101st Airborne Division. As a result, the 2nd Panzer Division and Panzer Lehr Division bypass the city to reach their main objective of the Meuse River crossings. By 21 December Bastogne is cut off.

Note gridlines are shown at intervals of 1 mile/1.61km

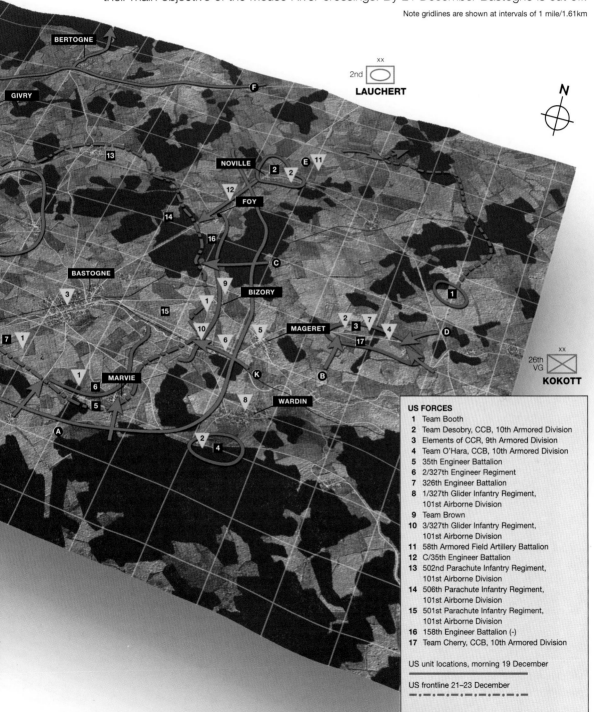

US FORCES
1 Team Booth
2 Team Desobry, CCB, 10th Armored Division
3 Elements of CCR, 9th Armored Division
4 Team O'Hara, CCB, 10th Armored Division
5 35th Engineer Battalion
6 2/327th Engineer Regiment
7 326th Engineer Battalion
8 1/327th Glider Infantry Regiment, 101st Airborne Division
9 Team Brown
10 3/327th Glider Infantry Regiment, 101st Airborne Division
11 58th Armored Field Artillery Battalion
12 C/35th Engineer Battalion
13 502nd Parachute Infantry Regiment, 101st Airborne Division
14 506th Parachute Infantry Regiment, 101st Airborne Division
15 501st Parachute Infantry Regiment, 101st Airborne Division
16 158th Engineer Battalion (-)
17 Team Cherry, CCB, 10th Armored Division

US unit locations, morning 19 December

US frontline 21–23 December

Although the 116th Panzer Division managed to break into Hotton, they were pushed out by headquarters elements of the 3rd Armored Division. This is a PzKpfw IV tank of II/Panzer Regiment 16 knocked out during the fighting on the afternoon of 21 December. (NARA)

Two tanks helped buttress the US defense of Hotton on 21 December and this M4 of Co. G, 33rd Armored Regiment was knocked out in the fighting. (NARA)

light tanks in the process. In all, about 100 US vehicles were abandoned or destroyed, including 23 M5A1 and M4 tanks, 15 M7 105mm self-propelled howitzers, 14 armored cars, 30 jeeps and 25 2¹/₂ ton trucks. The destruction of this trapped column distracted the lead elements of the Panzer Lehr Division from their main assignment of Bastogne.

The next element from the CCB, 10th Armored Division, to encounter Panzer Lehr was Team O'Hara, located near Wardin, covering the south-eastern approach to Bastogne. An attack by KG Fallois pushed them out of Wardin and back towards Marvie on the afternoon of 19 December, but **130** further German attacks were stymied.

On the afternoon of 19 December, the corps commander, General Lüttwitz, visited Bayerlein to discuss the best approach to dealing with Bastogne. Lüttwitz was extremely agitated by the number of new US units showing up in Bastogne, and feared that if the corps did not race to the Meuse now and bypass Bastogne, that the Americans would soon receive more reinforcements. Bayerlein argued that Bastogne was indispensable to any future operations and that it would continue to pose a threat even if bypassed. Bayerlein ordered a night attack by Kampfgruppe Poschinger from Neffe starting at 19.00hrs, which would coincide with a similar advance by the 26th VG Division towards Bizory. Neither attack proved fruitful and both encountered growing resistance. The outer defenses of Bastogne had been soft and relatively easy to penetrate; now they had hit a solid defense line.

While Panzer Lehr and the 26th VG Division were conducting their fruitless attacks on the southeastern edge of Bastogne, the 2nd Panzer Division had raced to the northeast outskirts with the intention of heading west. Around 04.30hrs, reconnaissance units had discovered the outer perimeter of Team Desobry, the third of the CCB, 10th Armored Division, outposts. Lauchert radioed to Lüttwitz to get permission to bypass the roadblocks near Bourcy and Noville in order to head west to the Meuse River, and the corps commander agreed. The German armored columns advanced in the fog, one of the columns moving across a ridge southeast of Noville. The fog occasionally lifted, leading to sharp, close-range duels between the Panzers and the US tanks. Realizing he was seriously outgunned, Desobry asked for permission to withdraw. This was denied as the 101st Airborne needed time to get its rifle companies into the line. When paratroopers of the 1/506th PIR arrived in the early afternoon, the aggressive paratroopers staged a counterattack, but it was quickly suppressed by tank fire. The 2nd Panzer Division responded with an infantry attack backed by two companies of tanks, but the German Panzers wisely decided to avoid tangling with the paratroopers and their bazookas in the ruins of Noville. The town could not be easily bypassed since the fields were too muddy to support the trucks following the lead Panzer columns. The attacks resumed at 05.30hrs on the morning of 20 December, cutting off Noville and pushing the paratroopers out of neighboring Foy. McAuliffe recognized that the Noville force stood no chance, and so gave permission for them to withdraw while other paratroopers tried to retake Foy. The column started to move out around dusk and, to their good fortune, fog settled, which hid their movement from surrounding German troops. The 2nd Panzer Division continued its race east, and captured a bridge over the Ourthe River near Ourtheville. But the lead columns were so short of fuel that they had to wait nearly a day for supplies to catch up.

Bayerlein resumed his attempts to crack through the Bastogne defenses near Bizory on the morning of 20 December. Small arms fire and artillery put an end to the Panzer Lehr attack, forcing Bayerlein to look elsewhere. Kampfgruppe Poschinger and infantry from the 26th VG Division attempted to fight their way further south, near Neffe, but a strong response from US artillery broke up several attacks. By 21 December, it was becoming obvious that Panzer Lehr Division was being wasted in costly attacks against the Bastogne defenses. The 2nd Panzer Division had already skirted around Bastogne to the north, and finally Lüttwitz gave Bayerlein permission to try the same to the south. But KG Hauser was left behind to reinforce the attacks by the 26th VG Div., thereby significantly weakening the division's attempt to reach the Meuse. The Panzer Lehr Division, with KG Fallois in the lead, set out for the Ourthe River near St Hubert on 22 December. In combination with the 2nd Panzer Division's advance to the Ourthe the preceding day, this left Bastogne surrounded.

While Manteuffel focused most of his attention on the Bastogne sector, Krüger's 58th Panzer Corps had encountered prolonged delays in executing its breakthrough on the Tailles plateau. Although the 112th Infantry had been pushed northward after three days of fighting, the 116th Panzer Division, had been very slow to exploit the rupture in the American lines. Poor bridges, traffic jams and the ensuing lack of fuel proved as nettlesome as the US Army. Manteuffel was so upset that on 19 December, he told Krüger he was thinking of relieving the divisional commander. His attitude changed during the day as the fortunes of the division abruptly improved. US defenses in the area around Houfallize were extremely thin, as units were tending to coalesce around St Vith to the north and Bastogne to the south. In the early morning, the divisional reconnaissance reported that Houfallize was not occupied by US forces and that the bridges were intact. The divisional commander, General von Waldenburg, decided to bypass Houfallize to the south, and the division reached Bertogne and the main road from Marche to Bastogne by evening. Indeed US resistance was so weak, that even the unmotorized 560th VG Div. was making good progress, passing by Houfallize to the north. Now the concern was no longer the corps' slow advance, but the open flank to the south as the 58th Panzer Corps outpaced its southern neighbor, Lüttwitz's 47th Panzer Corps around Bastogne. One of the unit officers recorded that "the Americans are completely surprised and in substantial turmoil. Long columns of prisoners march toward the east, many tanks were destroyed or captured. Our *Landsers* are loaded with cigarettes, chocolates, and canned food, and are smiling from ear to ear."

Reassessing the Plans

On 18 December, Patton met with Bradley at his Luxembourg headquarters. When asked what the Third Army could do to help the First Army in the Ardennes, Patton asserted that he could have two more divisions on the move the following day and a third in 24 hours. Patton was not happy to give up Operation Tink, but he ruefully remarked "What the hell, we'll still be killing Krauts." Unwilling to gloat in view of Bradley's anguish, Patton did not mention that his ability to shift a corps into the Ardennes was precisely because his staff had anticipated the German attack and had already prepared a set of contingency plans, while Bradley's had failed him. The following day, Eisenhower held a conference of all the senior US commanders in Verdun. The atmosphere was glum except for Patton who was his usual cocky self.

US Army doctrine suggested that the essential ingredient to countering an enemy offensive was to hold the shoulders. This objective seemed to be well in hand. Units on the northern shoulder on the Elsenborn Ridge had rebuffed every German assault, and the battered 4th Division was holding steady in the hills of Luxembourg. Eisenhower's short-term objective was to prevent the Germans from crossing the Meuse. Once forces were in place to hold the river line, Eisenhower wanted to begin a counter-offensive, and he turned to Patton asking him when he could start. Patton promptly replied that he could begin with a corps of three divisions within two days, on the morning of 21 December, to which Eisenhower blurted "Don't be fatuous, George", thinking that it was merely Patton's usual bluster. The other officers present were equally skeptical, recognizing the enormous difficulties of reorienting a corps 90 degrees, moving it in winter conditions, and keeping it supplied along a tenuous supply line. In the ensuing discussion, Patton made it quite clear that his plans had been well considered. Eisenhower, who had just received his fifth star, quipped to Patton: "Funny thing, George, but every time I get a new star, I get attacked." Patton smiled and responded, "And every time you get attacked Ike, I pull you out", referring to his role in redeeming the US Army after the Kasserine Pass debacle in 1943.

Patton's actual dream for this campaign would have been to allow the Germans to penetrate 40 or 50 miles (60–80km), and then cut them off in an envelopment operation. But he realized that the senior US commanders were too cautious for such a bold plan, especially under the present confused circumstances. Curiously enough, Patton's notion of a deep envelopment battle was the worst nightmare of the senior Wehrmacht commanders. Model was concerned that the US Army would wait until after the Wehrmacht had reached or even crossed the Meuse before launching a major counter-offensive, trapping most of Army Group B and ending the war in the West.

On 20 December, under pressure from his senior aides, Eisenhower decided to temporarily shift control of the elements of the US Army in the northern sector, including First and Ninth Army, from Bradley's 12th Army Group to Montgomery's 21st Army Group. The ostensible reason was the fear that the Germans were about to capture a vital communications

A tank patrol of the 3rd Armored Division scans for signs of the 116th Panzer Division near Houfallize on 23 December. The tank to the left is an M4A1 (76mm) while the one to the right is an M4A3E2 assault tank. (NARA)

junction that would have severed the landlines between Bradley's HQ in Luxembourg and the northern commands. But there were also concerns that the First Army staff was still in disarray and that Bradley had not been vigorous enough straightening out the problems. The switch caused enormous resentment due to past problems between Bradley and Montgomery in North Africa and Sicily, and Montgomery's persistent efforts to poach units from Bradley to reinforce his infantry-weak 21st Army Group. The short-term effects were beneficial, and Montgomery's take-charge style impressed American officers fighting in the St Vith salient. In the long term, the switch in command would prove to be troublesome due to Montgomery's maladroit control of the US corps.

Montgomery showed up at First Army HQ in Chaudfontaine on the afternoon of 20 December "like Christ come to cleanse the temple". After Hodges explained the current dispositions, Montgomery responded that he wanted to redeploy the forces, create a reserve, and use this reserve to counterattack once the German attack had run out of steam. The US officers strongly resisted giving up any ground, and wanted to begin counter-offensive operations immediately. Montgomery accepted the current dispositions, and ordered the transfer of Collins' VII Corps, which would form the northern counterattack force, from the idle Ninth Army sector. British officers on Montgomery's staff thought that Hodges looked like he had "been poleaxed" but when Montgomery tried to relieve him the following day, Eisenhower told him to be patient. The matter was dropped, but Hodges' performance over the next few weeks was underwhelming and the First Army staff depended heavily on his chief of staff, MajGen William Kean.

The mobilization of the two heavy armored divisions, the 2nd and 3rd Armored, stationed north of the Ardennes was already under way, and these were assigned to Collins' corps. Since the 3rd Armored Division was more easily redeployed than the 2nd, on 18 December its CCA was detached and sent to V Corps, taking part in the fighting against the spearhead of the 1st SS-Panzer Division, Kampfgruppe Peiper, near La Gleize in the northern sector. The remainder of the division arrived around Hotton on 20 December. The two heavy divisions followed the old 1942 tables of organization and had six tank battalions instead of the three found in all other US armored divisions. The divisions were tank-heavy and infantry-weak, so they were usually paired with infantry divisions for a more balanced force with an infantry regiment added to

An armored dough of the 3rd Armored Division mans a roadblock with a bazooka near Manhay on 23 December, hours before the 2nd SS-Panzer Division attack. (NARA)

A Panther Ausf. G of 2nd SS-Panzer Division knocked out in a fork in the road between Manhay and Grandmenil during the fighting on 23 December 1944 with the 3rd Armored Division.

When the advance guard of Panzer Lehr Division pushed into Neffe in the pre-dawn hours of 19 December, the lead Panther tank of Feldwebel Dette struck a mine, blocking the road and ending the initial attack. This shows Dette's tank later in the month after it had been pushed off the road during subsequent attacks. (MHI)

each of their three combat commands. Collins' VII Corps deployed two infantry divisions, the green 75th Division and the more experienced 84th Division, in this role.

On the evening of 18 December 1944, a series of telephone conversations were held between the senior Wehrmacht commanders. In separate conversations with Rundstedt and Jodl, Army Group B commander Walter Model told them that the offensive had failed due to the inability of the SS divisions to move forward, and the slow progress of Manteuffel's 5th Panzer Army. He indicated that not only were the "Grand Slam" objectives out of reach, but that he doubted that even "Little Slam" could be achieved since the Panzer spearheads were so far from the Meuse. This sentiment gradually permeated the various headquarters in Berlin, and on 20 December 1944, when Heinz Guderian visited Hitler's HQ and the OB West offices, he tried to pry away some of the prized Panzer divisions in the Ardennes to reinforce threatened sectors on the Russian Front. Hitler would not hear of such a thing and scorned the generals for their pessimism. Due to the dissension in the high command as well as difficulties in moving reserve units forward, Model was slow to reorient the focus of the offensive. Even Dietrich and the 6th Panzer Army staff understood the problems, and on 20 December suggested to Model that either all the Panzer divisions be directed towards Dinant to exploit the breakthrough of the 2nd Panzer Division, or alternately to reorient their own attack away from the stubborn Elsenborn Ridge, towards the central route being spearheaded by 116th Panzer Division, Houfallize–La Roche–Liege.

At noon on 20 December, the II SS-Panzer Corps was ordered to begin moving forward. Since there was still a slim hope that I SS-Panzer Corps might secure a breakthrough in the northern sector, no decision was made whether its SS-Panzer divisions would be committed to the 6th Panzer Army as planned, or shifted to exploit the successes of Manteuffel's 5th Panzer Army. Manteuffel later argued that it was this indecision in these critical few days that prevented the success of "Little Slam", since an early commitment of the several Panzer divisions in reserve could have provided the added impetus needed to push to the Meuse. But Model recognized that until the American salient at St Vith was eliminated, there was no maneuver room to shift the SS-Panzer divisions into the central sector. The German appreciation actually became more optimistic in the days before Christmas. The OB West intelligence briefing of 22 December asserted that a major Allied counterattack by the US Third or Seventh Army from the south was unlikely before the New Year, and that limited intervention along the flanks would probably not start for a week. In conjunction with the reduction of the American salient at St Vith, the German high command began to take steps to redeploy the II SS-Panzer Corps away from the northern sector and into the center where it could support the penetration by the 5th Panzer Army.

The stage was now set for some of the largest and most bitter battles of the Ardennes campaign. The fighting through Christmas in the southern sector was concentrated in three main areas: Bastogne, the approaches to the Meuse River near Dinant, and the road junctions along the Tailles plateau beyond Houfallize.

THE DEFENSE OF BASTOGNE

The decision to free Panzer Lehr Division to race for the Meuse reduced the strength of the German forces around Bastogne. Although Lüttwitz had ordered Bayerlein to leave Kampfgruppe Hauser behind to reinforce Kokott's 26th VG Div., this meant that the attack was only being conducted by a reinforced division. Even after two days of futile fighting to penetrate into Bastogne, Kokott had not lost hope. When he accompanied a reconnaissance battalion in a move towards Sibret, he continued to see evidence of US troops retreating out of the city towards the south, an area not yet firmly in German hands. If he could not break into Bastogne, at least he could choke it. From 20 to 22 December, Kokott continued to draw the cordon around Bastogne with GR.77 on the north and east side, Kampfgruppe Hauser the southeast and GR.39 the southern flank around Sibret. Even though his forces did not yet firmly control the western side of Bastogne, word from the neighboring corps was that the 5th Fallschirmjäger Div. was making good progress, and so would presumably take care of this sector.

When the road to Neufchateau was cut on the night of 20 December, Bastogne was effectively surrounded, even if the Germans did not control the western sector in any force. Until that point, command within the city was disjointed, with Colonel Roberts controlling CCB, 10th Armored Div., General McAuliffe commanding the 101st Airborne, with a number of separate corps units and groups of stragglers. Middleton decided that it was time to unify the command in Bastogne and so it was turned over to McAuliffe. The scattered stragglers were formed into Team SNAFU, a GI jibe against the fondness of the Army for acronyms, meaning "Situation Normal All F'ed Up". Team SNAFU was broken up into security patrols and used where needed around the city. The German repositioning on 21/22 December gave McAuliffe time to better organize the defenses.

At 11.30hrs on 22 December, two Panzer Lehr officers and their drivers walked up the road from Remonfosse under a white flag. Under

Lüttwitz's direction, they were to offer the Bastogne defenders an honorable surrender. They encountered an outpost of the 327th Glider Infantry and the officers were taken to McAuliffe's HQ in blindfolds. When told of the surrender demands, McAuliffe laughed and said "Aw, nuts". The idea of surrendering seemed preposterous to him as the Germans had proven unable to break into the city after four days of fighting. McAuliffe was at a loss as to how to reply to the formal surrender demand, however, until one of his staff suggested that his first reaction was fine. So they typed out "Nuts" on some stationery, thereby creating one of the legends of the Ardennes campaign. When the response was handed over to the German officers before they returned

LEFT **Newly arrived paratroopers of Ewell's 501st Parachute Infantry Regiment, 101st Airborne Division, head out of Bastogne towards Mageret on the morning of 19 December. It was the appearance of this column that dissuaded Bayerlein from launching a raid by Panzer Lehr Division into Bastogne that day. (NARA)**

BELOW **Paratroopers of the 1/506th PIR, 101st Airborne Division, set off from Bastogne for Foy in the late morning of 19 December to reinforce Team Desobry near Noville. (NARA)**

to Lüttwitz, they expressed puzzlement at the answer, to which the 327th Glider Infantry commander, Colonel Harper responded "If you don't understand what 'Nuts' means in English it is the same as 'go to hell', and I'll tell you something else – if you continue to attack we will kill every goddam German that tries to break into this city."

The success of the Bastogne garrison in repulsing repeated German infantry attacks was closely tied to the field artillery battalions that had accumulated within the Bastogne perimeter. But ammunition reserves were becoming dangerously low by the evening of 22 December. This led to restrictive instructions on the use of the howitzers, frustrating the

Surviving troops of the 28th Division and stragglers from other units were used to form Team SNAFU to conduct security patrols around Bastogne like this 28th Division patrol on 20 December. (NARA)

A view inside Bastogne on 26 December shortly before the relief column from the 4th Armored Division arrived. In the background is an M4A3 tank, probably of the 10th Armored Division.

CHRISTMAS IN BASTOGNE, 1944 (pages 54–55)
In the early morning of Christmas Day, Kampfgruppe
Maucke of the newly arrived 15th Panzergrenadier
Division launched an attack against the positions of the
502nd Parachute Infantry (1) and the 327th Glider Infantry
on the northern side of the Bastogne perimeter. The attack
was beaten decisively in a series of savage skirmishes in
the woods and villages outside the city. This scene shows
the aftermath of the skirmish as the paratroopers attempt
to reinforce their positions for a possible renewed German
onslaught. The most vivid memory for most American
veterans of the Battle of the Bulge was the misery of life in
the foxholes. It was commonplace for a unit to move every
few days, and sometimes even more than once a day. Each
move was accompanied by the need to dig another set of
foxholes and defensive positions (2). While foxholes were
useful in providing protection from German infantry attack,
the main killer in the Ardennes fighting on both sides was
artillery. Artillery was particularly deadly in wooded areas,
since detonations in the trees tended to spray the area with
wood splinters. Not only were these splinters deadly
against unprotected infantry, but even if the infantryman
was only wounded (3), the small splinters of wood were
difficult for medics (4) to find and remove and so often led
to life-threatening infections. The best protection against
this scourge was the foxhole. The standard US Army
practice was a two-man foxhole, deep enough to stand in. If
a unit was stationary for any period of time, the practice
was usually to create two sets of defenses – a deep fighting
foxhole, and a long, shallow trench for sleeping, preferably

with overhead cover such as logs. GIs were issued either
the pre-war style of "T" handled entrenching shovel, or the
later M1943 type (5) that had a folding blade. Neither was
particularly effective, especially in frozen ground full of
tree roots. The 101st Airborne Division was hastily
deployed to the Ardennes after months of fighting in the
Netherlands. By this stage, their distinctive paratrooper
garb had given way to the same types of uniforms worn
by other US infantry. This was especially true of new
replacements and the glider infantry. One of the major
scandals of the Ardennes was the poor preparation of the
US Army in providing adequate winter clothing. A particular
problem in the winter of 1944–45 was the inadequate
supply of water-resistant winter boots. This led to
high levels of trench foot in US infantry units. In the
background are a pair of burning PzKpfw IV tanks (6).
Although overshadowed by the larger Panther tank, the
PzKpfw IV was still the workhorse of the Wehrmacht, and
the most common German tank type in the Ardennes
fighting. Hidden in the tree line is a M18 76mm gun motor
carriage (7). This tank destroyer was the fastest tracked
combat vehicle of World War II, designed to fulfill the
Tank Destroyer Command's motto of "Seek, strike,
destroy". In fact, by the time it entered service, its
effectiveness was undermined by the inadequate
performance of its gun against the new generation of
German armored vehicles such as the Panther and
the Jagdpanzer IV/70. The more powerful M36 tank
destroyer with its 90mm gun was the preferred choice
in the winter of 1944–45. (Peter Dennis)

paratroopers and infantry along the front line who would often see 'the Germans moving about in the open without any response. The situation became so bad that one regimental commander pleaded with McAuliffe for artillery support only to be told; "if you see 400 Germans in a 100-yard area and they have their heads up, you can fire artillery at them, but only two rounds!" McAuliffe's primary concern was that ammunition would run out before Patton's Third Army arrived.

After two days of skirmishing, significant German attacks resumed on 23 December. In the late afternoon, Kampfgruppe Hauser made another attempt to push into Marvie on the southern side of the city, supported by GR.39 to the west. German infantry attempted to stealthily probe past the scattered US outposts and once in position, a pair of assault guns came clanking up the road but were halted by a wrecked half-track that blocked the approach. A platoon from G/327th Glider Infantry was overwhelmed on Hill 500 after dark, and the attack penetrated into Marvie. Two M4 tanks from Team O'Hara discouraged any further advance into the village, but German attacks continued in earnest until midnight, and controlled the southern fringe of the village through the following day in spite of US efforts. Kampfgruppe Hauser had a hard time reinforcing the operation with any armor, as the area was heavily wooded with only a single road into the village.

On the night of 22/23 December, a "Russian High", a high-pressure front bringing cold weather and clearing skies, arrived and changed the fortunes of war. The next morning, a wave of 16 C-47 transports appeared over Bastogne, dropping the first batch of supplies. By dusk, 241 aircraft had flown to Bastogne dropping 441 tons of supplies. Drops the following day by 160 aircraft added 100 tons of supplies.

Kokott was convinced that any further assaults into the southern sector of Bastogne would be futile, so he proposed to Manteuffel that the next attack would be conducted where he suspected the Americans were

Paratroopers of the 101st Airborne Division recover supplies after the airdrop of 27 December along the Bastogne perimeter. (NARA)

The catastrophic effects of an ammunition fire and explosion are all too evident from the shattered hulk of this PzKpfw IV of Kampfgruppe Maucke, 15th Panzergrenadier Division knocked out north of Bastogne during the engagement with the 101st Airborne Division at Christmas Day.

weakest, in the northwest. He hoped that he would be able to use whatever armor was available, since the terrain in the northwest was much more favorable for tanks, and the cold weather was hardening the ground. In fact, the US defenses were probably best in this sector. Impressed by Kokott's determination, Manteuffel promised that the 15th Panzergrenadier Division would be put at his disposal for this attack. The 15th Panzergrenadier Division had recently arrived from the Italian Front, and was both experienced and well-equipped. The attack was scheduled for Christmas Day and Manteuffel grimly relayed Hitler's message that "Bastogne must be taken at all costs." The lead elements of the 15th Panzergrenadier Division arrived on the northern side of Bastogne shortly

Trench foot was a significant cause of US casualties in the Ardennes fighting that could be prevented by proper foot care. This corporal of the 327th Glider Infantry is drying his feet while serving along the Bastogne perimeter.

before midnight on Christmas Eve. The reinforcements included Kampfgruppe Maucke with two battalions of infantry, a tank battalion with about 30 tanks and tank destroyers, and two artillery battalions. Kokott decided to launch the attack in the pre-dawn hours since otherwise the armor would attract the attention of American fighter-bombers that were now swarming over the battlefield in the clear skies. With so little time to deploy, many of the troops of Panzergrenadier Regt.115 rode the Panzers into the attack zone.

McAuliffe received first news of the attack at 03.30hrs on Christmas Day, when A/502nd PIR in Rolle reported that the Germans were on top of them and then the line went dead. The regimental headquarters alerted the rest of the companies with orders to send reinforcements to Rolle. The battalion HQ hesitated to rush another company into the fight in the dark until it became clearer where the Germans were actually attacking and in what numbers. At dawn, this became clear when tanks of Kampfgruppe Maucke were spotted moving near the junction of the 502nd PIR and the 327th Glider Infantry. There were three principal thrusts, the 15th Panzergrenadier Division attack furthest west between Champs and Hemroulle, an initial GR.77 attack in the center coming down the road into Champs, and a smaller attack by GR.77 that began around 05.00 when Germany infantry infiltrated through some woods between Champs and Longchamps. The most serious threat came from the Panzer attack that rolled right over A/327th GIR. However, the Panzergrenadiers did not drive out the infantry, and when the next wave of Panzergrenadiers approached the Co. A positions on foot, they were greeted with intense rifle fire. The 15th Panzergrenadier Division tank attack split up, some tanks heading towards Hemroulle and others to rear of the B/502nd PIR. Two M18s from 705th Tank Destroyer Battalion knocked out a few of the advancing Panzers but were in turn knocked out when they tried to withdraw. Before reaching the woods where C/502nd PIR was deployed, the tanks veered northward towards Champs, exposing

Another PzKpfw IV named *Lustmolch* (Happy Salamander) of Kampfgruppe Maucke, 15th Panzergrenadier Division abandoned in Champs during the fighting with the 502nd IR on Christmas Day.

their flanks to rifle fire from the woods and to a pair of M18s from 705th Tank Destroyer Battalion. The Panzergrenadiers on the tanks took the worst beating from intense small arms fire, while three PzKpfw IVs were knocked out by gunfire and two more by bazookas at close range. A single PzKpfw IV broke into Champs but was stopped by 57mm anti-tank gunfire and bazookas.

The group of tanks and Panzergrenadiers that had split off earlier towards the 327th GIR received a far hotter reception. Four tank destroyers were located between Cos. A and B, and Co. C received support from a pair of M4 tanks that arrived shortly before the German attack. None of the German tanks survived the encounter, two being hit point-blank by 105mm howitzers, and the rest being knocked out by tank destroyers and bazookas. Not one of the 18 PzKpfw IV that started the attack survived, and most of the Panzergrenadiers were either killed or captured. The Christmas attack was the last major assault until Patton's relief column arrived.

The Air Campaign

The weather for the first week was too poor for the Luftwaffe to have any significant impact on the battle and only 170 sorties were conducted on the first day of the offensive. On 17 December, 600 daylight sorties were flown including some strafing missions, and these were followed after dark by over 250 ground-attack missions by night-fighters striking at major communication centers such as Liege. The plan was to keep at least 150 fighters in the air at all times during daylight to provide an aerial umbrella for the Panzer divisions, but this was seldom achieved and the number of sorties continued to decline. The US 9th Air Force also had its close-support operations hampered by the weather as well, and it was distracted by the unusually large numbers of German fighters active over the battlefield. Its two tactical air commands (TAC) flew about 450 tactical sorties daily for the first week of the offensive, mainly fighter sweeps with few ground-attack missions. When the weather finally cleared on 23 December, both the IX and XXIX TAC turned out in force including 669 fighter-bomber sorties. Medium bombers from IX Bomber Command conducted interdiction missions against German supply lines, but were met by furious resistance from German fighters, losing 35 bombers and suffering damage to 182 more out of the 624 that took part. As a result, on Christmas Eve, the 8th Air Force conducted 1,400 bomber sorties against 12 Luftwaffe airfields over the Rhine to dampen down Luftwaffe activity. Four of the airfields suffered little damage, but the other eight were shut down on average for eight days. On Christmas Day, American air activity reached levels not seen since the August missions against the Falaise gap, totaling 6,194 tactical sorties including 4,281 fighter sorties. Oberst Ludwig Heilmann of the 5th Fallschirmjäger Division grimly recalled that by nightfall, the attacking *Jabos* had left "an uninterrupted trail of burning vehicles extending like a torchlight procession from Bastogne all the way back to the Westwall … in my opinion, the Ardennes offensive was irretrievably lost when the Allies sent their air forces into action on 25 December, a fact that even the simplest soldier realized."

The Luftwaffe was powerless to stop this, as their inadequately trained fighter pilots suffered disproportionate losses in encounters with the more numerous US fighters. Allied fighters claimed to have shot down

On 19 December, the 353rd Fighter Squadron attempted to bomb the headquarters of the 116th Panzer Division but was bounced by about 40 Luftwaffe fighters. In the ensuing melee, the outnumbered but more experienced squadron downed nine German fighters while losing three Thunderbolts. This is *Big Jake*, the P-47D of Lt Lloyd Overfield, credited with two fighters that day, and seen here taxying at Rosieres during the Battle of the Bulge. (NARA)

718 German aircraft from 17 to 27 December, while losing 111 aircraft to German fighters and 307 more to other causes. A post-war RAF history of the Luftwaffe pungently noted that "bad servicing of the Luftwaffe's aircraft was becoming more widespread, and the pilots were all too ready to seize on the slightest excuse for returning early from their missions. Many pilots, insufficiently trained as they were, had no zest for facing the heavy Allied air onslaught which was carried out during the four days of good weather, December 24–27." A total of 346 fighter pilots were lost between 23 and 27 December, including 106 on Christmas Eve, the worst losses during a very costly month for the Luftwaffe fighter force. By the beginning of January, the Allied air forces had conducted about 34,100 missions including 16,600 tactical sorties over the Ardennes compared to 7,500 for the Luftwaffe. The Wehrmacht received little solace from the heightened Luftwaffe activity since so few of the missions were ground-attack.

The last great Luftwaffe operation in the west was conducted on New Year's Day when Jagdkorps 2 finally staged Operation Bodenplatte two weeks late. The attack included every serviceable fighter in the west, totaling about 1,035 aircraft including pathfinders. The attack caught the Allied air bases in Belgium and Holland napping, and 144 American and British aircraft were destroyed on the ground, 62 damaged, and a further 70 lost in aerial combat. But it was a Pyrrhic victory for the Luftwaffe. Over a third of the attack force was lost, some 304 aircraft, including 85 shot down by their own flak. A total of 214 aircrew were killed or captured, including three Geschwader commanders, all six Gruppe commanders, and 11 Staffel commanders – an irreplaceable loss. Bodenplatte had a crippling effect on subsequent Luftwaffe operations in the west; in contrast Allied losses were replaced quickly from depots and few aircrew had been lost.

OPERATION *BODENPLATTE*, NEW YEAR'S DAY 1945
(pages 62–63)

At 09.30hrs on New Year's Day, the Luftwaffe staged its long delayed attack on Allied airfields, codenamed *Bodenplatte* (baseplate). Among the participants were the Me-262A-2a fighter-bombers (1) of KG51, one of Hitler's new wonder weapons. Twenty-one of these aircraft took part in attacks on RAF airfields at Eindhoven and Heesch in the Netherlands. The Eindhoven strike was conducted in conjunction with Bf-109 and FW-190 fighters (2) of Jagdgeschwader 3 and was the more successful of the two missions, destroying or damaging about 50 of the Typhoons (3) and Spitfires stationed with the three wings there. The attack on Heesch with Jagdgeschwader 6 had little effect and one Me-262 was lost to ground fire. Kampfgeschwader 51 was the principal Luftwaffe unit operating the fighter-bomber version of the Me-262 at the time, and it was responsible for the majority of Me-262 sorties in late 1944. The I Gruppe flew from the Rheine and Hopsten airbases while II Gruppe flew from Hesepe. These fighter-bombers were used repeatedly in ground-attack missions in the Ardennes, though there is little evidence to suggest they were very effective in this role given the difficulty of delivering unguided bombs at high speed and at low altitude. KG 51 lost a total of five aircraft during the Ardennes missions in December: four to fighters and one to flak. The origins of the fighter-bomber version of the Me-262 were controversial. Although the aircraft had been designed from the outset as a fighter, Hitler was insistent that the aircraft be used as a fighter-bomber as well. This version could carry two 550lb bombs (4) under the nose and additional fuel to extend its range. However, two of its four 30mm cannon were deleted to save weight (5). It was far from ideal as a fighter-bomber, since the pilot had a difficult time aiming against the target except in low-altitude strikes or from a shallow dive. The first of these aircraft were deployed with Erprobungskommando Schenk (test detachment Schenk) in France in late July 1944, becoming redesignated as I/KG 51 in mid-August. The handful of aircraft were used in occasional ground-attack missions against Allied forces throughout August, and one of the new jet fighter-bombers was spotted and forced down by a US P-47 fighter on 28 August 1944 near Brussels. The Me-262A-2a seen here wears the distinctive markings of KG 51. The unit markings include the white tip on the nose and tail (6). The unit codes on the fuselage side (7) are the four-letter style, in this case 9K+CP with the 9K identifying KG 51, the third enlarged letter identifying the individual aircraft, and the final letter indicating the Staffel (H, K, L, M, N, P). The camouflage finish is typical of this period: RLM 76 light blue on the undersides, with RLM 81 brown-violet and 82 dark green on the upper surfaces and extending down the sides in an irregular spray-painted mottled pattern. (Howard Gerrard)

PATTON STRIKES BACK

The Third Army began moving its III Corps towards Arlon on 19 December. The spearhead of the northern attack was Patton's favorite, the 4th Armored Division. Muscle came from the 26th and 80th Divisions, reinforced by three field artillery groups. The attack was launched in the late afternoon of 21 December by all three divisions, with the corps advancing from three to five miles. The following day, the 4th Armored Division reached Martelange 13 miles south of Bastogne, the 26th Division moved up alongside it to the east and the 80th Division took Heiderscheid. As the III Corps approached Bastogne, German resistance intensified. By 23 December, elements from Brandenberger's 7th Army were finally approaching the southern outskirts of Bastogne, and the 5th Fallschirm-jäger Division was assigned to cover the main road from Arlon through Marvie into Bastogne. Combat Command A took this route, but was halted by determined German resistance around Livarchamps. Recognizing that this route was the one most likely to be contested, the two other combat commands were sent up alternate routes. CCB went across country from Habay-la-Neuve but was stopped near Hompré. CCR was redeployed on Christmas, and after a 30-mile road march to the west, resumed its attack along the narrow Cobreville–Assenois road into southwestern Bastogne.

By the morning of 26 December, CCR was the closest of the three combat commands to Bastogne, and by mid-afternoon fought its way to within a short distance of the Bastogne defense. A task force was formed under Captain William Dwight consisting of Co. C, 37th Tank Battalion, and Co. C, 53rd AIB, which set off for Assenois at 16.10 after a preliminary artillery strike. The tanks proceeded into the village even before the artillery fire had lifted, avoiding much German resistance. Once the artillery lifted, the German defenders tried to disable the armored infantry column by throwing Teller mines underneath their half-tracks, blowing up one with mines, and knocking out three more with Panzerfaust anti-tank

Patton's initial assault against the 7th Army by the 80th Division led to a series of sharp battles along the Luxembourg border with the 352nd Volksgrenadier Division, supported on 23 December by Panzers of the Führer Grenadier Brigade. This StuG III assault gun is inspected by GIs of 2/319th Infantry in Heiderscheid a few days later. (NARA)

A Kampfgruppe of the Führer Grenadier Brigade attacked Patton's 80th Division in Heiderscheid on Christmas Eve and amongst its losses were the StuG III to the left and this SdKfz 251 half-track, one of the rare SdKfz 251/17 variants with a turreted 2cm autocannon. (NARA)

A group of prisoners from the 1/GR.914, 352nd Volksgrenadier Division, captured near Mertzig on 24 December by the 319th Infantry, 80th Division during Patton's drive to relieve Bastogne. (MHI)

rockets. But the American infantry drove out the defenders in bitter house-to-house fighting and 428 prisoners were taken. By late afternoon, Captain Dwight was greeted by the commander of the 101st Airborne, General McAuliffe in the outskirts of Bastogne. Shortly after midnight, the task force attacked the woods north of Assenois and by 03.00, the road was clear for vehicular traffic. The light tanks of Co. D/37th Tank Battalion escorted a relief column into Bastogne consisting of 40 supply trucks and 70 ambulances later in the day. While CCR had managed to break into Bastogne, it would take several more days of hard fighting to secure and widen the corridor. However, German forces in this sector were the weakest of the siege force, and the corridor was never seriously threatened. While this was not the end to the fighting for Bastogne, clearly the momentum was shifting in favor of the US Army.

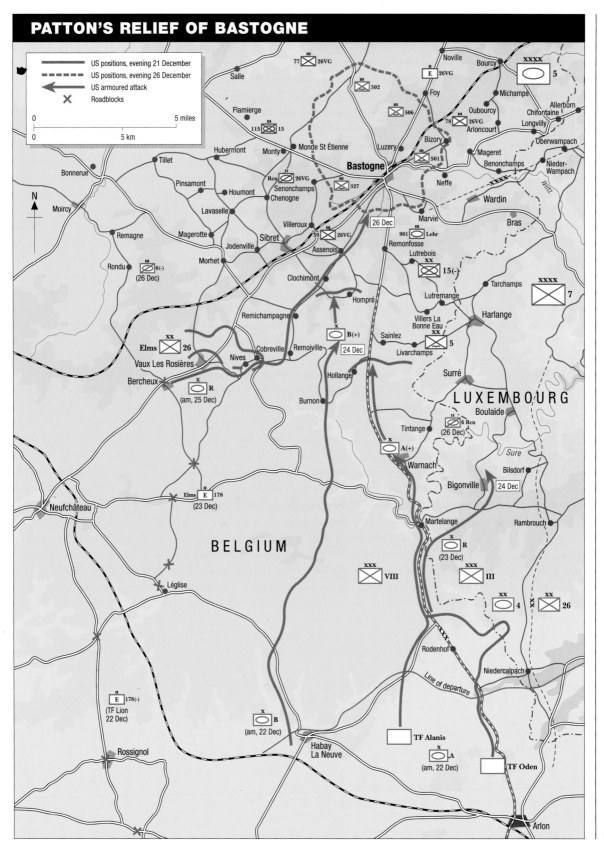

Legend:
- US positions, evening 21 December
- US positions, evening 26 December
- US armoured attack
- Roadblocks

0 ____ 5 miles
0 ____ 5 km

N

Salle
Flamierge
Hubermont
Tillet
Bonnerue
Pinsamont
Houmont
Moircy
Lavaselle
Remagne
Magerotte
Jodenville
Sibret
Morhet
Rondu
6(-)
(26 Dec)

77 26VG
Monde St Étienne
115 15
Monty
Luzery
Bastogne
Senonchamps
Chenogne
Villeroux
327
39 26VG
Assenois
Clochimont
Hompré
Remichampagne
Remonville
Cobreville
Nives
B(+)
24 Dec

Noville
Bourcy
E 26VG
Foy
506
Michamps
Oubourcy
78 26VG
Arloncourt
Bizory
501
Mageret
Benonchamps
Neffe
Marvie
26 Dec
Marvie
Remonfosse
901 Lehr
Lutrebois
15(-)
Lutremange
Villers La
Bonne Eau
Sainlez
Livarchamps
5

Allerborn
Chifontaine
Longvilly
Oberwampach
Nieder-Wampach
Wilz
Wardin
Bras
5
Tarchamps
7
Harlange
Surré

LUXEMBOURG

502
506

xxxx 5

xxxx 7

Elms 26
Vaux Les Rosières
Bercheux
R
(am, 25 Dec)
Burnon
Hollange

6 Rcn
(26 Dec)
Boulaide
Tintange
A(+)
Warnach
Bilsdorf
Sure
Bigonville
24 Dec

Neufchâteau
Elms E 178
(23 Dec)

BELGIUM

Léglise

E 178(-)
(TF Lion
22 Dec)

Rossignol

B
(am, 22 Dec)
Habay
La Neuve

Martelange
R
(23 Dec)
Rambrouch

xxx VIII

xxx III

4
xx 26

Rodenhof

Niedercalpach
Line of departure

TF Alanis

A
(am, 22 Dec)

TF Oden

Arlon

153

The first US tank into Bastogne was this M4A3E2 assault tank named Cobra King of Lt Charles Boggess from Co. C, 37th Tank Battalion, 4th Armored Division. (Patton Museum)

A column of tanks from the 4th Armored Division move through Bastogne with an M4A3E2 assault tank, possibly Cobra King, in the lead. (MHI)

The Struggle for the Tailles Plateau

When the "Russian High" arrived on the night of 22/23 December, the rain-soaked, muddy fields began to harden. This improved the prospects for German mobile operations since the Panzer columns were no longer trapped on the roads, and no longer obliged to fight for every village and road junction. While the cold weather restored some fluidity to the battle, it also led to clearing conditions that permitted Allied fighter-bombers to return to the fray, with frightful consequences for exposed German supply columns in the Eifel. The change in the weather had an immediate and dramatic impact on the fighting in the central sector of the Ardennes front, the battle for road junctions along the eastern edge of the Tailles plateau stretching towards Marche. This road net roughly paralleled the front line running from Trois Ponts in the north, west through Bra, Manhay, Grandmenil, Erezée, Hotton, and finally to

Marche. These road junctions were a German tactical objective since they controlled access to routes leading north and west towards the Meuse.

Krüger's 58th Panzer Corps made the initial breakthrough in this sector, with the 116th Panzer Division pushing past Houfallize on 19 December and reaching Hotton on 21 December with the 560th VG Div. to its right. Hotton was weakly defended by headquarters elements of the 3rd Armored Division, but the advance guard of the 116th Panzer Division was not strong enough to capture the town. Likewise, task forces of the 3rd Armored Division at Soy and Amonines stopped the 560th Volksgrenadier Division. Although Model had hoped to commit the II SS-Panzer Corps into this sector to reinforce this breakthrough since 20 December, lack of fuel and the continued hold-out of US forces in the St Vith salient blocked access from the northern sector of the Ardennes

RIGHT **One of the classic images from the Battle of the Bulge as two armored doughs from the 10th Armored Infantry Battalion, 4th Armored Division take aim at targets in the field outside Bastogne on 27 December 1944. (NARA)**

BELOW **A company of the 10th Armored Infantry Battalion, 4th Armored Division approaches Bastogne on 27 December and an explosion can be seen in the distance. (NARA)**

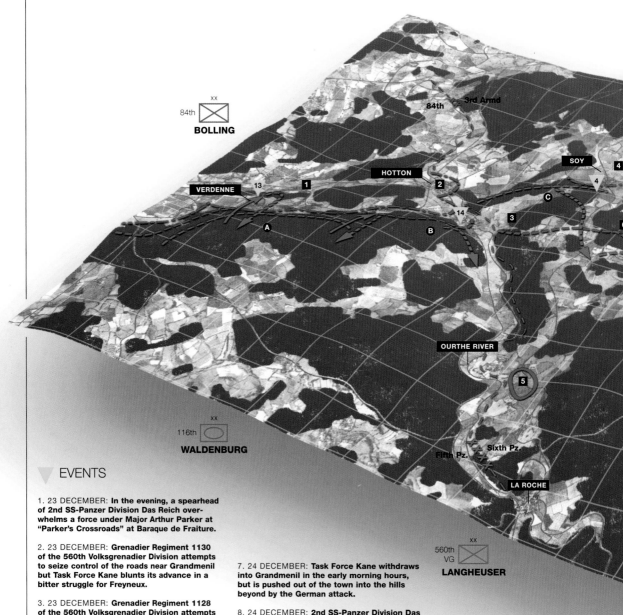

84th XX BOLLING

84th 3rd Armd

SOY 4

HOTTON

VERDENNE 13 1 2

4

C

14

A B

OURTHE RIVER

5

116th XX WALDENBURG

Fifth Pz. Sixth Pz.

LA ROCHE

560th XX VG LANGHEUSER

▼ EVENTS

1. 23 DECEMBER: **In the evening, a spearhead of 2nd SS-Panzer Division Das Reich overwhelms a force under Major Arthur Parker at "Parker's Crossroads" at Baraque de Fraiture.**

2. 23 DECEMBER: **Grenadier Regiment 1130 of the 560th Volksgrenadier Division attempts to seize control of the roads near Grandmenil but Task Force Kane blunts its advance in a bitter struggle for Freyneux.**

3. 23 DECEMBER: **Grenadier Regiment 1128 of the 560th Volksgrenadier Division attempts to take Amonines, but is beaten back by Task Force Orr of CCB, 3rd Armored Division.**

4. 23 DECEMBER: **Grenadier Regiment 1129 of the 560th Volksgrenadier Division attempts to take Soy, but is forced to retreat by elements of the CCR, 3rd Armored Division. These attacks continue through Christmas.**

5. **Elements from the 7th Armored Division, including a C/40th Tank Battalion are overwhelmed in the dark by the spearhead of the 2nd SS-Panzer Division Das Reich moving on Manhay, losing 21 of their 32 tanks.**

6. NIGHT, 23 DECEMBER: **Before they can conduct their planned withdrawal, Task Force Brewster is already outflanked by an attack of a Kampfgruppe of SS-Panzergrenadier Regiment 3, 2nd SS-Panzer Division. The troops abandon their vehicles and escape on foot.**

7. 24 DECEMBER: **Task Force Kane withdraws into Grandmenil in the early morning hours, but is pushed out of the town into the hills beyond by the German attack.**

8. 24 DECEMBER: **2nd SS-Panzer Division Das Reich fights its way into Manhay but fails to gain access to the Liege road beyond.**

9. 25 DECEMBER: **The battle turns to a stalemate on Christmas day when attacks by the 289th Infantry and Task Force McGeorge against Grandmenil and CCA, 7th Armored Division fail, as do efforts by the 2nd SS-Panzer Division to break out of the town towards the west.**

10. 26 DECEMBER: **An attack by SS-Panzergrenadier Regiment 4 against the 325th Glider Infantry in Tri-le-Cheslaing fails.**

11. 26 DECEMBER: **Task Force McGeorge and Panzers of the 2nd SS-Panzer Division clash again in the first skirmish of the day, but renewed American attacks later in the day in conjunction with the 3/289th Infantry puts the US partly in control of Grandmenil by dusk.**

12. 26 DECEMBER: **The 3/517th Parachute Infantry, 82nd Airborne Division, finally regains Manhay after nightfall.**

13. 26 DECEMBER: **After its Kampfgruppe Bayer is trapped north of Verdenne in a failed attack on 24 December, the badly weakened 116th Panzer Division tries to relieve them, but is beaten back again by the 334th Infantry. Kampfgruppe Bayer is given permission to escape after dark.**

14. **The Fuhrer Begleit Brigade joins the attack on the road junctions trying to seize Hotton, but is stopped. At dusk, it is ordered to back up and head for Bastogne to join the siege there.**

BATTLE FOR THE ROAD JUNCTIONS

23–27 December 1944, viewed from the southeast. When US forces withdraw from the St Vith salient on 23 December, they permit the injection of the II SS-Panzer Corps into the battle for the key road junctions on the Tailles plateau. In a series of bitter skirmishes around Christmas, the Waffen-SS Panzer units fight their way into several of the key towns while neighboring units of the 5th Panzer Army do likewise further west. But in the days after Christmas, US counter-attacks push them back out of these towns.

Note gridlines are shown at intervals of 1 mile/1.61km

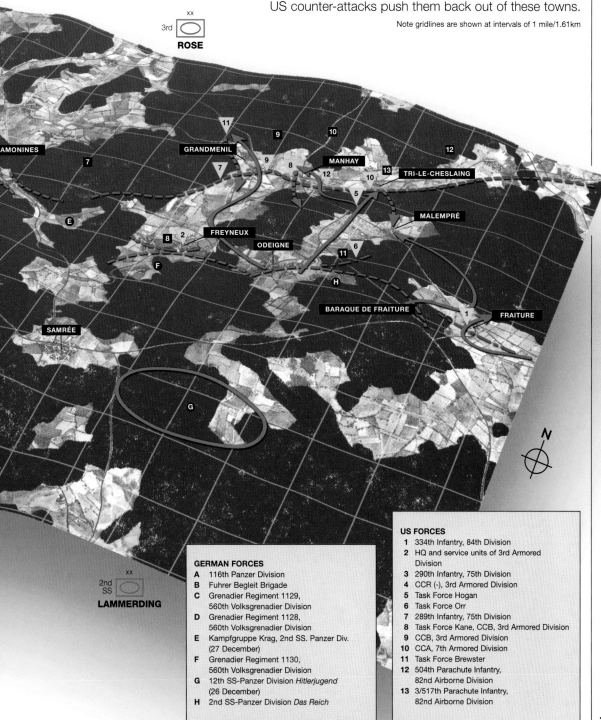

3rd xx **ROSE**

AMONINES
GRANDMENIL
MANHAY
TRI-LE-CHESLAING
MALEMPRÉ
FREYNEUX
ODEIGNE
BARAQUE DE FRAITURE
FRAITURE
SAMRÉE

2nd SS xx **LAMMERDING**

GERMAN FORCES

- **A** 116th Panzer Division
- **B** Fuhrer Begleit Brigade
- **C** Grenadier Regiment 1129, 560th Volksgrenadier Division
- **D** Grenadier Regiment 1128, 560th Volksgrenadier Division
- **E** Kampfgruppe Krag, 2nd SS. Panzer Div. (27 December)
- **F** Grenadier Regiment 1130, 560th Volksgrenadier Division
- **G** 12th SS-Panzer Division *Hitlerjugend* (26 December)
- **H** 2nd SS-Panzer Division *Das Reich*

US FORCES

- **1** 334th Infantry, 84th Division
- **2** HQ and service units of 3rd Armored Division
- **3** 290th Infantry, 75th Division
- **4** CCR (-), 3rd Armored Division
- **5** Task Force Hogan
- **6** Task Force Orr
- **7** 289th Infantry, 75th Division
- **8** Task Force Kane, CCB, 3rd Armored Division
- **9** CCB, 3rd Armored Division
- **10** CCA, 7th Armored Division
- **11** Task Force Brewster
- **12** 504th Parachute Infantry, 82nd Airborne Division
- **13** 3/517th Parachute Infantry, 82nd Airborne Division

into the central area between the Salm and Meuse rivers. From the Allied perspective, the salient had been held far longer than expected, and with the defenses on the verge of collapse, Montgomery authorized a withdrawal.

When the ground froze on the night of 22/23 December, the trapped CCB, 7th Armored Division, and the other units in the St Vith salient could finally pull back over the Salm. With the obstruction posed by the St Vith salient removed, Obergruppenführer Bittrich's 2nd SS-Panzer Corps began to flood into the vacuum created by the US withdrawal into the area from the Salm to the Ourthe river. The objective of the II SS-Panzer Corps was to further rupture the US defensive lines in the La Gleize–Bra–Erezée–Marche area with a secondary, if somewhat hopeless, mission of relieving Kampfgruppe Peiper trapped in La Gleize. With the prospects for the I SS-Panzer Corps growing increasingly poor, it was becoming clear to Berlin that the failure of Dietrich's 6th Panzer Army was having a ripple effect by exposing the advances of Manteuffel's 5th Panzer Army, since their lines of communication were now vulnerable to US reinforcements pouring in from the north. Model and Rundstedt wanted the II SS-Panzer Corps to gain control of the road net on the Tailles plateau to weaken US armored attacks against the 5th Panzer Army from the north.

The 2nd SS-Panzer Division *Das Reich* began moving over the Salm River on 23 December heading for the Baraque de Fraiture crossroads, while the neighboring 9th SS-Panzer Division *Hohenstaufen* moved to its right, against the withdrawing St Vith garrison and the 82nd Airborne Division. The roadblock at Baraque de Fraiture was held by a small detachment from the 589th Field Artillery led by Major Arthur Parker, and reinforced by some tanks from TF Kane of the 3rd Armored Division. The crossroads was at a key junction between the 3rd Armored Division and 82nd Airborne Division, but was weakly held due to a lack of resources. On the afternoon of 23 December, "Parker's Crossroads" was pummeled by German artillery for 20 minutes and then assaulted by a Panzergrenadier regiment supported by two tank companies. As this

position was overwhelmed after nightfall, it opened the door to Manhay, which controlled access to the road leading to Liege.

The 560th VG Div., the easternmost element of the 5th Panzer Army began the push against Manhay from the western side, attempting to seize villages on the approaches to the town. GR.1160 attempted a two-pronged attack on Freyneux, held by Task Force Kane of CCB, 3rd Armored Division. Although supported by assault guns, the attacks were beaten back by tank fire and the regiment suffered such heavy casualties that it was no longer effective. Further west, GR.1129 advanced towards Soy and Hotton, but the attack was held up by other elements of the 3rd Armored Division.

The American defenses around Manhay were in a confused state with elements of the XVIII Airborne Corps, including the 7th Armored Division withdrawing from the St Vith salient, intermingled with newly arrived and scattered task forces of the 3rd Armored Division under Collins' VII Corps. Field Marshal Montgomery was very unhappy about the weak and exposed defensive positions of the 82nd Airborne Division and on the morning of 24 December, he instructed Ridgway's XVIII Airborne Corps to pull back the scattered paratrooper detachments to a more defensible perimeter along the road from Trois Ponts to Manhay that night. Likewise, the 3rd Armored Division reorganized its defenses, reassigning elements of the 7th Armored Division to the defense of Manhay. Amidst this confusion, the 2nd SS-Panzer Division began its attack up the Manhay road.

SS-Oberführer Heinz Lammerding of *Das Reich* delayed the attack towards Manhay until a key bridge at Odeigne could be completed. With the new bridge in place, he waited until nightfall to begin the attack to avoid being pummeled by American *Jabos*. Christmas Eve in this sector was a clear, moonlit night with the ground frozen hard and covered by a thin layer of snow, in other words excellent for tank movement and well suited to night operations. SS-Panzergrenadier Regiment 3 *Deutschland* began moving up the road from Odeigne around 21.00hrs towards a roadblock of CCA, 7th Armored Division, which was in the process of pulling back as part of the reorganization. One of the German columns was led by a captured Sherman tank, and in the dark, the American tanks

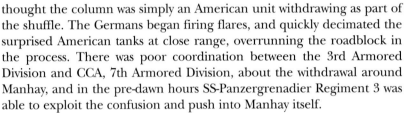

LEFT **A GI from the 3/289th Infantry, 75th Division examines one of the Panther Ausf. G of the 2nd SS-Panzer Division in the ruins of Manhay on 30 December. (NARA)**

ABOVE **A GI of the 325th Glider Infantry armed with an M3 "grease gun" .45cal sub-machine gun takes cover near a German supply trailer during the fighting on 3 January 1945. (NARA)**

thought the column was simply an American unit withdrawing as part of the shuffle. The Germans began firing flares, and quickly decimated the surprised American tanks at close range, overrunning the roadblock in the process. There was poor coordination between the 3rd Armored Division and CCA, 7th Armored Division, about the withdrawal around Manhay, and in the pre-dawn hours SS-Panzergrenadier Regiment 3 was able to exploit the confusion and push into Manhay itself.

TF Brewster, the most exposed of the US outposts, began to withdraw not realizing that the area between them and the rest of the 3rd Armored Div. had been flooded by advancing German troops. When the two lead tanks were knocked out and blocked the retreat route, Brewster ordered his troops to abandon their vehicles and infiltrate back to US lines as best they could. Task Force Kane pulled back more successfully, but were forced to give up Grandmenil due to the shortage of infantry. Fortunately, infantry reinforcements from 289th Infantry, 75th Division, arrived shortly afterwards and blocked the roads leading out of Grandmenil. When 2nd SS-Panzer Division *Das Reich* attempted to push out the west side of town, again using a captured Sherman tank in the lead, they were halted when a lone bazookaman knocked out the lead tank. The road was constricted on either side by steep slopes, so *Das Reich*'s column was effectively stopped for the moment.

Although the *Das Reich* assault had managed to thoroughly disrupt the planned American reorganization around Manhay, it fell far short of its objectives of gaining the road exits out of Manhay and neighboring Grandmenil northward, which were still firmly in American hands. On Christmas Day, Obergruppenführer Bittrich received new orders. Instead of pushing up the road to Liege, he was to turn his corps westward, down along the road towards Erezée and Hotton, to strike the flank of Collins' VII Corps, which at the time was closing in on the spearhead of Manteuffel's 5th Panzer Army near the Meuse River. *Das Reich* spent most of Christmas Day attempting to gain room to maneuver in the

A patrol by the 23rd Engineer Battalion on 7 January near the scene of the earlier fighting for "Parker's Crossroads" at Baraque de Fraiture. (MHI)

An armored dough of the 36th Armored Infantry, 3rd Armored Division mans a M1919A4 .30 cal Browning light machine-gun near Amonines while behind him is one of the division's M4 medium tanks.

Manhay–Grandmenil area prior to their new drive west, while the US forces attempted to reestablish a cohesive defense and push *Das Reich* out of Manhay and Grandmenil. An attempt to retake Grandmenil on Christmas afternoon by the 289th Infantry backed by tanks from TF McGeorge faltered when US aircraft accidentally bombed the US tanks. An attack into Manhay by CCA, 7th Armored Division, was stopped in the late afternoon after the lead tanks encountered road obstructions and were knocked out by German anti-tank guns. *Das Reich* had no more success in its efforts, as the hills overlooking the towns were peppered with US artillery observers who called in repeated howitzer strikes every time the Panzers attempted to move. When the artillery let up, the towns were hit by repeated US airstrikes, and Manhay and Grandmenil were turning into a killing ground. Plans to move the other main element of the corps, the 9th SS-Panzer Division *Hohenstaufen*, to the Manhay area to reinforce the planned drive on Erezée also failed. The fighting for the crossroads was turning into a bloody stalemate, but one that favored the Americans since they could move in more reinforcements. By Christmas, the US Army had 17 field artillery battalions in the area from the Aisne to the Lienne rivers, and much of this was within range of the stalled *Das Reich*.

To the west, the battered 560th VG Div. continued its attempts to win control of the road west of Erezée around Soy and Hotton from overextended elements of the 3rd Armored Division. TF Orr reported that on Christmas Eve, the German infantry had made 12 separate attacks to break through their defenses and that "if they'd have had three more riflemen, they'd probably have overrun our positions." The American defenses along the key road gradually began to solidify as the green 75th Division came into the line. Although the inexperienced troops took heavy casualties during their hasty introduction into combat, the added rifle strength considerably bolstered the American lines.

By 26 December, *Das Reich* could not wait any longer for the arrival of the 9th SS-Panzer Division, and early that morning deployed SS-Panzergrenadier Regiment 4 *Der Führer* against the 325th GIR to the east at Tri-le-Cheslaing. This attack was stopped cold. The main attack was a two-pronged effort emanating out of Grandmenil, one group straight down the main road towards Erezée and the other up a narrow **161**

The fields around Amonines are littered with the wrecks of SdKfz 250 half-tracks of the 116th Panzer Division, destroyed during an encounter with Task Force Orr of the 3rd Armored Division. The vehicle to the left is an unusual variant with a 2cm cannon.

path towards Mormont intended to outflank the American defenses if the first attack did not succeed. The German attack out of Grandmenil coincided with an effort by TF McGeorge to retake the town, and a head-on tank duel ensued. The M4 tanks of TF McGeorge stood little chance in a direct confrontation with the *Das Reich* Panthers, and lost all but two M4 tanks in the brief encounter. However, the tank duel derailed the main German attack. The northern probe towards Mormont was stopped when a German tank was knocked out in a narrow gorge, blocking any further advance. Grandmenil was subjected to a barrage by three artillery battalions, and then assaulted again by 16 M4 tanks of TF McGeorge and 3/289th Infantry. The US infantry captured about half of Grandmenil and the access to the road to Manhay. The 7th Armored Division made a half-hearted attempt to reach the Grandmenil–Manhay road at the same time, but the badly battered unit could not put enough strength into the field, and the attack was halted by German tank fire. After Manhay was softened up with fighter-bomber strikes, the village was attacked by 3/517th PIR in the evening, and by dawn the paratroopers had pushed *Das Reich* out. By this stage, Bittrich realized that any effort to force open the road through Grandmenil was futile, and on the morning of 27 December, *Das Reich* was withdrawn. Furthermore, the operational objective of the attack, to relieve pressure on the 5th Panzer Army spearhead near the Meuse, had become pointless after the 2nd Panzer Division had been trapped and crushed in the days after Christmas by the US 2nd Armored Division. Further attacks were attempted, including an assault on Sadzot on 28 December, but the II SS-Panzer Corps had reached its high-water mark days before, and in early January Berlin began stripping SS-Panzer units out of the Ardennes to reinforce the threatened Russian front.

THE HIGH-WATER MARK

Late on the evening of 23 December, the reconnaissance battalion of the 2nd Panzer Division reported that it had approached to within nine kilometers of the Meuse River near Dinant. This would prove to be the high-water mark of the Ardennes offensive. The reconnaissance battalion of 2nd Panzer Division had reached and crossed the Ourthe River at Ourtheville on 21 December, followed by Panzergrenadiers later in the day. The advance beyond was slowed for more than a day by a lack of fuel. By 23 December, the division was again on the march in two columns, the main one along Route N4 to Marche and a smaller column to Hargimont. Present with the division was the impatient corps commander, General Lüttwitz, who relieved one of the regimental commanders when the pace of the advance was slowed by a weak American roadblock. While Hargimont was captured, Marche was stoutly defended by arriving elements of the 84th Division. Lüttwitz ordered Lauchert to turn the bulk of his division west towards Dinant and the Meuse, and to leave only a blocking force towards Marche. He hoped to deploy the 9th Panzer Division near Marche once it arrived. The division was preceded by Kampfgruppe Böhm consisting of its reconnaissance battalion reinforced with a few Panzers. On the night of 23/24 December, KG Böhm raced up the highway towards Dinant, finally reaching the woods near Foy-Notre Dame. It was followed on 24 December by the advance guard of the division, KG Cochenhausen, consisting of Panzergrenadier Regiment 304 and 1/Panzer Regiment 3.

Radio reports of the advance caused jubilation in Berlin. Hitler personally congratulated Rundstedt and Model, and freed up the 9th Panzer and 15th Panzergrenadier Divisions to reinforce the 5th Panzer Army. Model was under few illusions about reaching the "Grand Slam" or "Little Slam" objectives, but Panzers reaching the Meuse was enough of an accomplishment that it would help the Wehrmacht save face from all the disappointments of the campaign. Model immediately directed the 9th Panzer Division to follow the 2nd Panzer Division and protect its right flank from advancing American forces. As noted earlier, he ordered the entire 15th Panzergrenadier Division into the area north of Bastogne to finally crush the resistance there.

An M4A1 (76mm) of Task Force B, CCA, 2nd Armored Division carries infantry into an assault near Frandeux on 27 December during the attempts to contain the Panzer Lehr Division near Rochefort. (NARA)

SPEARHEAD TO THE MEUSE (pages 78–79)

Kampfgruppe Böhm races to the Meuse in the days before Christmas 1944. This battlegroup was based around the 2nd Panzer Division's reconnaissance battalion, Panzer Aufklärungs Abteilung 2, but its combat power was reinforced by a few Panther tanks from the division's Panzer regiment, Pz.Rgt.3. This was necessary as its reconnaissance battalion had been only partially refitted prior to the Ardennes operation. Its first company was absent and still refitting, while its third company was equipped mainly with bicycles. Ill-equipped or not, one of the reasons for the success of 5th Panzer Army in penetrating deep behind American lines was the more effective use of their reconnaissance units. Model's Army Group B headquarters was critical of poor use of reconnaissance units by the neighboring Waffen-SS Panzer divisions, which usually employed them like any other Panzer or Panzergrenadier formation. The regular army Panzer divisions had learned from hard experience that the primary job of the reconnaissance elements was to move fast and avoid unnecessary combat in order to fulfill their mission. The armored patrol seen here is led by a SdKfz 234 Puma armored car (1). This was one of most effective scout vehicles of World War II, armed with a 50mm gun (2).

Each of its eight wheels was independently sprung, and it had excellent mobility for a wheeled vehicle in terrain, and high travel speeds of over 50 mph when on roads. In the Ardennes, the division had ten of these armored cars as well as two of the related SdKfz 234/1 armed with a 20mm cannon, and two SdKfz 233 armed with a 75mm short gun. Following behind the Puma is a Panther Ausf. G tank (3). The 2nd Panzer Division started the offensive with 51 Panthers and 29 PzKpfw IV tanks. Behind the Panther is the lead SdKfz 251 armored half-track (4). Although more commonly associated with the Panzergrenadier regiment, this jack-of-all-trades was also used by scout units and there were 13 of these on hand at the beginning of the offensive. The more common armored half-track in the reconnaissance battalion was the SdKfz 250 light half-track with 33 in service in December 1944. The vehicles seen here mostly lack any distinctive tactical unit insignia since the division was re-equipped so soon before the start of the offensive. The Panther and Puma lack the usual tactical numbers on the turret, and the division's distinctive trident emblem is nowhere to be seen. The use of foliage for camouflage was common in the Ardennes, especially after 23 December when the clear weather marked the return of the dreaded American *Jabos*. (Peter Dennis)

A pair of GIs from the 207th Engineer Combat Battalion prepare a bazooka by fitting a battery into the launcher during the fighting near Buissonville on 29 December. (NARA)

But by this late date, the advance of the 2nd Panzer Division no longer had any strategic significance. There was no operational value in reaching the Meuse at Dinant, as the town was backed by high cliffs and could be easily defended by the Allies. Namur was even less attractive and its fortifications posed a substantial hurdle for any attacker. The spearhead Panzer divisions were exhausted, short of functional tanks and dangerously short of fuel. This was not immediately apparent to Hitler or the Allied commanders.

The threat of German units crossing the Meuse prompted Field Marshal Montgomery to begin redeploying his reserve, the British XXX Corps, on 19 December to cover the exits over the river. This took time, but by 23 December, the major river crossings at Givet, Dinant and Namur were each covered by tank battalions from the 29th Armoured Brigade, each reinforced by a rifle company.

By the time that KG Cochenhausen approached the Meuse, Allied reinforcements were becoming a growing threat. Its attack was constantly diluted by the need to detach units to fight off flank attacks by American units appearing in the area. One of its Panzer columns was wiped out in the pre-dawn hours when it stumbled into an advancing column from CCA, 2nd Armored Division, along the Ciney–Rochefort road. To make matters worse, the division was threatened from the rear when the 335th Infantry of the 84th Division began an attack near Marche that at one point captured the main supply road. Although elements of the 2nd Panzer Division managed to hold the road open, American pressure was increasing as more reinforcements arrived.

On the night of 23/24 December, a single captured jeep with a scout party of three German soldiers approached the bridge at Dinant, but were blown up when they ran over a mine planted by the British defenders. The advance of KG Böhm was finally brought to an end on the morning of 24 December. As one of its columns began probing towards the river crossing, their lead PzKpfw IV tank was destroyed by a Sherman 17-pdr of the British 3rd Royal Tank Regiment that had taken up defensive positions on the east bank of the river the day before. Later in the morning, two more Panthers were knocked out, and the 3 RTR roadblocks established the farthest advance point of the Wehrmacht during the Ardennes offensive. CCA, 2nd Armored Division, advanced down the Ciney–Rochefort road for most of Christmas Eve, joined up with the British tankers, and pushed on to Buissonville in the afternoon, threatening to isolate KG Cochenhausen.

By late on Christmas Eve, it had become clear to Lüttwitz that the advance had come to an end. By now he recognized that he was facing major opposition in the 2nd Armored Division and 84th Division. Instead of ordering the long-delayed Panzer Lehr Division to Celles to join with the 2nd Panzer Division to race for the Meuse, Lüttwitz realized he would need to block any further advance of the Americans to buy time for the vulnerable 2nd Panzer Division to return to the corps bridgehead at Rochefort. He hoped to take Humain and Buissonville,

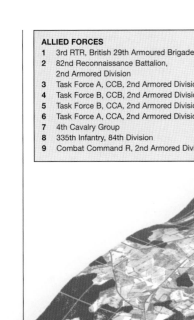

ALLIED FORCES

1   3rd RTR, British 29th Armoured Brigade
2   82nd Reconnaissance Battalion,
    2nd Armored Division
3   Task Force A, CCB, 2nd Armored Division
4   Task Force B, CCB, 2nd Armored Division
5   Task Force B, CCA, 2nd Armored Division
6   Task Force A, CCA, 2nd Armored Division
7   4th Cavalry Group
8   335th Infantry, 84th Division
9   Combat Command R, 2nd Armored Division

MEUSE RIVER

1

DINANT

1

FOY-NOTRE DAME

2

A   2

4

CELLES   6

3   B

5

11

C

WANLIN

▼ EVENTS

1. 23 DECEMBER: **The British 29th Armoured Brigade deploys its forces along the Meuse to prevent a German advance across the river.**

2. 24 DECEMBER: **The reconnaissance spearhead of 2nd Panzer Division, reaches the high water mark of the German Ardennes offensive near Foy-Notre Dame by dawn on Christmas Eve.**

3. 24 DECEMBER: **Kampfgruppe Cochenhausen, the advance guard of the 2nd Panzer Division, reaches the area around Celles on Christmas Eve. It has already encountered elements of the US 2nd Armored Division and is desperately short of fuel.**

4. **The 3rd RTR deploys some of its tanks to the east of Dinant, and destroys the forward Panzer patrols.**

5. **Task Force B of CCB, 2nd Armored Division cuts behind Kampfgruppe Cochenhausen in an advance from the Ciney area.**

6. **Task Force A of CCB, 2nd Armored Division joins up with Task Force A near Celles, trapping Kampfgruppe Cochenhausen in the woods east of Celles. Over the next few days, these trapped forces will be gradually squeezed and the pocket overwhelmed.**

7. 25 DECEMBER: **Task Force B of CCA, 2nd Armored Division departs Leignon on the morning of Christmas Eve and by Christmas Day is poised to cut off the 2nd Panzer Division from their staging area in Rochefort.**

8. 25 DECEMBER: **Task Force A, CCA, 2nd Armored Division pushes to the east of Task Force B, securing Buissonville on Christmas Eve and shielding the 2nd Armored Division from attacks by Panzer Lehr Division on Christmas Day.**

9. **The 4th Cavalry Group secures the gap between the 2nd Armored Division and the neighboring 84th Division.**

10. **The 335th Infantry, 84th Division defends the approaches to Marche against attacks by elements of the 2nd Panzer Division and Panzer Lehr Division.**

11. **Kampfgruppe Holtmayer stages a last ditch attempt to break through to the trapped advance guard of 2nd Panzer Division around Celles, but is beaten back by CCB, 2nd Armored Division with heavy losses.**

12. **Panzer Lehr attempts to relieve 2nd Panzer Division but is thwarted in a running series of encounters with CCA, 2nd Armored Division.**

13. 26–27 DECEMBER: **The 9th Panzer Division is added to the fray west of Marche leading to major tank skirmishes around Humain with CCA and CCR of the 2nd Armored Division.**

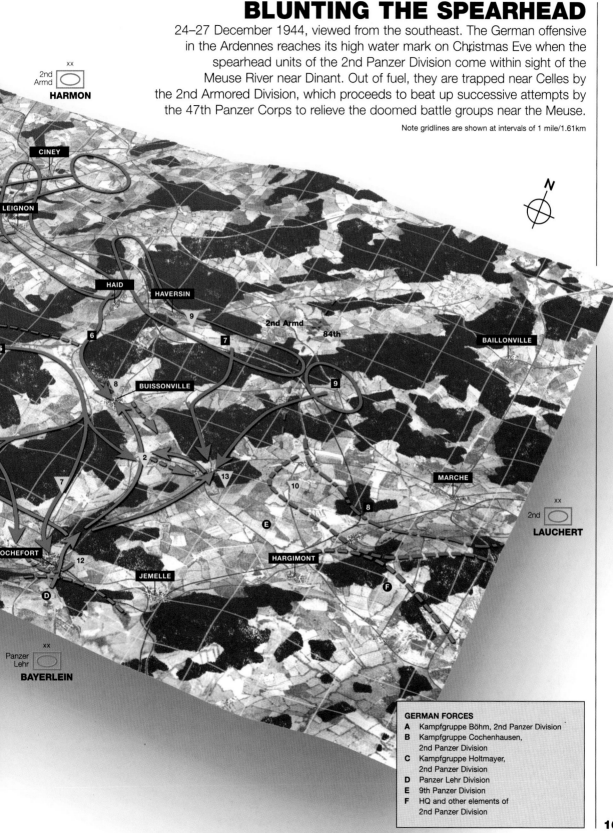

BLUNTING THE SPEARHEAD

24–27 December 1944, viewed from the southeast. The German offensive in the Ardennes reaches its high water mark on Christmas Eve when the spearhead units of the 2nd Panzer Division come within sight of the Meuse River near Dinant. Out of fuel, they are trapped near Celles by the 2nd Armored Division, which proceeds to beat up successive attempts by the 47th Panzer Corps to relieve the doomed battle groups near the Meuse.

Note gridlines are shown at intervals of 1 mile/1.61km

2nd Armd XX — **HARMON**

2nd XX — **LAUCHERT**

Panzer Lehr XX — **BAYERLEIN**

CINEY

LEIGNON

HAID

HAVERSIN
9

2nd Armd
84th

BAILLONVILLE

6

7

8

BUISSONVILLE

9

2

13

10

MARCHE

8

7

E

OCHEFORT

12

JEMELLE

HARGIMONT

F

D

GERMAN FORCES
A Kampfgruppe Böhm, 2nd Panzer Division
B Kampfgruppe Cochenhausen,
   2nd Panzer Division
C Kampfgruppe Holtmayer,
   2nd Panzer Division
D Panzer Lehr Division
E 9th Panzer Division
F HQ and other elements of
   2nd Panzer Division

169

Lt Robert Boscawen, commander of 2 Troop, the Coldstream Guards sits in a Sherman (17-pdr) guarding one of the bridges over the Meuse at Namur on Christmas Day. British armored units were deployed along the Meuse River in the days before Christmas to prevent a possible German crossing. (NARA)

thereby relieving pressure on the beleaguered 2nd Panzer Division. The desperately needed and long-delayed 9th Panzer Division was still behind schedule and lost another day when fuel could not be provided.

General Ernest Harmon of the 2nd Armored Division was itching to attack KG Cochenhausen after it was spotted by aerial reconnaissance. US units had intercepted German radio messages that made it very clear that the German units were seriously short of fuel. The opportunity to crush the Wehrmacht spearhead was almost thrown away. Montgomery was still concerned that the Germans were planning to throw their weight through the center and continue the advance towards Liege. Hodges had visited Collins on 23 December and knew that he wanted to attack the 2nd Panzer Division spearhead with the 2nd Armored Division. Yet in the wake of the fighting around Manhay, precipitated by the confused withdrawal on 23 December, Montgomery talked to Hodges about withdrawing VII Corps back to the Andenne–Hotton–Manhay line, not pushing forward. Montgomery's preoccupation with "tidying-up" the northern sector of the front so alarmed Bradley that he sent a note to Hodges that warned that while he was "no longer in my command, I would view with serious misgivings the surrender of any more ground". The following day, Montgomery reiterated his intent for the VII Corps to go over to the defensive. Hodges and the First Army staff were not enthusiastic to rein in Collins. A senior staff officer was sent to VII Corps headquarters with Montgomery's instructions, but First Army consciously neglected to forbid an attack, anticipating that the aggressive Collins would use his discretion to destroy the German spearhead. As Hodges' staff hoped, Collins ordered an attack. This decision proved timely as it allowed the 2nd Armored Division to beat up the weakened Panzer divisions of Lüttwitz's corps piecemeal rather than having to confront them simultaneously.

The 2nd Armored Division's main thrust on Christmas Day was conducted by CCB against KG Böhm and KG Cochenhausen, while CCA and the 4th Cavalry Group blocked Panzer Lehr Division and the newly

This Panther Ausf. G from the Panzer Lehr Division was knocked out during the attacks on Buissonville in the days after Christmas in the fighting with the 2nd Armored Division on the approaches to the Meuse. (NARA)

arrived 9th Panzer Division further east. CCB launched an enveloping attack out from Ciney in two task forces joining at Celles in the mid-afternoon and clearing the town. This trapped two large concentrations of 2nd Panzer Division units in the woods north of the town. Panzer Lehr Division attempted to push CCA out of Buissonville with an early morning attack at 07.50, but was repulsed with the loss of eight tanks, an assault gun and numerous infantry. A Panzergrenadier attack 40 minutes later was also hit hard, putting an end to attacks that day. Another battalion from Panzer Lehr was more successful at Humain, pushing a troop from the 4th Cavalry Group out of the village early on Christmas Day, and holding it against further attacks.

Lauchert formed KG Holtmayer from remaining elements of 2nd Panzer Division near Marche in hope of relieving the Celles pocket, and it departed Rochefort on the night of 25/26 December. It reached to within a kilometer of the Celles pocket but, without significant armored support, it was shattered by artillery and then roughly brushed off by CCB, 2nd Armored Division. To further seal off the pocket, on 27 December elements of the 4th Cavalry Group established a blocking position near Ciergnon and CCA, 2nd Armored Division, pushed south from Buissonville, reaching the 2nd Panzer Division's main assembly area in Rochefort. CCB, 2nd Armored Division, spent 26/27 December reducing the Celles pocket. At 15.30hrs on 26 December, the 2nd Panzer Division headquarters radioed survivors in the pocket to destroy any remaining heavy equipment and attempt to fight their way out. The trapped German units made two major break-out attempts on 26 December, but on 27 December the pocket began to collapse and about 150 tanks and vehicles were found destroyed or abandoned and 448 prisoners were taken. About 600 soldiers escaped from the woods on the nights of 26 and 27 December. By the end of December, the 2nd Panzer Division had been reduced in strength from about 120 tanks and assault guns to only about 20 and was no longer combat effective.

Panzer Lehr Division, reinforced by elements of the 9th Panzer Division, continued attempts to hold back the VII Corps attack. Harmon committed both CCA and CCR against Humain on 27 December, finally retaking the town from the 9th Panzer Division shortly before midnight. The neighboring 335th Infantry pushed down out of Marche, further sealing off the main highway onto the Marche plateau. Manteuffel by now realized that any further attempts to reach the Meuse would be futile, and his two best Panzer divisions were too weak for further offensive operations, with only about 50 operational Panzers.

SECURING BASTOGNE

The corridor between Patton's Third Army and Bastogne was precarious for the first few days, and was initially located on poor secondary roads. The last week of December was spent trying to gain control of the main roads, while at the same time both Manteuffel's 5th Panzer Army and Brandenberger's 7th Army desperately tried to sever the corridor. Manteuffel still held out hope that the "Little Slam" objectives might be reached, first by eliminating American resistance in Bastogne, then swinging back northwest toward Dinant. Model and Rundstedt agreed, adding a new 39th Panzer Corps headquarters under Generalleutnant Karl Decker to manage the units scraped together from elsewhere in the Ardennes. The Führer Begleit Brigade was assigned to the attack south of Bastogne, and other units moving into the area, included the badly decimated 1st SS-Panzer Division *Leibstandarte SS Adolf Hitler*, the 3rd Panzer Grenadier Division and the Führer Grenadier Brigade. The first attempt by Remer's Führer Begleit Brigade (FBB) was aborted after the unit was pounded by American fighter-bombers. On the US side, the CCA, 9th Armored Division, began a push out of Bastogne on the morning of 27 December to clear the western side of Bastogne, and spent three days grinding into the German defenses.

There were several strategic options for eliminating the "Bulge" in the Ardennes. Patton proposed the most ambitious, an attack by his Third Army from the area of Luxembourg City with a corresponding First Army lunge from the northern shoulder, joining at St Vith and entrapping as much of the 5th and 6th Panzer Armies as possible. This

GIs from the 84th Division dig in after a skirmish along a tree line near Berismenil on 13 January that left the GI in the foreground dead. The division advanced as far as Grande Morment the next day, before halting to recuperate after weeks of hard fighting in the Ardennes.

A patrol from the 101st Airborne Division moves out of Bastogne during the fighting on 29 December. (NARA)

A .30cal. machine-gun team of the 3/289th Infantry, 75th Division has set up in a house in Salmchateau on 16 January during the fighting to link up with Patton's Third Army. (NARA)

operation was never seriously entertained by Bradley or Eisenhower as there were serious doubts that such a mobile operation could be supported in the winter months over the restricted road network in Luxembourg and in the Elsenborn Ridge/Hohes Venn area as well as the recognition that the Germans could withdraw faster than the US Army could advance. Both Collins and Ridgway were anxious to start offensive operations after Christmas, but Montgomery remained fearful that the Germans might still break through somewhere along the First Army's extended defensive perimeter. The First Army Corps commanders doubted the Germans had the resources and held a more realistic appreciation of the solidity of the First Army defenses. When pressed by Collins about a possible attack from the Tailles Plateau towards St Vith to cut off the German offensive at its base, Montgomery said: "Joe, you can't supply a corps along a single road" to which Collins "in disrespectful exasperation" replied "well Monty, maybe you British can't, but we can." Patience with Montgomery's stalling of offensive operations by the First Army made Eisenhower rue the day he had turned over command of the First Army to him. Collins offered Hodges three options for closing the Bulge, the least ambitious of which was a push by VII Corps to coincide with Patton's offensive, meeting forces near Houffalize. While it would cut off any German forces in the deepest pockets of the Bulge to the northwest of Bastogne, most senior commanders realized it would trap few German forces. Eisenhower approved the plan on 27 December with Patton's Third Army to jump off on 30 December and First Army to start counterattacks on 3 January. This approach meant pushing the Germans out of the Bulge, rather than trapping them within and counted on attrition rather than envelopment to destroy Wehrmacht units.

After several days of inconclusive skirmishing around the Bastogne perimeter, and considerable repositioning of forces, both sides planned major attacks on 30 December. Middleton's VIII Corps had been reinforced and consisted of the 87th Division to the west, the newly arrived and green 11th Armored Division in the center and the 9th Armored Division at the base of the corridor. The aim of this attack was to begin to push the German forces away from the western side of Bastogne. At the same time, Manteuffel planned a three-phase assault, beginning with an attack by the 47th Panzer Corps against the corridor from the northwest and the new 39th Panzer Corps from the southeast.

Both sides exchanged heavy artillery fire in anticipation of the attacks, and both the 11th Armored Division and 87th Division made modest gains. Remer's Fuhrer Begliet Brigade hardly got past its start point and the neighboring 3rd Panzergrenadier Division was tied down in defensive operations for most of the day. The attack by the 39th Panzer Corps with a Kampfgruppe of the 1st SS-Panzer Division and the newly arrived 167th VG Div. struck the US 35th Division around Lutrebois. The US infantry defended tenaciously, and were backed by divisional artillery, the artillery of the 4th Armored Division and significant close air support. General Höcker of the 167th VG Div. reported that his lead battalion was "cut to pieces … by tree smasher shells", the new and secret US Army proximity fuses debuted at Bastogne that detonated at predetermined altitudes over the ground, substantially improving their lethality against exposed infantry. When the main Panzer column of the 1st SS-Panzer

An M4 medium tank of the 4th Armored Division takes part in operations to push out of Bastogne on 3 January 1945 with a .30cal. machine-gun team in the foreground. (NARA)

Division Kampfgruppe moved into action around noon, it was pummeled by air attack along the Lutremange-Lutrebois road. A Panzer company that escaped the *Jabos* stumbled into an ambush of the 4th Armored Division and was stopped after losing about a dozen tanks and three assault guns. By the end of the day, the German attacks had completely failed and the momentum was clearly shifting to the American side.

A planned 6th Armored Division attack on 31 December from the eastern side of the corridor, became trapped by icy roads and the congested road network. The attack began in earnest on New Year's Day, making good progress with the capture of Bizory and Mageret, and progress was even better on 2 January. The division's neighbor, the 35th Division, was slow in joining the attack due to the need to clear out remaining pockets of German resistance from the attack the preceding day. The VIII Corps continued to push up along the right side of Bastogne, with the tanks of the 11th Armored Division slugging it out in a series of skirmishes with Remer's Führer Begleit Brigade. In four days of fighting, the 11th Armored Division advanced only six miles at a cost of 660 casualties, 42 M4 and 12 M5A1 tanks. Nevertheless, the VII Corps had stopped the 49th Panzer Corps attack cold, and its capture of the road junction at Mande-St Etienne threatened to cut off the German forces on the northwest side of Bastogne.

With his own prospects for offensive action now gone, Manteuffel was so worried that the American advances on the west side of Bastogne might trap the 47th Panzer Corps that he recommended a general pull-back to the line Odeigne–La Roche–St Hubert. While Model agreed, he knew that Hitler would countenance no retreat. In later years, Manteuffel pointed to the 3 January 1945 fighting as the final turning point in the Ardennes

A view inside Bastogne on 20 January as a truck column of the 90th Division passes through. (NARA)

when the strategic initiative passed entirely to the US side. After this date, the Wehrmacht was never again able to stage a significant attack in the Ardennes and for the most part endured a series of grinding defensive battles.

ERASING THE BULGE

By late December, even Hitler had given up hope of victory in the Ardennes. On 27 December, the 6th Panzer Army was ordered to go over to the defensive. Hitler's enthusiasms turned in another direction, to Alsace, hoping to exploit the overextended defensive lines of the US 6th Army Group there, which had been stretched to cover part of the line formerly held by Patton's Third Army. Operation Nordwind was launched on 3 January 1945, gaining some initial successes. But it had no strategic consequences, and little impact in the Ardennes beyond placing even more stringent limits on German reinforcements and supplies. Manteuffel asked Model on 2 January to authorize a general withdrawal from the Bastogne vicinity to a more defensible line hinged on Houfallize, but Model knew of Hitler's opposition to any withdrawal and so refused. Hitler instead ordered another attack on Bastogne for 4 January, which fizzled after only minor gains. The US First Army began its offensive operations to join up with Patton's Third Army on 3 January 1945. On 5 January, Model was forced to pull out two of the Panzer divisions from the Bastogne sector to reinforce the badly pressed 6th Panzer Army, ending any further attempts against Bastogne.

From the American perspective, the early January fighting was as much against the weather as against the Germans. The snowy conditions grew progressively worse, and the struggles for the many small road junctions between Bastogne and Houfallize were bitter and costly for both sides. On 8 January, Hitler recognized the obvious, and authorized a withdrawal to prevent German units from being trapped by the slow but steady American advance. But the withdrawal did not proceed as planned, and La Roche was captured sooner than anticipated. Hitler planned to gradually have the 5th Panzer Army take over the 6th Panzer Army sector, with the 6th Panzer Army serving as a reserve to counter an anticipated Allied attack at the base of the Bulge, the type of operation proposed by Patton that was not in fact in the works. However, other events intervened. The fighting in the Ardennes became irrelevant on 12 January 1945 when the Red Army launched its long-expected winter offensive. With the Red Army on Germany's doorstep, there were no longer any resources for Hitler's foolish gambles in the west.

On 14 January, Rundstedt himself pleaded with Hitler to permit a withdrawal in stages all the way to the Rhine, but Hitler would only countenance a withdrawal to the Westwall. On 16 January, the US Third and First Armies met at Houfallize, marking the end of the first phase of erasing the Bulge. It would take until 28 January to recapture all of the territory lost to the German offensive.

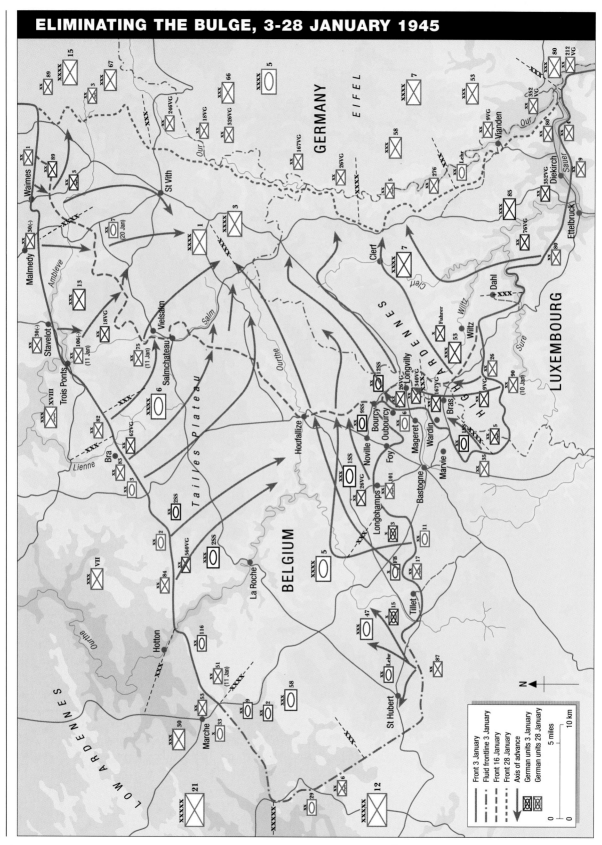

THE AFTERMATH

itler's final gamble in the West had failed within its first week when the 6th Panzer Army was unable to secure the Meuse River bridges at Liege. Although the 5th Panzer Army had far greater success in penetrating the American defenses in the central and southern sector, this was a race to nowhere that was operationally irrelevant as it neither destroyed any significant US forces nor did it secure any vital terrain. At best, the Ardennes attack disrupted the pace of Allied offensives into western Germany, but even this is debatable since the attrition of the Wehrmacht in the Ardennes weakened later defensive efforts in 1945. The most significant strategic effect of the Ardennes offensive was to distract German attention from the growing threat of Soviet offensive actions. The drain of resources to the west prevented the creation of viable reserves to counter the predictable Red Army assault into central Germany in mid-January 1945, helping to ensure the disaster that followed.

From a tactical perspective, the performance of Manteuffel's 5th Panzer Army clearly outshone Dietrich's 6th Panzer Army. When the US Army in 1995 used historical data from the Ardennes offensive to test one of their computer war game simulations, the war game concluded that the 5th Panzer Army had performed better than expected, and the 6th Panzer Army more poorly than its resources would have suggested. The Waffen-SS continued to suffer from mediocre leadership at senior levels, which was particularly evident in offensive operations such as the Ardennes. In contrast, the regular army continued to display a high level of tactical excellence even under the trying circumstances of the Ardennes operation, epitomized by Manteuffel's superior leadership in preparing and executing the badly flawed Ardennes plan. Nevertheless, the emaciated Wehrmacht of late 1944 did not have the combat

For months after the battle, the Belgian countryside was littered with wrecked armored vehicles. This is a knocked-out German Sd.Kfz. 251/9 (7.5cm) "Stummel" used to provide fire support for Panzergrenadier units, and photographed by the US Army Howell mission. (NARA)

effectiveness in offensive operations of years past. The head of Rundstedt's staff later wrote that the Ardennes had "broken the backbone of the Wehrmacht on the western front". A meeting at Model's headquarters after the fighting concluded that morale had plummeted since the defeat, and "the German soldier is in general fed up." The head of the Luftwaffe fighter force, Adolf Galland later wrote that the Luftwaffe was "decimated in the large air battles, especially during Christmas and finally destroyed" during the Ardennes campaign. As the diarist of the Wehrmacht High Command, P.E. Schramm later noted, "The abortive (Ardennes) offensive had made it clear not only the aerial but the armored superiority of the enemy."

Losses in the Ardennes fighting were heavy on both sides. US casualties totaled 75,482 of which there were 8,407 killed, 46,170 wounded and 20,905 missing through the end of January. The British XXX Corps lost 1,408 including 200 killed, 239 wounded and 969 missing. Estimates of German losses vary from about 67,200 to 98,025 casualties depending on the parameters. In the case of the lower of the figures, this included 11,171 killed, 34,439 wounded and 23,150 missing. The Wehrmacht lost about 610 tanks and assault guns in the Ardennes, or about 45 percent of their original strength, compared to about 730 US tanks and tank destroyers.

Although the US Army suffered from some serious mistakes by senior commanders at the outset of the offensive, at the tactical level, its units performed well. The only division to be completely overwhelmed, the 106th Division near St Vith, was a green unit in an exposed and badly overextended position, overwhelmed by more numerous enemy forces. The American response to the German offensive was timely and effective, exploiting the US advantage in battlefield mobility to quickly shift units to block the German advance. The stalwart defense by US infantry, armor and engineer units, backed by ample artillery support, stopped the German offensive.

From an operational perspective, the Allied response after Christmas was lackluster with the exception of Patton's prompt relief of Bastogne. Bradley and Eisenhower suffered a blow to their confidence by failing to anticipate the German offensive. Combined with the unfortunate decision to allow Montgomery to control the US forces in the northern sector of the front, the Allied counterattack was timid and failed to exploit the potential either to trap significant German forces or at least to force a less organized withdrawal. In spite of these problems, the US Army's defeat of the Wehrmacht in the Ardennes crippled the Wehrmacht in the West and facilitated the offensive operations into northwestern Germany in February and March 1945.

The Ardennes campaign precipitated a crisis in Allied command after Montgomery made a number of tactless remarks that exaggerated his own role in the victory. Montgomery had been campaigning for months to be named the supreme land forces commander as part of a broader effort to shift Allied strategic planning towards his view that the offensive against Germany should be conducted on a narrow front by his own 21st Army Group. Eisenhower considered asking for his resignation as the best solution to this nagging problem and Montgomery backed down, largely ending the Allied debate about the strategic conduct of the war in northwest Europe in Eisenhower's favor.

BIBLIOGRAPHY

Due to its importance, the Battle of the Bulge has been the subject of hundreds of books, especially from the American perspective. The northern sector has received far less treatment than Bastogne and the southern sector, and the focus here is on a selection of books dealing with this sector rather than on the many general histories of the campaign. The defense of Bastogne has been the focus of a disproportionate share of the books, not only because of the drama of the story, but due to the tendency to pay special attention to the units remaining under Bradley's control and less to those units under Montgomery.

This book was heavily based on unpublished material as well. The best perspective on the German side is provided by the scores of interviews conducted with nearly all the senior German commanders by the US Army after the war as part of the Foreign Military Studies effort. Copies of these are available at several locations including the US Army Military History Institute at Carlisle Barracks, Pennsylvania, and the US National Archives in College Park, Maryland. Some of these have been reprinted in two books edited by Danny Parker: *Hitler's Ardennes Offensive* and *The Battle of the Bulge: The German View* (Greenhill and Stackpole, 1997, 1999). The US Army MHI has an extensive collection of interviews with senior US commanders, and the several interviews conducted after the war with Gen Bruce Clarke are particularly illuminating about the fighting for St Vith. Besides the many wartime after-action reports, there are a large number of unpublished US Army studies of the battle including *The Defense of St. Vith, Belgium 17–23 December 1944: An Historical Example of Armor in the Defense* (US Armored School, Ft. Knox, 1949) and *Tank Fight of Rocherath-Krinkelt 17–19 December 1944* (OCMH, 1952). There is a very useful Master's history dissertation prepared by a veteran of the fighting, Frank Andrews, *The Defense of St. Vith in the Battle of the Bulge, December 1944* (NYU, 1964). Besides the many wartime, after-action reports, there are a large number of unpublished US Army studies of the battle including *Armor under Adverse Conditions: 2nd and 3rd Armored Divisions in the Ardennes* (Ft. Knox, 1949) and *Armor at Bastogne* (Ft. Knox, 1949). There are numerous divisional histories of the units fighting in the Ardennes, and Battery Press has reprinted many of the best of these including the superb 101st Airborne history *Rendezvous with Destiny* and other useful accounts such as the 28th Division history.

Statistical data on the battle comes from a number of sources including "Ardennes Campaign Statistics: 16 December 1944–19 January 1945" prepared by Royce Thompson (OCMH: 1952). In addition, in the early 1990s, the US Army Concept Analysis Agency commissioned the creation of a very large statistical database on the campaign to test its computerized Stochastic Concepts Evaluation Model, a computer war simulation program. This database was based on extensive archival research and provides day-by-day data on personnel, casualties, and weapons strength on both sides.

Cavanagh, William *Krinkelt-Rocherath: The Battle for the Twin Villages*, (Christopher Publishing: 1986). A detailed account of the battle from the US perspective by an Ardennes expert.

Cavanagh, William, *A Tour of the Bulge Battlefield*, (Leo Cooper, 2001). A good, short history of the Ardennes campaign along with useful information on making a battlefield tour by one of the acknowledged experts on the battle.

Cole, Hugh, *The Ardennes: Battle of the Bulge*, (OCMH: 1965). This US Army official history in the Green Book series still remains the best single volume on the battle, and is still in print through the US GPO.

Doherty, J.C., *The Shock of War*, (Vert Milon: 1997). A survey of the northern sector based around many anecdotal accounts of the fighting from the perspective of US veterans.

Dupuy, Ernest, *St. Vith: Lion in the Way*, (Infantry Journal: 1949; also Battery Press reprint). The semi-official history of the ill-fated 106th Division.

Gaul, Roland, *The Battle of the Bulge in Luxembourg*, (Schiffer, 1995). A highly detailed two volume account of combat operations in Luxembourg with Volume 1 covering the Germans and Volume 2 the Americans.

Guderian, Heinz Gunther, *From Normandy to the Ruhr*, (Aberjona, 2001). A candid and highly detailed account of the 116th Panzer Division by a veteran of the unit and son of the famous German Panzer commander.

Jung, Hermann, *Die Ardennen-Offensive 1944/45.* (Musterschmidt, 1971). The classic German account of the Ardennes campaign.

Koch, Oscar, *G-2: Intelligence for Patton*, (Schiffer, 1999). The memoirs of Patton's intelligence chief which reveals the controversy about the Allied intelligence blunders at the beginning of the Battle of the Bulge.

Koskimaki, George, *The Battered Bastards of Bastogne*, (Casemate, 2003). A collection of interviews with veterans of the 101st Airborne about the defense of Bastogne by the radio operator of the divisional commander.

Macdonald, Charles, *Company Commander*, (Burford Books: 1947, 1999). A classic memoir of a young infantry officer of the 23rd Infantry, 2nd Infantry Division who fought at Krinkelt-Rocherath and later became a senior US Army historian.

Meyer, Hubert, *The History of the 12.SS-Panzerdivision Hitlerjugend*, (Federowicz: 1994). An English translation of the classic study by an officer of the division.

Marshall, S.L.A., *Bastogne: The First Eight Days*, (Infantry Journal 1946, 1988 GPO reprint). A detailed account by the army historian, based on battlefield interviews with the American participants.

Neill, George, *Infantry Soldier: Holding the Line at the Battle of the Bulge*, (University of Oklahoma: 1999). An excellent new memoir by a former BAR gunner with the 99th Division that provides an intimate portrait of the experiences of an average rifleman in the fighting in the northern sector.

Pallud, Jean Paul, *Battle of the Bulge: Then and Now*, (After the Battle, 1984). The definitive photographic history of the battle by the well-known specialist, that combines extensive historical photos with contemporary photos of the same scenes. A smaller companion volume by Philip Vorwald was published in 2000.

Parker, Danny, *To Win the Winter Sky*, (Combined Publishing: 1994). An excellent account of the air war over the Ardennes.

Reynolds, Michael, *The Devil's Adjutant*, (Sarpendon, 1995). A biography of Jochen Peiper with a detailed account of Kampfgruppe Peiper in the Ardennes.

Reynolds, Michael, *Men of Steel: I SS Panzer Corps* (Sarpendon: 1999) This presents a German perspective on the fighting.

Reynolds, Michael, *Sons of the Reich: II SS Panzer Corps*, (Casemate, 2002). An account of the II SS-Panzer Corps in 1944–45 with extensive coverage of the Ardennes campaign.

Ritgen, Helmut, *The Western Front 1944: Memoirs of a Panzer Lehr Officer*, (Federowicz, 1995). A first hand account of Panzer operations by a colonel of the Panzer Lehr Division, including operations in the Ardennes.

Rush, Robert, *Hell in the Hürtgen*, (University of Kansas: 2001). A stimulating account of the campaign preceding the Ardennes which provides the best examination to date of the state of American and German infantry at this stage of the war.

Rusiecki, Stephen, *The Key to the Bulge: The Battle for Losheimergraben*, (Praeger:1996). A detailed account of the fighting for Losheimergraben with balanced coverage of both the US and German sides.

Vannoy, A and Karamales, J, *Against the Panzers: US Infantry vs. German Tanks 1944–45*, (McFarland: 1996). This account of US infantry actions against German tank attacks contains a particularly good description of the Krinkelt-Rocherath battle.

Wijers, Hans, *The Battle of the Bulge: The Losheim Gap-Doorway to the Meuse*, (Brummen: 2001). An excellent collection of personal accounts from the German and American veterans about the fighting in the northern sector during the first days of the campaign.

Winter, George, *Manhay: The Ardennes, Christmas 1944*, (Federowicz, 1990). A short but informative monograph on the fighting between the 7th Armored Division and the 2nd SS-Panzer Division based on interviews with veterans from both sides.

INDEX

181